T0269869

FARLEY AND CLAIRE

An Intimate Portrait of
Claire and Farley Mowat

**MICHAEL
HARRIS**

Farley

AND

Claire

A Love Story

DAVID SUZUKI INSTITUTE

GREYSTONE BOOKS

Vancouver / Berkeley / London

For everyone who ever got a second chance at love,
and the ones who gave it to them.

Greystone Books Ltd.
greystonebooks.com

David Suzuki Institute
www.davidsuzukiinstitute.org

Cataloguing data available from Library and Archives Canada
ISBN 978-1-77164-977-3 (cloth)
ISBN 978-1-77164-978-0 (epub)

Editing by Nancy Flight
Copy editing by Brian Lynch
Proofreading by Jennifer Stewart
Jacket and text design by Jessica Sullivan
Jacket photograph by Ray Allan / *Vancouver Sun*

Printed and bound in Canada on FSC® certified paper at Friesens. The FSC® label
means that materials used for the product have been responsibly sourced.

Greystone Books thanks the Canada Council for the Arts, the British Columbia
Arts Council, the Province of British Columbia through the Book Publishing Tax Credit,
and the Government of Canada for supporting our publishing activities.

Canadä

BRITISH
COLUMBIA

BRITISH COLUMBIA
ARTS COUNCIL
An agency of the Province of British Columbia

Canada Council
for the Arts

Conseil des arts
du Canada

Greystone Books gratefully acknowledges the xʷməθkʷəy̓əm (Musqueam),
Sḵwx̱wú7mesh (Squamish), and səlilwətaɬ (Tsleil-Waututh) peoples on
whose land our Vancouver head office is located.

Contents

Foreword

MARGARET ATWOOD

Memories of Farley:

Farley floating on his back in the Bay of Pigs, Cuba, making spouts like a whale, his little round tummy sticking up above the waterline, while telling a story to a mesmerized ten-year-old.

"I went into a radio station to do an interview," he said. "They introduced me live on air. 'Here with us today is . . . Fartley More-fat!'" Delight all round. The radio people must have been in the habit of calling Farley that behind his back, and one of them had slipped up.

Farley running out into the Cuban night, waving his arms and shouting, "It's the CIA! My toilet is boiling! They're trying to kill me!" Indeed, all the toilets in the minimalist chalets assigned to our bird-watching group were percolating. Our leader—Graeme Gibson, a long-time friend of Farley's—had intimated to the tourist officials of Cuba that North Americans liked warm showers rather than the cold ones on offer. The warm showers had duly been arranged, but no OFF thermo-stat had been installed, so the water had reached boiling point during the night. Also, the toilets had somehow been hooked up to the shower systems. "Tried to scald my balls off!" said Farley. "It was a plot!" Farley was making a joke, though the episode was in fact reminiscent of some of the efforts made to eradicate Fidel Castro in those years.

This was in the late 1980s, on our first-ever birding trip to Cuba. It had taken Graeme a couple of years to convince the Cuban authori-ties that not all North Americans with binoculars were spies and that dedicated birders would actually pay money for a chance to see the endemic Cuban birds, over twenty at that time, and counting. Graeme had gathered together a dauntless band willing to drive around Cuba in a bus without any glass in the windows, with another one following in case of breakdowns—a wise precaution.

To mark the debut of this initiative, a special dinner was laid on at the Bay of Pigs venue, and officials were present to make solemn protocol speeches. Farley had been selected to reply. "I've got my speech in here somewhere," he began, rummaging around in his satchel. "Nope! It's my dirty underwear!" (He pulled this out and displayed it.) "Must have lost the speech. Let's have a drink!" The gathering dissolved into laughter, and the Cubans began talking about what really interested them, which was their horoscope signs.

Farley started waltzing my seventy-eight-year-old mother around the room. "What're you doing with that old poop?" he said, indicating my eighty-year-old father. "Run off with me!"

One of the Cubans pressed a butter knife into my father's hand. "Kill heem!"

Throughout all of this, Claire was quietly keeping watch over the shenanigans. She knew Farley was a rascally cut-up and mischievous performer: whenever Farley was in a group, there was fun and unpredictability. She also knew what was behind the stage curtain: the romantic, the melancholic, the Second World War vet who'd seen first-hand how terrible human beings could be to one another. She knew there were delirious highs and highjinks in the life of Farley: she knew also that there would be lows, and that the lows could get quite low indeed.

I first met Farley through Jack McClelland of McClelland & Stewart, who published both of us. The year was 1972. I was thirty-two, and Farley was already a legend. I had two books out that year, a novel—*Surfacing*—and an ordinary readers' intro to Canadian literature called *Survival*, because up to that date there hadn't been one. I was attracting a certain amount of press attention. Farley gave me two pieces of advice. He said I would need a public persona—a sort of act I could use when being interviewed on radio shows and the like—and that this version of myself would be a kind of shield. He also said, "Now you're a target, and people will shoot at you."

Both of these statements were based on Farley's own experience. The wisecracking, kilt-flipping, devil-may-care, Fuck Them Farley was sure to get the attention of media types, as well as being characteristic of a certain kind of war vet—irreverent, curious, questioning of authority, not too interested in colouring inside the politeness lines. Such vets, benefitting from the education on offer, enlivened university campuses in the decade after 1946. (My own generation, entering universities in the mid- to late 1950s, was considered dull by our professors, who missed the uproar.) If you're a freelance author—as Farley was—you need to promote your books, because they are your only source of income. You won't have a guaranteed income, you won't get promotions, you won't retire with a pension.

The other Farley was the serious one, focused on justice for neglected and maltreated human and animal life alike. It was this Farley that was targeted early on by government bureaucrats and big resource concerns, angry that Farley—in books such as *People of the Deer* and *Never Cry Wolf*—had drawn attention to their incompetence and, in some cases, their greed, their exploitation of Indigenous lands, and their inhumanity. Farley was very early on the scene in his advocacy for Indigenous peoples who lived on the land, who at that time had no means of reaching the Canadian public except through intermediaries like Farley. The response of the enraged officials at that time was twofold: block Farley's access whenever possible, by—for instance—cutting off research funds, and claim he was lying. Some even went so far as to say he had simply *made up* a whole group of people—the Ihalmiut. They said that these people simply did not exist.

These early attempts did not shut Farley down—the accusations did not at that time go, as we say, viral—but Farley was never out of the crosshairs of the enemies he'd made, and a later attempt very nearly squelched him permanently. I speak of the notorious *Saturday Night* article of 1996, with a cover showing a Pinocchio-nosed Farley. The aim was the same: discredit a trusted advocate for northern Indigenous peoples by painting him as a liar. Maybe then people would conclude that the peoples he'd described didn't really exist, and it would be full steam ahead for land grabbers.

All this under the guise of "investigative journalism," a weighty-sounding descriptor. But two can play at that game. Michael Harris is himself an investigative journalist. He's taken a dive much deeper than the shallow, trust-destroying takedown effort displayed by *Saturday Night*.

Farley and Claire is a love story, a biography, a Tale of Two Farleys, or perhaps three: the public one, the private one, and the secret one. But it's also a vindication. Who, in the end, should be awarded the biggest Pinocchio nose?

One of the last times I saw Farley and Claire was on Pelee Island, where they had come to help support our migratory bird efforts at the annual SpringSong gala. Farley had done the full song and dance for his enchanted audience: no kilt-flipping, but lots of jokes and anecdotes, and some punchy messages. He was, as they say, rapturously received.

The next night we took Farley and Claire out to dinner. It was Farley's birthday. To celebrate, he howled like a wolf. A party trick, yes. An attention-grabber for radio show hosts.

But also a cry of infinite longing and mournfulness. A goodbye to what Farley saw as an increasingly diminished and dying natural world.

Introduction

NOBEL LAUREATE Gabriel García Márquez once observed that "everyone has three lives: a public life, a private life, and a secret life."

At the time of Farley Mowat's death, in 2014, a great deal was known about his public life. He was a trailblazer on two issues that currently dominate the cultural reality of Canada: the environment and the plight of Indigenous peoples.

Mowat the naturalist, the voice of Canada's North, wrote forty-two books, published in 550 editions during his lifetime. His defence of whales and wolves was so compelling that some of his books, such as *Never Cry Wolf*, were made into movies that became box-office hits. With more than fourteen million books sold throughout the world, Farley Mowat was a literary superstar.

In championing the rights of Indigenous peoples and environmental issues while those causes were still in their infancy, Mowat also inspired people like the young David Suzuki to follow in his footsteps. Margaret Atwood has observed that many people now advocating for Indigenous peoples often forget who was the first to take on the challenge in books such as *People of the Deer*—Farley Mowat.

We know a lot about the author's private life because he wrote about it so well. But Mowat also disguised his private life with a carefully cultivated public persona of the hard-drinking rowdy-man who scandalized people at parties by flipping his kilt and loudly declaimed what others might think but would never say.

It was pure marketing, designed to support his image as the bad boy of Canadian literature. The real man was very different. He listened to Bach, not bagpipes, while he wrote, was extremely well-read from an early age, and despite his incredible literary output sometimes fell victim to paralyzing self-doubt.

Then there was his secret life, rarely if ever penetrated in the portrayal of a man as complex as Farley Mowat. In 1960, Mowat found the love of his life in a chance meeting on Saint-Pierre, the small French island off the south coast of Newfoundland. Claire Angel Wheeler changed the arc of Farley's journey.

Their passionate love affair was complicated by the fact that Farley was a married man with two children, though his marriage had been unhappy for many years. Claire brought him back to love and to life, and Farley inspired her to develop her own considerable skills as a writer in her journals and in six published works. The course of true love never runs smooth, but run it did, for an incredible fifty-four years of love and creation.

If this book gives readers a rare look into the secret lives of two remarkable people, the credit goes to Claire Mowat. It was Claire who opened the embargoed Mowat Archives at McMaster University to me and also shared the couple's stunning private journals. But it is their marvellous love letters, published here for the first time, that illustrate why theirs was a love affair for the ages.

1 | The Quiet One

FARLEY MOWAT MOVED silently through the darkened house and softly kissed his sleeping family goodbye. After lingering over the beds of his two sons, Sandy and David, he opened the door of the log house he had built in Palgrave, Ontario, and slipped outside. It was time to hit the road.

It was 6 a.m. and the morning was fresh and fine. His jeep, Lulu, was packed with all of his personal gear. It also held supplies for the *Happy Adventure*, a sailboat he had bought with his Canadian publisher, Jack McClelland, as co-owner. The equipment for his boat, which was waiting for him in Newfoundland, included a seventy-five-pound anchor. Anxious to get the dust of Ontario off his wheels, he drove hard all day, finally stopping at a small motel just east of Quebec City at 8 p.m. It was June 27, 1960, and Canada's rising literary star was in the thirteenth year of a marriage that was pulling him down like quicksand.

On the road by 6:30 the next morning, Farley felt exhilarated. His spirits always improved when he was travelling to the East Coast. It was raw, unpretentious, and inarguably authentic, something like Farley himself. That night, he camped by invitation in someone's backyard, just outside Chatham, New Brunswick. The drive along Nova Scotia's stunning western shore was like a tonic, leaving him deeply calm and content—feelings that had been missing for a long time. The next day, he made it to North Sydney just in time to board the night ferry, *William Carson*. The vessel reached Port aux Basques in Newfoundland the next morning, shrouded in fog.

From there, Farley drove relentlessly to Freshwater Brook, then on to St. George's, heading to Corner Brook. When Lulu lost her muffler, Farley rewired it. When she had a flat tire, he fixed it. Farley Mowat was what they call in Newfoundland "handy," a person who could fix things on his own. Farley stopped just outside Humber Gorge for the night, but was off again at dawn on July 1. Breakfast was fresh trout from a nearby pond, a meal that two locals shared with him. Fried in fat back, the "scoff" of trout reinforced Farley's feeling of being at home again.

When he reached St. John's, Farley looked up his friend Harold Horwood at the Teamsters office, and they headed to the small town of Fermeuse to check on the *Happy Adventure*, a thirty-foot-six-inch schooner built in 1956 as an inshore fishing boat and named after a pirate ship. The work on the boat, including the addition of a deck-house, was supposed to be finished by now, but had only just begun. So Farley returned to St. John's, where he visited Mike Donovan, a war buddy, who was now director of public libraries for Newfoundland. Mike decided to take a day off work to help Farley shop for equipment for the boat.

Jack McClelland was due at Torbay Airport on July 12 but was a no-show, so Farley stayed up most of the night trying to get a coat of paint on the inside of the cabin to make it more presentable. Jack arrived the next day in his usual spectacular style, driving a huge rental car. He brought the mainsail and jib with him, as well as the water and fuel tanks.

The boat was lying at Philip Brophy's stage in a protected cove next to the Moore fish plant, where the stench overpowered Farley's Toronto guest. Jack seemed equally unimpressed by the cod tongues Farley fried up for their dinner. The business of fitting out the boat seemed eternal, but Jack was, as usual, a trouper. They painted the *Happy Adventure* together and fitted lockers and cupboards below deck.

Helped by locals who had originally built the boat, the two took a week—and a combination of slavery and desperation—to complete the job, relieved by the occasional slosh of rum. The maiden voyage of the *Happy Adventure* was made on July 24. "The morning devoted to frigging jobs, mostly in the rigging," Farley wrote in his diary, "but at 14:00 Jack and I looked at each other and mastering my trepidation, which was enormous, we decided to go for a sail."

They found the compass to be wildly inaccurate, but they eventually made a fine public display, running down the harbour under full sail as the crews of homebound skiffs waved and cheered enthusiastically. By late afternoon, the wind had come up and wisps of fog began to obscure Cape Ballard. Farley could not get the rigging of the schooner to work, and despite Jack's best efforts, the engine kept cutting out. After they finally docked at dusk, a sodden-hearted Farley wrote, "I was wet with sweat and had lost all confidence in myself and in the boat."

As the inexperienced skipper of the *Happy Adventure*, Farley knew they needed someone to help them if they were to sail around Cape Race at the southeastern tip of Newfoundland. A local man agreed to come aboard. For three or four hours, life was sheer bliss as they skimmed across the ocean. The boat began taking on water as they rounded Mistaken Cape into Trepassey Bay, but they made it to the town of Burin.

Jack had to return to his day job, saving Canadian publishing, so Farley waited in Spoon Cove, in the majestic Burin Inlet, for his friend Mike Donovan to join him. It was Mike's first passage on any sort of boat other than a troop ship, but true to character, he proved a worthy first mate.

Mike had been one of Farley's lieutenants and closest friends during the war, when they were in northwestern Europe together. Their intelligence team assembled examples of the best enemy armaments for shipment back to Canada, including a forty-five-foot v-2 rocket, which Farley theorized had been designed to carry a nuclear warhead. As soon as the rocket arrived by ship, it was spirited off to the Defence Research establishment at Valcartier, Quebec, where its components were disassembled, photographed, and blueprinted.

When the heavy fog finally lifted, they set sail for Saint-Pierre and Miquelon. The islands had a long history in the fishery, with a European presence there for more than 350 years. Although the archipelago was just eighteen miles from Newfoundland, across Fortune Bay, when visitors entered it, they entered France.

By the time the two friends arrived in the inner harbour at 8 in the evening on August 7, the *Happy Adventure* was taking on water at an alarming rate, and proving to be great inspiration for one of Farley's most famous books, *The Boat Who Wouldn't Float*. Farley decided to have the vessel hauled up on dry dock for badly needed repairs.

They discovered the stopwaters were gone, and an entire plank had rotted out. A new brass bolt was found for the stuffing box, and the ship was recaulked with oakum. The compass proved to be as reliable as the boat itself; when they were bearing sw, the needle pointed to NNE. Great for the accident of discovery, but no way to navigate the Northwest Atlantic.

Tuesday, August 9, threatened rain, so they decided not to repaint the boat. Local Martin Dutin came on board with a sketch of the Basque flag they would fly when the boat was relaunched. "Many visitors this morning," Farley observed. "Basques, Spaniards, Newfoundlanders and St. Pierreaise. All charming. All helpful. All interested, and all civilized. If my roots were not dehydrated and blunted with scar tissue I would attempt to dig them in here I think."

After lunch, the skies cleared and the *Happy Adventure* was invaded by hordes from the inaugural Canadian French summer school on the island, who made themselves at home and proceeded to get drunk. Children tracked paint here and there, and some of the adults behaved like "pseudo-Yanks," as Farley called them. The antics drew sorrowful headshakes from the men working on the boat.

The presence of this group of Canadians was a new phenomenon on Saint-Pierre. Some professors of French at the University of Toronto had vacationed on the French island in 1959 and had had a wonderful time. They were impressed that the old provincial ways and customs had been preserved. Life was quiet, and the inhabitants were genuinely friendly and hospitable. They also spoke excellent French. Clarence Parsons had spent fifteen years of his youth on Saint-Pierre, and after returning to Toronto from vacation, he and his fellow professors decided to found a French summer school on the island. That decision, made in a city Farley hated, would change his life forever.

The University of Toronto Division of University Extension announced an inaugural oral French course from August 1 to August 29, 1960. Thirty-five people came the first year, including spouses and children. Some families even brought their dogs. Students ranged in age from eighteen to sixty-four and included high-school teachers, university students, and even the president of a large publishing firm. They boarded with local host families and enlivened the social scene with their raucous parties each summer, which became legendary.

FROM THE FIRST TIME she noticed it in an atlas, a tiny little dot of an island off the coast of Newfoundland, Claire Wheeler had always wanted to go to Saint-Pierre, and now her dream had come true.

She was twenty-seven and loved travelling. Claire had been to England twice, once with her mother to meet family and once on her own for four months, after a breakup with a boyfriend, with side trips to Paris and Rome. She longed to get away from the dullness of life in upscale Rosedale in Toronto and from her job in an office at Simpsons-Sears, a downtown department store. The company would have paid to send her to Quebec City for French lessons, but she wanted to go to Saint-Pierre instead and paid for the course herself.

Claire had become friends with three or four other girls at the school. One of them mentioned that there was a famous Canadian author moored in the harbour, and they decided to take a look at his boat. They hung around for ten minutes, hoping to catch a glimpse of him.

At the time, the thirty-nine-year-old Farley was the author of seven books, with an eighth due out that fall. His first book, *People of the Deer*, had been published in 1952 and had made the January cover of the *Atlantic* magazine in the United States, no small accomplishment for a first-time author. Using a blend of storytelling and reporting, Farley had perfected the art of the nonfiction novel, a style made famous fourteen years later, when Truman Capote published *In Cold Blood* to international acclaim.

Margaret Atwood would later say in a foreword to Farley's 2002 book *High Latitudes* that his early support for northern peoples in *People of the Deer* was "a wakeup call, the spark that struck the tinder that ignited the fire from which many subsequent generations of writers and activists have lit their torches, often ignorant of where that spark came from in the first place."

Atwood compared the impact of Farley's book to *Silent Spring*, Rachel Carson's seminal work that was the fountainhead for the environmental movement. Farley's book would also have a profound effect on the life of a young student who would blaze an impressive trail of his own on Indigenous and environmental issues—David Suzuki, who has said that Farley "was my inspiration and my teacher."

Shortly after arriving in Saint-Pierre, Farley was invited to a celebration dinner at the Detcheverrys', a local couple who were welcoming their son George home after a six-year absence. He was now first mate on a twenty-two-thousand-ton tanker. Farley liked a good party, but he went back early to the shipyard that night to prepare for the relaunch of the *Happy Adventure*. Perhaps her planned new name would bring her better luck. "The shipyard crowd is magnificent, and I love them dearly," he wrote in his journal.

Wednesday, August 10, 1960, was a sunny day, and Farley was doing some shipwork and painting. The cabin was in shambles, and Farley noted that it "looked as if a mobile whorehouse had been in operation." The Canadian students had been there enjoying a feast of boiled crabs and other delights. Some of them returned later to help clean up the mess.

Farley was informed that there was a female reporter outside and that his friend Paulo Lescoublet wanted to impress her. The stranger was not a reporter. Farley noticed a girl quietly sketching the *Sandy Point*, a large Newfoundland schooner that had been hauled out onto the cradle next to the *Happy Adventure*. He dimly recognized her as a member of the French school. Generally, they were an unruly crowd, but he was "so heartened by her silence that I gruffly invited her to have a drink and see the boat when she had time."

Farley went back to work but was "oddly aware of the quiet one," who had begun to sketch his boat. The beautiful young woman with the dazzling eyes and golden hair was Claire Wheeler. After graduating from the Ontario College of Art, she had briefly worked doing layout for a publishing company and then landed the job at Simpsons-Sears. She had originally applied to do catalogue page layout, but there were no openings. The company was, however, looking for a copywriter. "You needed English and imagination. I liked it," Claire recalled in an interview. Finding "adjectives to extoll the merits of bicycles, wrist watches and children's clothes was easy."

Claire liked writing and had kept a diary from the age of twelve, after receiving one for Christmas. On January 1, 1946, she started her journal with a list of things she could not live without. She was crazy about silver bangles, suede loafers, boogie-woogie, and a Grade 7 classmate named Jack.

A couple of weeks after she turned thirteen, Claire wrote about how she brushed the snow from the boy's jacket after he and a friend had tumbled off their toboggan. "There will never be another Jack as long as I live," she wrote. "I am in heaven when I touch him."

By fourteen, Claire had learned to type. "My capacity for prose exploded with the newfound ease of the typewriter and those big, empty pages of bond paper." Although she would turn more to drawing at seventeen, she later realized that words were her preferred medium. "They had always mattered more to me than color, line or texture."

Her fellow copywriters were much more interesting than the people who did the advertising art. Most were literary people with aspirations to be real writers. Everything they wrote had to be translated into French, so Claire became acquainted with the French-speaking writers and noted that a French translation took up more space in an ad. Her employers appreciated her eye for detail and marked her as an up-and-comer.

Although she was shy, Claire was also talented and personable, and she was soon promoted to the store's planning department. The company would be opening stores in Quebec, but no one in the department had any French. Claire had high-school French and had gone to night school at the University of Toronto to study the language further. That's where she learned about the French summer school in Saint-Pierre. Which is how she ended up on a dock sketching Farley Mowat's boat.

A BLOND PYRENEES SHEEPDOG had been following Claire around the harbour as she sketched, and when the giant wet animal bounded toward her, she stepped up on some planks to avoid it and protect her sketches. Farley saw her predicament and came to her aid. They talked about her drawing, and he invited her to come to the launch of his boat. She accepted.

Claire had not read any of Farley's books, but she remembered being moved after reading an excerpt from his 1959 book *The Desperate People,* in *Maclean's* magazine. She also remembered seeing him on a CBC television show called *Fighting Words.*

She read the newspapers, but a radio on the desk in her bedroom was her main source of news. She had the radio on while doing her projects for art college, and often listened to classical music. Claire spent a lot of time sketching at the Royal Ontario Museum, a place Farley loved as well. He also shared her love of classical music. Despite his public image as the kilted bad boy of Canadian literature, he didn't really care for bagpipes.

It was getting close to launching time, and Farley's friend Theophile Detcheverry arrived, followed by "the advance guard of the bellowing Canadians" from the French school. Farley invited Claire to stay on board for the launch while the rest of the students went ashore.

The bull engine refused to start once they were in the water, and they drifted for half an hour while Farley cursed and struggled. When they made it back to their mooring near the custom house, the compass adjuster was waiting to "swing the compass"—or check that north was really north. The boat had a huge compass the size of a dishpan that Farley had bought at a marine auction, the sort of gear you might find on a Great Lakes freighter. Farley returned to his mooring with an adjusted compass, a dry boat, and a pretty woman, all of which delighted him. Eros was fluttering closer.

Claire's first impression of Farley was that he was friendly and nice, though he looked decidedly scruffy with his unruly hair and paint splotches on his clothes. She also remembers that she was both intrigued by Farley and attracted to him. He was funny and interesting, though he smelled awful because he worked hard on the boat and hadn't had a bath in ages. His idea of cleaning up was going for a swim in the ocean, using saltwater soap he had bought at the same auction where he acquired his compass. Farley had a large personality. "He wasn't a person you could ignore," Claire recalled. "I don't know what I was doing. When you really feel an attraction to another person you are not thinking logically."

Farley had mesmerizing blue eyes. He was amusing, articulate, and brave—or foolhardy—to be sailing in this small boat. He was unlike anyone Claire had ever met. She had dated men who talked down to her, convinced that they were smarter than she was. Farley was obviously intelligent but did not flaunt it. Claire noted that he also had great emotional intelligence. She knew nothing about Farley's private life when they met, but she understood from the beginning that she was playing with fire. By the end of her time on Saint-Pierre, she knew he was married.

Farley, Claire, and Mike joined Martin Dutin at his home for dinner that night. Farley wrote in his diary: "A magnificent evening, with good food, good liquor, good people and much conviviality." He returned to his boat to find the Canadian students having an informal party on board without permission and he chased them away.

Farley was up at dawn the next morning to prepare for the official blessing by a Dominican priest, who showed up with a terrible cold and a gallon of holy water. Theo had painted the new name on the bow: *Itchatchozale Alai*, a Basque name that was all but unpronounceable. Farley promptly shortened it to "*Itchy.*"

After a lunch of anchovies, tuna, cognac, and rum, Farley decided to take a nap. Mike shook him awake and whispered that a Miss Wheeler had arrived for the launch ceremony. "Contrary to custom, and to my not inconsiderable surprise I roused hurriedly, brushed my hair, combed my beard, and smiled," Farley wrote in his journal.

The celebration that evening included much Izarra, a Basque drink. Farley recorded what happened afterwards in his journal: "Feeling very warm and in love with all the world, suggested that we make a passage to Miquelon over the weekend, and no trouble signing on a crew. Miss Wheeler appeared to be close at hand during all of this days revels, and I find this pleasant. I am a fool."

When a friend brought Farley a fine, big codfish as a gift, Farley decided to invite Claire aboard *Itchy* for a Newfoundland dinner. He walked to her rooming house, where he was "transfixed and pierced by the most landladyish landlady" and told sternly to sit in the parlour.

There was much scurrying upstairs. The high-pitched whispers from above made Farley break into a cold sweat and wonder what he was doing there. "I had only need of a batch of posies clutched in my hot little paw to complete an idyllic picture," he noted. But when he saw Claire, radiant and graceful, he didn't care if he was entering his second childhood.

The two of them went shopping for kitchen utensils for the boat. Dinner on board was a success. He recorded that "my general malaise seems to have lifted noticeably since our arrival here and I am settling contentedly into this feckless, beachcomber sort of life. I feel slightly like a deserter to my ship, for she grows dirty and unkempt, as all ships do who lie in harbor. I feel that we should gird our loins and sail again, and maybe we will in a day or two. Maybe."

At 1 o'clock on August 13, the guests arrived for the planned sail to Miquelon, full of gaiety, their picnic hampers laden with food and wine. Farley worried about appearing incompetent in front of "the quiet one" and was unmanned by this discovery. "It has been so long since I have given <u>that</u> kind of damn," he wrote. They had dinner that night in a local restaurant. Farley and Claire were appointed Maman and Papa for the evening. People were noticing.

The guests chose to stay on shore for the night, but Farley returned to the boat. "It was a miraculous night, full of strange happenstances, and tea parties in the grey light before the dawn." At dawn, Farley swam in the white sea with some porpoises, which at first he had thought might be sharks.

"Shivering slightly, and warming myself with brandy, I sat on the end of the dock and waited for morning to bring life to Miquelon." It had been only a week since he and Mike arrived on Saint-Pierre. "I am humbled and not a little bit afraid. Renewals and rebirths are painful things."

The sound of bells pealing from the old church disturbed his thoughts. The dogs howled in unison, and Farley went in search of his crew. They had arranged to depart at noon. "A day of loveliness, with a slightly hazed sky and a gentle breeze." They left the dock under sail, "as all ships should leave." Farley wrote a poem on Miquelon for Claire, to commemorate the voyage:

"For Wisdom's Sake"
You are most wise to spurn love's latest avatar,
Since woman's wisdom in you has discerned afar
The foredoomed setting of one unborn star.
Thus, being wise, you'll rest in wisdom. Sans regret.
Sans knowledge . . . of the stars which never set.

When *Itchy* returned to Saint-Pierre, Theo and Mme Detcheverry were on the dock to greet the boat. Their son George was on board, and she was delighted to see that he was safe. All night, she had dreamed of corpses. She was so overjoyed at their return that she invited everyone to supper.

"Much later," Farley recorded, "Claire and I reconnoitered at the Zazpiak Bat,* and the Old Gods smiled, and came to their decision." Monday, August 15, was the Feast of the Assumption, and the day that Farley and Claire became lovers, five days after their fateful meeting. For Farley "it meant an end and a beginning, and that's enough to say."

In celebration, they dressed the rigging of the boat with multi-coloured signal flags. The Basque flag flew above the jack. None of the other vessels followed their example. So there *Itchy* bravely lay, "small, green, flamboyant, and with her own secrets: and if no one else knew why she was dressed so gaily (or if they thought it was for the Assumption), that did not matter," Farley wrote.

Farley joined Claire to watch the parade from the square, a procession of children in white, "a conglomeration of shambling clericals,

* A Basque sports club

followed by a milling horde of soberly dressed adults, followed by a jackal-fringe of tourists." Claire and Farley looked at each other solemnly and went into the Café l'Escale for a drink.

Later, Farley took a real bath at his friend Martin's house. But there were apparently no secrets in Saint-Pierre. Word of the couple's connection was getting around. There was an elaborate dinner party at Mme Dutin's, but Farley recalled nothing of it, "My eyes were lost in eyes, and my tongue clove to the roof of my mouth."

Mike, the soul of consideration, elected to sleep on shore that night. The night was calm and the air sweet. It was a quiet scene, "with no sounds save the lapping of waters and the occasional explosive bark of a champagne cork bouncing against the cabin roof." Although Claire was shy in public, in private she felt free to express her gaiety and sense of fun, which Farley loved.

The plan had been for *Itchy* to sail the twenty-six miles to Fortune, Newfoundland, on August 16, but Farley decided to stay. His mornings were long and dreary because the French school had classes all morning. By the time Claire joined him, "the sun was high and warm." They walked through the cemetery. "Then we climbed the old mountains behind the town, deep in a tangle of scrub that smelled richly of Arctic flowers, dwarf birch and Labrador tea."

On the crest, they reached a sunny hollow that offered a striking view of the island looking out to sea. With heavy hearts, the lovers descended slowly through the back of the town, knowing they would soon be parted. Claire went to her boarding house. Farley dropped in to l'Escale. There, it was noted by others that he had small blue lupins threaded in his beard.

Farley still did not want to sail. He found himself in one of those rare sweet spots he refused to leave. "Life settled into a delight of little things. Dawn on the quay after a walk through a sleeping town... Coffee with Ella Giradin in Cafe L'Escale. The smell of sewage and salt cod... of many things of consequence, and not of any. But most of all, the dark hours with the little vessel moving gently under us." To ward off inquiries, Farley printed a sign saying that *Itchy* would not sail that day and nailed it to the mast.

After lunch on August 17, the couple hired one of the island's five hundred cars to take them swimming at the beach at Savoyard. They ignored the enclosed bathing area and chose instead a more private stretch of rock and shingle. "Here we lay in much wind and sun, drank champagne from little bottles, instead of Coca Cola, and even swam—a little."

The details melted and ran together in Farley's slow dream of his new love, leaving him melancholy: "There is one sad thing about this life. The waiting which I do each morning for the appearance of a quiet one in the companionway."

August 18 was St. Claire's Day, and Claire the student was delayed. Farley spent the afternoon aboard *Itchy*, moping in the cabin. Friends arrived to find out why he had vanished for three nights. "Then suddenly she came and all was well."

Only temporarily. On Friday, August 19, Mike departed for Fortune on board the ferry *Spencer II* for a tour of library duty in his car. Farley was to meet him there the following Monday. "Hellish thought," he noted.

ALTHOUGH HIS HEAD was in the clouds, Farley had practical matters to attend to. He decided to keep *Itchy* in Saint-Pierre for the winter. He also planned to install a new diesel engine and enlarge the bunks. Maybe he would even install a biffy. But now he began the task of preparing his little ship to sleep for the winter, packing gear and stripping down the gay flags.

As their time together guttered down like a dying fire, Farley and Claire grew less careful about concealing their secret. They held hands through a French comedy put on by the Lions Club and a farce staged by the French school. "The enemy," as Farley named those who did not approve of their relationship, glared daggers, "and the quiet one held her head high and walked in dignity and beauty, and I was desperately proud of her."

A friend had to lend Farley twenty dollars so he could buy a ticket on the *Spencer II* and then make the drive back to Ontario. Theo and Martin invited Farley and Claire for a farewell sail to the Grand Barachois, a lagoon south of Miquelon Island, on board the *Oregon*, a boat that had "the lift and sweep of a Viking longboat," according to Farley. They saw the capelin fishers packing up for the season. Things were ending, but Farley revelled in every fleeting delight.

"The Barachois was at its most magical this morning. The mist was there, but not tangible, and the sun stood clear above our heads. There was no distance, and things wavered and retreated, swimming slowly into sight again so that perspective and distance both became illusionary."

No one bothered the seals in the lagoon. But they roused wild ghost horses near the shore who went "streaming through the shallows to the dunes beyond." Despite losing the propeller and being hauled back to Saint-Pierre by another boat in advance of a hurricane, they ended the day listening to classical music after a seven-course dinner at Theo's house. Farley wrote in his journal, "So ended as good a day as any I have known in many a long year."

The next day, August 21, 1960, was perhaps the worst. Farley had to board the *Spencer II* for the trip to Newfoundland. Claire was also leaving the island. They had had twelve magical days together before having to return to the world as it had been before—Claire to her job at Simpsons-Sears in Toronto and Farley to his wife and sons and a troubled marriage in Palgrave. It was like walking the plank.

They decided to spend their last evening pub-crawling, but the joy went out of it when they discovered mobs of "Yankee" soldiers everywhere, making insulting remarks about the "natives." A U.S. naval ship had also come into port to shelter from the hurricane.

"And so to a last night aboard the little ship. She was stripped bare, but still friendly to those who loved her and still able to give comfort to those in need thereof," Farley wrote.

The next morning, Farley dragged his gear to the ferry like a condemned man. Before they parted, he gave Claire a poem. Then he glumly waited, listening for the sound of her Dakota taking off from Saint-Pierre's unpaved runway. Silence.

Presently, a car arrived at the dock, and the quiet one descended like a spectre in the mist. Claire's plane had been grounded by fog. A blessed, if brief, respite from separation. After a last drink—on the house at their favourite café, l'Escale—Farley's boat to Fortune was ready to shove off. "The lines were let fly, and we drew out into the stream and the fog closed in on a small figure waving from the quay... and then nothing much except the surf beating over the green graves of L'Enfant Perdu."

There may be sadder sights than a ship pulling out of harbour with someone you love, but not many. Claire's emptiness while watching Farley disappear into the fog, not knowing if she would ever see him again, not really knowing if he loved her, was something she had never experienced before. Her only solace was his promise that he would call her—that, and the poem he had pressed into her hand at the very last:

> Your straight eyes looked on me, unguarded,
>   and they said:
> "Awake, my love." And I, who had been too
>   long dead,
> Put by the cerements of my self-sought grave,
> Held out my arms—and took the girl you gave.

Farley spent most of the crossing to Newfoundland sitting in the bow of the ferry, drinking Napoleon brandy and singing softly to himself. He watched a pod of pilot whales surging through the grey waves and thought of Claire. He wrote her a letter he dated "One Day Without You." It read, "And the night began, and I knew for the first time the nature of loneliness, the essential nature of it, and I wept for you in my foolishness... I wish you were here, and do not know how I shall endure the long hours and the long miles ahead."

Stocked with three bottles of rum, three tins of Basque sardines, and a sleeping bag, Farley Mowat began the long drive to Toronto, where he planned to tell Jack McClelland what had happened. While still in Newfoundland, he picked up a hitchhiker headed to Toronto with thirteen cents in his pocket. Farley put his companion in a motel when they stopped for the night, while he slept in the car.

Driving west just outside Grand Falls on his way to Port aux Basques, Farley saw a rainbow that seemed to cover half the world. "Thank god I am a romantic," he wrote. "I could do nothing but wonder and be thankful, for this was a sign, surely."

2 | Stolen Evenings

IT WAS PAST TIME to be getting home, but Farley couldn't resist one final chance to see the Quiet One. So, on his way back from the East Coast, he drove to Toronto rather than Palgrave, putting off his return for as long as he could.

True to his word on Saint-Pierre, he called Claire at her office. She was "astonished and bewildered." Years later, when asked what was the most surprising thing Farley had ever done, Claire replied, "He called me at Simpsons-Sears."

Thanks to Farley's publisher, the couple had a private trysting spot. Jack McClelland's parents were vacationing, and he gave Farley the keys to their Toronto home. Farley stayed in the city for three days. Jack could see how happy he was and enabled the affair however he could. Inevitably, the mooring lines of Farley's previous life drew him back to Palgrave, his wife, Frances, his young boys, the chickens, and the dog, Kippy. But Claire and memories of Saint-Pierre held him like a spell. There was no honest way to act as if nothing had changed. And so began the period of stolen evenings, love letters, and lies.

In late September 1960, Claire was at her parents' cottage in Muskoka, sunbathing and drying her hair in the sun. As she wrote to Farley, it was good to see her parents again. "They are well and happy and still talk remotely of the day I will 'marry and settle down'. And I wonder at their reaction were I to evade both these conventions."

Muskoka was the perfect place for the long thoughts of a lonely lover with a secret. To Claire, it was the best time of the year, when the cottagers abandoned their motorboats to watch football and left the untroubled lake mirroring the sky. A quivering silence, ready to amplify any sound—voices over the water, a fish jumping—fell over the beauty of it all. It had rained the night before, and Claire had slept upstairs directly under the roof. She listened to the raindrops while reading *People of the Deer*. Then she drifted into a glorious sleep, thinking of *Itchy* and of Farley, writing to him that the day "is as nearly perfect a day as possible for me without you."

That first letter from Claire brought Farley to tears and laughter. He read it in a small trailer he had christened *Itchatchozale Alai II*, which was "anchored" in the back forty of a neighbour's farm, Twin Elms, not far from Farley's home. His writing trailer was actually more spacious than its namesake, and there was no doubt about how Farley planned to use it.

"There is peace here, for love and for gentleness and, to defend it, I have placed fierce signs all along the approach routes, and am contemplating the use of bear-traps and trip-guns," he hyperbolized. "Oh, my loved one, I wish—I wish . . . but then there is tomorrow, and an uncounted number of tomorrows." How much did he love her? "Let the stars speak of it, for I cannot. Till Friday. F."

Farley sent Claire a detailed map of how to find *Itchy II*, moored in an imaginary place he christened "Cognac Cove." The map marked a culvert and a narrow bridge before the turnoff to the little track that led to the field. "Shoal waters" were marked so she could avoid them, including "Mowat Morgue," Farley's sardonic name for his family home.

In late September, Farley told Claire that he had begun work on a war book. The idea had come to him after he found some old war files from 1946 in a forgotten trunk. Clipped to them was a note saying, "Holy Jesus, Squib, you'd better burn these things!"

Looking at the files in 1960, Farley told Claire that he could not believe how he had escaped a court-martial, syphilis, or an untimely death. "I enclose the author's disclaimer which will precede the libelous, pornographic, and eminently illegal tale."

In the satirical disclaimer for the book, Farley asked that librarians refrain from demanding he tell them under which section of the Dewey Decimal System the book should be classified.

Although Farley loved talking to her, calling Claire on the telephone was a problem. "All the local phones leak," he said. He had to go all the way to Bolton, seven miles away, to find one that didn't. "And, bleakly, I cannot prophesy my next trip youward. Wednesday I am trapped. Thursday will be hell. The weekend looks black and useless. And without you I am useless as the proverbial tits on a mythical bull. I lack all desire to do anything, and so just sit and glum. I half-envy you your job—at least it fills in the hours." He ended the letter, "I love you deeply, dearly and most distractedly."

They were already dreaming of next summer and their planned return to Saint-Pierre. "Damn your terrible and beautiful eyes," Farley wrote, "this is intolerable! And I'm an intolerant little fellow. And very much in love."

Farley had been having trouble with his war book. When he dropped his professional guard as a writer, Claire kept creeping into the narrative, a distraction that threatened to turn what was supposed to be a tale of war into a love story, hardly what his publisher was expecting. "Jack will go bankrupt," Farley joked. Although he eventually managed thirty thousand words on the novel, it would be many years before Farley could bring himself to write about his war years in *And No Birds Sang*.

Now the author of eight books, Farley was inching away from being well-known toward being outright famous. In its November 7, 1960, edition, *Time* magazine favourably reviewed his new book, *Ordeal by Ice*. He joked to Claire that he had been referred to in the *Caledon East Illustrated Canadian News Magazine* as one of Canada's "foremost gentlemen." "Gawd! What will they call me next?"

Fame dragged a scorpion's tail behind it. With the acclaim came public responsibilities that made it harder to see Claire. There was always something he had to do, someone he had to meet. The director of the Grenfell Mission of Labrador was flying in from New York to meet Farley, or he had to go to Toronto for a publicity affair to celebrate playwright Leonard Peterson's new play, *The Great Hunger*. Then there was a TV panel debate between Farley and an Ottawa bureaucrat on the plight of the Inuit.

Farley was so desperate to see Claire that he invited her to attend that event, though he warned her that the panel would be dull. He then worried that if she did attend, he would have the unbearable urge to leap over the footlights to join her in the audience. And if there was no time with her, he predicted dire consequences. "I shall become a beast, savage and of murderous inclinations."

WITH ECSTATIC INTERLUDES, the "beast" would have to control himself until spring. In the meantime, they agreed to keep their affair secret from Frances and from Claire's parents. That meant a dual charade— Claire pretending at home that she didn't know Farley, and Farley going through the motions of being married back in Palgrave. It was taxing to the maximum Claire's distaste for lies and Farley's innate impulsiveness. "This whole damned existence is becoming most unsatisfactory. I want you," he wrote Claire. "Not in an isolated hour, but all the bloody time. Right now, and every now. Hell!"

It was getting harder and harder for Farley to come up with plausible excuses for travelling to Toronto to steal a few precious hours with his lover. It was easier to tell Frances that he was at the trailer working on his new book, *Owls in the Family.* He hated to ask Claire to come to him there, but she was glad to make the thirty-nine-mile trip, though she did not go there often. "A letter from you and I am at peace with the world," she wrote. "I'm filled with longing—and love for you."

Farley soaked up her words but began to feel the first wisps of despair about their situation. On October 16, 1960, he wrote, "This is a footling life, and lousy. All that holds me to it is you. I could no more leave you now than I could outcry the Gods. Loving you is all there is."

Two days later, he described how his passion for her was affecting his work: "How the devil can I render deathless literature and you not by? How the devil, indeed, can I do anything save mope. But, on the other hand, with you beside me how the devil can I do anything but make love to you? Either way, the reading public will have to be content with Hemingway."

Making life even more difficult, Palgrave was worse than he remembered it. The fake life with an increasingly depressed Frances, the chaos of the children, demands from his public and publisher, and the aching desire to be with Claire plunged him into a desperate entropy.

"My days here are aeons in a vacuum. Only in writing is there surcease, and the writing isn't much good either for when it becomes an escape it becomes shoddy and uncertain. I am here, but not here. Poised constantly for flight, teetering on a word, an act. And holding myself shut so that not even Sandy can be allowed entree. I am in Palgrave, but not of it—not 'of' anything."

It was the ancient agony of lovers kept apart. Claire made everything possible, yet impossible. In the moments when they were together, his sexual desires eclipsed everything else. He wrote that the "need is a tidal wave that overwhelms all else and quick snuffs out the best that ought to be between us; the gentleness, the simmering of love. There is surcease in the body's rapture, no solution to the elder need— the long, slow consumption of me in you, and you in me."

Farley was so anxious to draw Claire more deeply into his life that he began introducing her to his circle of friends, despite the couple's agreement to remain in the shadows until they could reunite on Saint-Pierre. Claire particularly liked journalist and activist June Callwood and her husband, Trent Frayne. But with each new acquaintance the risks multiplied. It was now only a matter of time before word of what was really going on between them got back to Palgrave and Rosedale.

In part, it already had.

With Claire's parents away at their cottage, Claire and Farley shared Chinese food and an afternoon dalliance in her Rosedale home. Someone unexpectedly turned up to use the workshop at the back of the house. Their dishes were still on the table, and they were upstairs in bed. "Oh my god, it's my brother," Claire gasped as she looked out the bedroom window.

Farley asked what his name was, wrapped a white towel around himself, and rushed downstairs to the front door. Offering his hand, he spoke plainly: "Fred, I'm Farley Mowat. And I love your sister." Claire's astonished brother didn't have the faintest idea who he was shaking hands with. That day, he told his wife about "this funny little guy with a beard and a bath towel" who greeted him at his parents' house. But she was the only person Fred told.

It was the second time a trip to Claire's home in Rosedale nearly outed the lovers. The first time, the Wheelers were having a lazy Sunday morning reading the weekend newspapers when Claire's mother remarked, "Here is an article about that Eskimo play by that fellow Farley Mowat—you know, Claire—the one who was in St. Pierre this summer." Before Claire could think of something to say, her nana added brightly that she knew him too. He had been there for tea!

"My heart faltered," Claire wrote to Farley. "How did she know? My mother looked curious and puzzled. 'Wasn't that the fellow's name, Claire?' Nana persisted. "'You remember, the one who was doing some writing?'"

"'Oh no, Nana,' I said with great assurance. 'That was Bill Moffat, don't you remember? He was a biologist.'" Claire's mother glanced at Nana piteously, thinking she was becoming confused. Claire had to leave the room. Nana, of course, was right.

With the separation proving unbearable for both of them, Farley began to doubt the wisdom of the motto they had adopted after meeting on Saint-Pierre. "No plans . . . no promises," he mocked. "*There* is a floating island of refuge for you, if you like. Held up by bright balloons on thin, thin, strings. Thin-skinned balloons. Fragile and tender in an untended air. How long can we two stand the gaff?" It would be infinitely simpler, he told her, if they could throw caution and convention to the wind the way other lovers did. "Take our fun where we can get it. Wriggle about under a pall of deceit and never feel the acid in it eating us away."

Time was not on their side, and they had few options. Divorce was difficult, and even if Frances was agreeable, it meant instant scandal for all of them. Farley could make a soft departure from Palgrave and find a place somewhere else. But without Claire, it would be a pit, not a sanctuary. The alternative was to remain in the semi-shadows and hold their breath until spring. When he put it all down in writing, Farley was astonished at himself. "Jesus! So much self-pity in so small a space. Sometimes I nauseate myself. You too, maybe." They needed more talk between them, much more talk. "Battle planning. It's time to dare the fates and plan, and promise too."

Deep down, they both knew the danger they faced. Either they exerted mastery over their situation or they would be washed away in a torrent of doubt and conventional imperatives. They had to have the courage to love all the way or risk the big goodbye.

So Farley told "Miss Valkyrie of 1960" to put her golden helmet back on and unship her spear. "And why fore all this? because, you lovely wench, because I love you. *That's* why. There are dragons to slay. Will you ride sidesaddle, or up behind me on the old warhorse? Hmmmm. I bite your ear."

On a more practical matter, Farley gave Claire some advice about keeping what was increasingly becoming their open secret. Not only were others listening in on their calls, but people at the post office could read their letters if they wanted to. "For Gods sake put some spit on your envelopes!" he advised her. "The last two have opened like lily petals before I could even lay a hand on them. You want to embarrass my postmistress?"

Just before Halloween 1960, Claire wrote to Farley about the very different demons besetting her because of their forced separation. There was no spouse she had to deceive, no children to look after, and no publisher or public to satisfy. But walled up behind her secret love for Farley, Claire had to put on an act for her parents and friends, at the same time that her job at Simpsons-Sears was growing increasingly empty: "My darling Farley, Just how we shall survive until Spring I don't know. A dark grey lassitude creeps over me this evening but I do not intend to pass it on to you."

It had been another week of "bureucratics" at the office, with nothing to justify it at week's end but a small packet of money. "I don't know if it is the futility of it all that I find discouraging or the loneliness. Hard to believe that a handful of souls can spend so many hours each day together with scarcely an honest exchange among them."

Life at the office was a little like a cocktail party, full of chatter rather than conversation, and of superficiality that bordered on the infernal. Claire got through the tedious days at Simpsons-Sears by rereading Farley's love letters. Observant fellow workers might have noticed that she regularly took a photograph out of her handbag and looked at it furtively. A photograph of a bearded man.

Like Farley, Claire did her best to buoy her lover's spirits, knowing that he depended on her every letter, as she did his. So she posed for him in words, describing what she was doing and what she was thinking. It was Friday night, she told him. Her cat, Georgette, was sitting on her lap purring, and Glenn Gould was playing the *Goldberg Variations* for the fifth time on the phonograph.

"I am sitting here telling myself that I am indeed fortunate to have a good job and a good home and a tidy little life and to stop complaining about it. But think, suppose I had not gone to St. Pierre, suppose I had never met you . . . No, this is as pre-destined as your turning the corner on Avenue Road at the precise moment of my arrival there. We shall make our escape together, what do you say? The weekend would be long and Monday would be Hallowe'en."

As it turned out, they were able to spend a few hours together the day before the ghosts and goblins hit the doorsteps with their loot bags. It was rapturous but temporary.

"Wasn't it wonderful though Farley? If it were only sufficient. If I could only be content with Sunday outings; or Monday outings or Friday nights, but damn it I want <u>you</u> and no half measures. This is a statement of pagan selfishness and causes me to reflect on the old Christian proverb 'Be grateful for whatya' got'. I shall try not to be," she said.

IN EARLY NOVEMBER Claire's job took her to Kingston, Ontario, where she was tasked with sprucing up the drab displays in the Simpsons-Sears store there. She joked to Farley that her car, which she now called "Mowat Minor," had the aroma of an old wine cellar. When all else failed, the couple used it as a mobile love nest. "Must have agreed with her though, for she assures me, she can be used as a country inn any old Sunday afternoon," Claire wrote.

Claire spent hours pacing the floors of Simpsons-Sears Kingston, trying to refurbish its moth-eaten, depressing decorations. The day started at 6 a.m. and ended with a solitary supper in the dining room of the Princess Hotel, where Claire was the only woman in a roomful of travelling salesmen. She read Farley's beautiful letters while she waited for her veal cutlet. They were "mine and mine alone, and I can feel sorry for everyone else in the world, for who has such a love as mine?" she wrote. "Oh I wish you were here! Miles from home and a cosy double bed and you in Palgrave."

She thought of calling Farley, then rejected the impulse. But she couldn't help her curiosity about the woman she was having nightmares about, the person who was keeping them apart.

"I wonder if F [Frances] would be as upset to hear you speaking with me as I am to hear you speaking with her? . . . So I shall pine no more, but think on our next meeting. And on the east, and all the others. I love you forever. I kiss your funny nose, C."

On November 8, Farley wrote Claire a letter from Palgrave, which he now referred to as "Corpsetown." He told her that a letter had arrived from Victor-Coventry Motor Works, confirming they would be delighted to deliver a new diesel engine to Saint-Pierre for the boat. Unfortunately, Farley explained, he could not shove the new engine aft to make room for a biffy. So he suggested they get Claire a potty of her own. Pink enamel.

And how would he pay for *Itchy*'s new bull engine? "I may have to sell my services at stud to pay the bill. How would I word the ad? Bearded Bull Begs Business? Let Billy Bash your Beautiful? Cut rates during the winter months!"

Claire returned to Toronto from Kingston on a Thursday, and she and Farley spent Friday evening together. Farley wrote to praise what he called Claire's "sorcery" and to sound a kind of warning.

"In Boston, a few centuries past, they would have hung you for a witch." Both of them had to be on guard, for he worried that "the ugly and brutal entity that lies insensate in the air in these parts, can be as deadly as any puritan mob intent upon fixing a living symbol on a gallows. You are aware of this all the time. I am not, but must remind myself, or be reminded."

As depressed as he was, Farley declared that he planned to hibernate and bury himself in work until the spring, promising a little ominously "to clean no more Lugers." He asked, "Can you conceive of the wonder which is you? And which was wrapped around me like a benison on Friday night? Thank God for it; thank God for you. Sleep well, my love. I have never been so much a part of you as I am now."

But his official life, including his marriage, kept pulling him back, sinking him more deeply into frustration and despair. Later in November, for publicity purposes, Farley and Frances had to drive to Buffalo, New York, where he appeared on a popular U.S. TV show called *Meet the Millers*. They would be baking a layer cake. Stars like Elizabeth Taylor and Tony Bennett had also appeared as guests, but Farley was appalled. He was terribly worried about what was becoming of him in his counterfeit life:

"The fact that this is me, doing this, is a fearful revelation of how totally careless I have become of me. I would not surprise myself overly much to wake some morning and discover that I had joined Rotary International." He felt degraded and promised Claire he would not think of her on the day of the show because "it would degrade you to involve you in my own degradation." But he would think of her tonight, "God how I shall think of you!"

Claire tried to write letters to Farley from work but found it increasingly difficult. And it wasn't just that her colleagues seemed to like reading over her shoulder; the atmosphere of the place conflicted with her love for Farley and the desire to express it. "So there it lies smoldering like a great volcano, until we are together."

As much as she mythologized their love, Claire voiced a practical concern that neither one of them could ignore. One of the classic arguments used by some wives to hang on to unhappy husbands is the negative effect a divorce would have on the children. Claire believed that for Farley to stay in Palgrave for the sake of his sons would be a tragic mistake:

"I feel that you, even more than I, cannot stay in your present situation forever. This viewpoint is doubtless selfish and biased. But my love for you is selfish. How can it be otherwise? Perhaps I could stay here, the bright young Miss Wheeler; until it will be the experienced, hard-bitten Miss Wheeler. There is not too much loss in this to anyone. But you my darling deserve and must have, at the very least, love. You'll never know how much I want to give it to you either. Sometimes I feel that the obstacles in our path are not as immense as we choose to imagine. Surely the biggest setback is, for me at any rate, the deliberate pain I might cause someone else. True, it would not be as big a pain as that which would befall me were I denied you entirely."

And she gave another reason why it would be unwise to sacrifice so much for the boys: "Because of course they do not appreciate it. More selfish reasoning, but with logic."

After stealing another steamy evening with Farley, Claire spent the next day cleaning her car, "placating" her mother by attending church with her, and sewing with Nana. That took care of her "semi-obligations" to her family, but Farley remained her obsessive preoccupation.

"Soon I will be in my bath, and the last little trace of you will be gone. Didn't wash deliberately last night and so it was that you stayed the entire night with me. Come to think of it, you must have been with me in church too! That's a disarming thought. In truth you are with me all the time. Do you remember, Farley, when you said to me 'no plans... no promises' and I nodded sleepily and said 'yes darling, no plans... no promises'. A curious thought is it not? One which I shall remember and forget at the same time."

By the end of November 1960, despite Claire's best efforts to give him supportive advice, Farley was bending under the enormous pressure of his divided existence. He was working on a children's book, *Owls in the Family*, and hoped to have half of it completed before he had to leave for Montreal for publicity duties. He was trying out chapters on Sandy, and as he told Claire, his son was a harsh taskmaster. "My audience is impatient. If I don't have a new chapter for Sandy each evening, he bitches something fierce."

In addition to an often brutal writing schedule, there were the domestic duties, which had recently multiplied. Frances was now losing the ability to function. Farley told Claire that his wife had taken to bed after downing most of a bottle of Scotch, the house was a pigsty, and he had to pick up Sandy from school and then "get supper for the brats"—always a term of endearment in Farley-speak.

Then Rose Kastner, a friend of Farley's who knew about Claire, called about a gala party she was organizing. Luminaries would be coming, including fellow authors Mordecai Richler and Pierre Berton. Farley told Rose that he had the flu, but his wife, Frances, wanted to come if she felt well enough. As for himself, his ailment was deeper than the flu. "Too damned depressed to contemplate a party of any sort," he wrote Claire.

Rose had been about to call Claire herself to invite her to the party and was somewhat shaken by Farley's announcement that Frances might attend. Farley explained himself to Claire. "I won't go unless you are there. Doubt if Fran will go now, but can't be sure. Why don't you go along anyway? Ought to be interesting. If Fran and I come, ought to be hell! If I come alone, will be sweet agony, but better than not seeing you at all." They were desperate words from a conflicted man, as his closing lines to Claire made clear. "I need direction. Hell, mainly, desperately, I need you. My God, but I love thee!"

Farley saw Claire again as November slid into December—another stolen evening in Toronto that offered fleeting ecstasy, followed by epic loneliness, which left him walking the city's empty streets and lying awake in bed staring at the ceiling. Rather than soothing him, their tryst reminded him of their miserable situation. Shakespeare had it right in Farley's case; increase of appetite for Claire grew by what it fed on.

"Goddamn it all. I'm developing a positive hatred of the hours after midnight. There are times when I would rather not see you at all, than have to envisage the agony of those too-early partings. When, in heaven's name, will there be a time for tenderness and the quiet touch? I am becoming honestly frightened for our love, in the face of these inevitable strains. Love will not suffer, but we will! All we have time for is each other's bodies, and without the rest of it, even the touch of bodies can grow stale in habit. And, oh my darling, though it may not sound much like it, I am aware that these strains are as great on you (and maybe greater) than on me. But then you are a brave spirit, and you keep quiet about such things. Without you, I, on the contrary, grow cowardly and fearful."

Claire might have been better at hiding it, but she, too, keenly felt the emptiness of their long days apart and uncertain future. She soldiered through boring days at the office, played the dutiful daughter at home, went to the cottage in summer, and did some weekend skiing in the winter. But her heart wasn't in it. Her heart was with Farley.

"Just how is it that I continue to love you this way? Pining like a demented school-girl? Or more curious—how do you continue to love this demented school-girl? Only the Gods must know. My waking and sleeping thoughts are filled with you. There is no escape. Even the diversion of reading are books written by you. Damn it—why couldn't you have been a lawyer? Or a plumber? I love you so much and your beard is tickling me now. Very soon now..."

In late November 1960, they had a glorious weekend together. She realized now that the Monday-morning dark cloud that moved in after times of great joy was the price of their temporary joy. She pondered the emptiness of her life without Farley: "Perhaps I dwell on this a little too much Farley, but you cannot know what you have done, and are doing, for me. A malady of mine, known as 'Creeping Hopelessness' is now clearing up very nicely thank-you, accompanied by a bout of good spirits. Despite our forbidding future, I find I am able to put my faith in Miracle cures."

That faith would be put to the test in December, when Farley sent Claire a six-page letter with shocking news. Frances had known about their love affair within a week of their return from Saint-Pierre and had remained silent about it for months. They had played the game of secret love. Now it was time for the game of public consequences.

3 | A Coward Loves You

HEART'S WINTER FOR FARLEY AND CLAIRE began auspiciously enough. On a Monday night in early December, just before going to bed, Claire was overwhelmed by the need to write to Farley. "My God, what would my life be without you? You are my only solace, my true love, my everything."

She also thanked Farley for his "woodsy Noel card. I love it and it makes me weep a little for I cannot imagine anything more idyllic than to live in such a place with you. Any place is idyllic with you my darling. It's just that it all looks so perfect ... so complete. I console myself that this is probably an illusion. Probably? No! Certainly it is an illusion."

Claire sprinkled in some good news. Now that ski season had arrived, "weekends away from Toronto are not so questionable," a reference to her ever-vigilant parents' inquisitiveness about their daughter's outings and company.

Farley replied that it would be fun to do a book of poems for children with silly animal verses, illustrated by Claire. "More fun than owls." Work was on his mind, and public obligations. That weekend, he had to do some publicity in Montreal. He wasn't looking forward to it. "I shall take benzedrine and chew mesquite buttons all day long." By nightfall, he told her, he would be as sharp as a tack. "That bemused looking imitation pillar that you will see, supporting the roof of Montreal's central station, will (if it has a beard) be me."

Claire wrote from work that she had attended a reunion with friends from the Ontario College of Art. She was impressed that they had retained their idealism after graduation. Of her fellow students she wrote, "None seemed lost to the world of split-levels and tail fins. Outwardly a few had accepted it, but none had become submerged by it." Two friends who were married were going to Europe with one-way tickets, prompting Claire to say, "Not a bad idea that."

And then, as if touched by clairvoyance, she added, "Last night produced a dream of weird dimensions, involving myself, the lady who comes between us, and you. I shall elaborate on this when I see you, for it frightened me greatly."

Back in Palgrave, things were far from good but, to Farley, seemed a little better. Misreading the situation, he had detected signs of what he took for improvement in his wife's state of mind. He told Claire that Frances had seemed happier and easier to live with during the past three months than at any time in recent years. All of which made his wife's sudden question, and the revelation that followed it, so stunning.

"Frances rallied from her depths and rather pitifully asked if I wished to sell the place and move away," he wrote to Claire. When Farley asked why, Frances blurted out that she had learned about his affair with Claire just a week after he returned to Ontario from Saint-Pierre. In other words, she had known about them for months and kept silent. As many unfaithful husbands discover, wives see a little more than they think.

Hurtful reports of Farley's affair had been coming to Frances regularly, including an account of their rendezvous in Toronto the previous Sunday. In Farley's words, troublemakers had been "nibbling" at her. By Monday afternoon, Frances knew about it, and now knew Claire's name and a little about her. But even more stunning than her knowledge of her husband's affair was her initial reaction to it. Frances had decided that she should be grateful to Claire "for having been able to give me love of a kind and nature that she could not give." For that, Farley wrote, "she is, I believe, honestly grateful to you though her woman's pride is obviously somewhat damaged."

There were no recriminations or attacks on either Farley or Claire. On the contrary, Frances admitted that her married life with Farley had not been good "and that much of it had been her fault." She was prepared to let Farley go to Claire for good but ultimately could not give up what she had. The old story: change without change.

"She says she loves me," he wrote to Claire. "Perhaps she does. It is no love like ours, but it is perhaps the best she has. She too, like us, is immured in loneliness." Frances did not plead, but under Farley's questioning, made it clear she "would like to have some part of me." She did not use the old arguments of what parting would do to the children. She was, in fact, "perhaps for the first time in her life, quite honest with herself."

Frances not only bore no ill will toward Claire, but according to Farley "several times seemed to have tears for you as well as herself." Farley suspected that his wife's empathy with Claire came from the depths of her own isolation and loneliness. She wished that she and Claire could meet, although the prospect terrified her. "I credit her with full sincerity when she said that you came out so badly in the whole affair, having so little of me, and little solidity" regarding a home and certainty. Frances carried the unexpected empathy for her rival a step further. Paraphrasing his wife's words, Farley wrote Claire, "If people are being hurtful to me, what must they be doing to Claire?" Farley believed her concern was genuine.

After months of deception, and with no choice, Farley finally laid his cards on the marital table. He told his wife that he loved Claire deeply and would go on loving her. Frances accepted this, "envying you a little, perhaps, but not hating." Farley also told her that he would continue to be with Claire. Frances accepted this too as a matter of course. Instead of appearing angry or aggrieved, she wondered if this arrangement would be enough for Claire. Farley also told his wife that he and Claire would be going back to Saint-Pierre in the summer. It was old news. Frances already knew they had met there and planned to return as a couple.

Finally, Farley made Frances a promise that troubled him deeply: he agreed to stay in Palgrave for the winter and then take Claire to St. Pierre in the summer—if she would still have him. Beyond that point, he wrote to Claire, "I could not and would not commit myself. Most unsatisfactory. From your point of view, perhaps, cowardly. And indeed, from my point of view as well. So a coward loves you."

Depressed and fearful of the future, Frances clung to a position that was conflicted and ultimately untenable. She did not wish to come between Farley and Claire, but at the same time she wanted to hold on to at least a semblance of her marriage. She was also desperate to keep her home and the boys. Even if it were only in name, she hoped to remain Farley's wife. Taken together, this was her sheet anchor, and Farley somehow understood that.

Farley now knew what his wife thought of his lover. But what would Claire think of him for agreeing to stay in Palgrave with a woman he didn't love? Although he hoped nothing in his bombshell letter would be misinterpreted or cause Claire pain, he realized that what he referred to as his cowardice in dealing with Frances could mean the end of them.

"What will you say, and do? I am afraid; but I cannot plead against you if you decide that you must wield the sword. I have no right to plead, having forfeited that right by failing to wield the sword myself." Farley asked that she not decide to make an end of it until they had talked together. If Claire refrained from doing "what sense, precedence, self-preservation, the world at large must inevitably dictate that you should do . . . it will be bitterly hard for you in the days immediately ahead."

Farley's warning was understandable. If Frances had been so well-informed about their affair, it was inevitable that Claire's friends and family and the people she worked with would all soon know about it too. "Some will be angry at you, some will be righteous, and worst of all will overtly pity you." Playing devil's advocate, Farley wanted to ensure that "you are fully aware of the torment I shall bring you." The last words of his six-page letter were, "My lips upon your breast, in love. F."

Claire remained devoted to him, but Farley was obsessed with the idea that he had ruined everything for all concerned. A brief talk on the telephone left Farley feeling that he had tortured rather than reassured Claire. "What a dreadful thing that telephone call was. So coldly, over so much space, at the end of your day and week in the grey confines of the city, to have me talk like that, a strange clipped voice from nowhere muttering unintelligibly of cataclysms."

Days later, Farley's own state of mind brought him to the point of "near hysteria" when he thought he had lost his precious photographs of Claire. "I had so well hidden my pictures of you that I could not find them. I grew quite desperate—as if it was you I could not find."

While ransacking drawers looking for the photos, he came across Claire's letters to him. He sat down and read them all from beginning to end. Instead of making him feel better, the letters catalogued the many blunders he believed he had made with Claire, some of which had probably tormented her. He was frightened that he had mistreated her one too many times and that he may have lost her. "And in that moment the loss—the sense of potential loss—was almost beyond bearing."

It was a worried and fearful Farley Mowat who wrote to Claire about how sorry he was for the two nights and days of turmoil and uncertainty he had caused her over the most recent events in Palgrave. He again worried that he had "tortured" her too many times during their love affair, and then suggested that a deep flaw in his own psyche might be responsible for all the misery. It was a variation on Oscar Wilde's observation that each man kills the thing he loves, sometimes with a flattering word, a kiss, or a sword.

"Sometimes I have thought that there is a perverse genius within me," Farley wrote, "that insists that I must place all things I love in constant jeopardy. For I love you most terribly and yet I thrust and cut at you as if you were some ancient enemy. Well, this time perhaps I have done it. And if I have cut a shadow's throat, then I have cut my own with the same stroke."

JUST A WEEK after revealing to Farley that she knew about his affair, Frances delivered another shocker. It came as he was trying to reassure his lover, coexist with his wife, and complete the manuscript for *Owls in the Family*, which had to be in the mail in just one more day. Frances cheerfully announced that she had changed her mind about giving Farley up. She now intended to compete with Claire for him. Farley thought of it as Bishop Strachan, his wife's private school, against Havergal, which was Claire's, with him as the playing field. He told Claire he didn't like being in the middle of that scrum. "Besides its un-natural and contrary to reality. Who the hell am I that women should growl above my helpless corse . . . I need your little paw upon my sweating brow, and badly."

With Christmas, a deadline, and two women bearing down on him, Farley contracted stomach flu, along with Sandy, David, and even their dog, Kippy. Farley was beginning to have a haunted feeling and was yearning for distant places and an escape from the world that was closing in on him—provided Claire was by his side.

Instead, he drew the assignment of shepherding the boys through Toyland in Eaton's department store and then looking after them at his in-laws' house while Frances did some Christmas shopping. A phone call to Claire, who was nearby at work, was impossible. It was frustrating to be so close to her without being able to see her. He wondered in a letter if she had felt his presence. An exhausted Farley began the long drive back to Palgrave at 10 o'clock that night, the car packed with wife, kids, and Christmas presents. He described to Claire the state he was in when they arrived. "Dead. Me, dead. They still energetic. It's hell being that close to you, and yet so far."

During the Christmas season, the mail moved even slower than the time remaining before they could return to Saint-Pierre. Deprived of her words, Farley kept writing to Claire with a growing sense of hopelessness. "Gloomily, I don't suppose this letter will reach you for years, if ever. I shall shoot either my wife or the Postmaster General, whichever is responsible for the drouth of Clairiana."

Farley did not make it to Montreal. He found he could not move farther away from Claire than Cornwall. Obligatory Christmas events filled the rest of the holiday calendar, including the children's Christmas party and an open house at his Palgrave home.

Frances had left the house alone in a bleak depression. Farley had seen her spiral down to rock bottom several times before, a process that usually took five days. Since he was obliged to look after the boys, he came to the conclusion that he wouldn't be able to see Claire until after Christmas. Even though he knew she was distressed by meeting in motels and inns, he wrote to her wondering if the two of them could get away for a full night and a day on Boxing Day. "Damn your panther soul—I love you so."

When Farley finally received a letter from Claire on Simpsons-Sears stationery just before Christmas, he discovered that she was as frustrated as he was. But there was a silver lining. Despite the pain of being separated at what was supposed to be a joyous time of year, she remained as madly in love with him as she had always been.

"Beloved, I am a trifle depressed. Damn that operator and her three minutes. It's not nearly long enough for me to croon all the sweet nothings to you I would. And damn the stultifying atmosphere of this place. Oh darling I want you so much and I wanted to say something loving to you on the phone just now, and I still want to for I love only you. And I won't let it corrode. None of the acidic influences will touch our love. For I shall always love you. Oh I want to cry. It's Christmas. Well let it be. The festive season indeed! . . . But we shall schedule the 27th and it will be ours. Let us hope for Thursday also . . . How can I live without you? What a morose question but it exists nevertheless. I will not live without you. We will be shot down in flames together. Oh come soon my love."

If Farley's spirits were raised by that letter from Claire, the one he received on Thursday, December 29, put him over the moon. Claire had attended a reunion of some of the people who had been on Saint-Pierre with them and said that Farley would have "wept" to see so many souls longing to see the place again. The gathering itself was "filled with good talk and booze, and not filled with enemy campers. All those present filled with nostalgia. Climax of the evening was home movie starring Canada's best-loved seafarer, author and TV personality Farley Mowat. How magnificent you were, wielding your green paint brush and shouting things at the camera." (There was no sound.) The next scene, in living colour, was the launching of the *Itchatchozale Alai*. "I thrilled at the sight. Little did the audience know I was concealed within. Bright comments sped around the room; 'Look, there he is' or 'Look at that beard!' or better still 'There's a hunk of virility for you!'"

Those who conjectured about Farley and Claire's relationship and approved of it asked to be remembered to Farley. Classmates hoped the couple would have a drink with them soon.

"1961 approacheth, and I am fading fast. Do you pause to reflect on the passing year? I don't. Yet one action gives me pause for reflection—the great tangle of prevarication under which I see you. This only I regret—deliberate, calculated lies. Black and nasty are they not? Yet possibly kinder than deliberate cruelty—the only alternative. On this note, I leave you. But be sure I love you, regret nothing and hope for everything. St. Pierre looms celestially on our horizon. And ecstasy looms on my horizon when I think of you. A Happy new year to my love, C."

It couldn't have been a worse New Year's for the man she loved. It was bad enough that they had missed Christmas together and would ring in 1961 apart. But just before the big night, a desperately depressed Frances took a handful of sleeping pills. Luckily, she washed the deadly potion down with Scotch and promptly threw up. Farley was upset, but his emotions were tempered by the fact that he had been through this many times before with his troubled wife.

"This day she lies, beset by gloom, dark and distraught. I might be more disturbed had I not gone through this self same exhibition a hundred times in the past years, and with no Claire to bring about the dramatics."

When Frances improved, Farley learned that she had been consulting friends about the "situation." Then she once again surprised her husband by telling him that she wished to give up "all this" and retreat to, of all places, Saint-Pierre. Farley was aghast. "The very prospect gives me cold shivers. Neither you nor I would ever be able to set foot upon the isles des paradis again. Don't know whether I can keep the top on the pot till spring. But I shall try, and mightily."

Claire was distressed by Frances's recent behaviour, knowing that it put further constraints on Farley. But curiously, she showed sympathy for her rival's situation, just as Frances had empathized with hers.

"A prolonged siege of this, followed by a long period of repentance; surely these are the waves which wear away the face of the cliff. Yet, damn it all, I am full of sympathy at the same time. I only know how I would feel if the same thing were happening to me . . . Let F. blame me, I say. Perhaps it will be easier for her to pin it on someone or something. Enough of this. Be brave and never forget that I love you."

4 | Heavy Fog, Vague Tomorrows

IN 1961, IT WOULD HAVE BEEN EASY to conclude that Claire Angel Wheeler had joined that loneliest club of all—that sad sorority of the mistresses of famous married men. There was no question that she had won the heart, along with the rest of the body parts, of Farley Mowat. There was no question that she had found the love of her life and was all in, body and soul, come hell or high water. But their planned return to Saint-Pierre, where they had met and fallen in love, shimmered like a mirage in the distance—part reality, part illusion, something you could reach out for but never quite touch.

Claire knew that the crazy love comes with no guarantees. She was well aware that Farley was still bound to Palgrave with hoops of flesh and blood. It was yet to be determined if they would ever be anything more than weekend lovers who wrote extraordinary love letters. What she had for certain was unconditional love for Farley and the snow-flake's kiss of his magical words. In wishing Claire a happy new year, Farley the "word-monger" cast his familiar spell, this time with a little humour: "What say we make it one? Hey? Did you know that I was in love? Damme, it's so! With who (with whom!)—why, with youm. Who else? (cold feet and all). All my love, my love, F."

Farley's words could always make Claire smile, but her heart must have cracked a little when she read his New Year's Eve note. It reminded her that they would both be ushering in 1961 with other peo-ple—Farley with Frances, and Claire with a blind date.

"Peace again descends upon us—an uneasy peace. Tonight we go to a New Year's party at which, who knows?, some fine handsome young fellow will fall wildly in love with my wife. I, on the other hand, will moodily gurgle at my glass and mutter incoherent nothings to myself as I contemplate the spectral image of you and your handsome young fellow gallivanting gracefully across some distant floor. I hope he trips and breaks a toe."

Farley needn't have worried. New Year's was the saddest day of the year for Claire. Shallow company, blowout whistles, and paper hats were no substitute for what she wanted. Her escort for the big celebration turned out to be underwhelming—an Englishman she found pompous and boring, "without an ounce of intelligence or fun in him."

She wrote Farley that she would be skiing with friends on the upcoming weekend, presenting a chance to see each other without the usual parental grilling at her end. But Farley was constrained by family duties these days and would be until his marital affairs were settled. He couldn't promise to come. Claire told him it was too bad that Frances had known about them from the beginning, but to "take heart my darling, for I am sure there are blacker days ahead for us before the flowers of Spring appear."

Claire was overjoyed to receive two letters from Farley in response. He told her that he was immersing himself in work to cope with the unbearable conditions at home. He worried that if her parents found out about the affair, their reaction might be so harsh that it would diminish her love for him. Claire, who in many ways was Farley's horse whisperer, put that fear to rest. "Most emphatically, fear not that my love for you could ever weaken. Even a howling ruckus could do nothing to dampen it."

But that didn't mean their life in limbo wasn't causing her distress. For one thing, despite her courageous words, she was concerned about her parents and what a scandal might do to them. After all, they were the Wheelers of Douglas Drive. "The long, long struggle to produce a nice daughter from a nice home may appear a little fruitless to them in the face of all that is to follow," she wrote. And then there was her job at Simpsons-Sears. It was boredom and loneliness all week, followed by sterile companions on those weekends without Farley.

Only rarely did her letters suggest a flight from responsible living. In one of them that did, Claire declared that with the slightest encouragement from him, she would quit her job and run away to sea. "Oh but I want to run away. Let's run away Farley!... What do you think of this my love? I am serious for I fear I cannot go on like this... Think on me my love. It is only the thought of you which keeps me alive. My delightful one, your angel sends you her heart."

Events in Palgrave prevented Farley from joining Claire during her ski weekend with friends, all of whom she suspected were virgins. But he was happy she was off in Nature and not imprisoned in Toronto, a grey city filled with grey people. "I can visualize you with such pleasure, and such ease, against white hills and mantled trees, but I cannot, ever, really see you against the frosted glass and varnished furniture of Simpsons-Sears. Have fun my darling. That windOwhipped whorl of snow behind you—that is me."

If she revelled in his every word, Claire's love letters were keeping Farley alive, he said, "sending the grey days hereabouts into a whirling vortex that spins toward spring. Faster and faster yet, still not fast enough." The war with Frances vacillated between fiery outbursts and stony silence, an emotional armistice that never lasted. Things between them grew so dysfunctional that Farley packed his bags and left them by the front door. He hoped Frances would get the message: there was only so much he could and would take.

The forces holding him to his homestead were complex, including the difficulty of getting a divorce in 1961. It would be seven years before Canada's archaic divorce laws would be reformed by a young justice minister from Quebec, Pierre Trudeau. But Farley's central restraint was guilt. What would a split mean for his young sons? He awakened one morning to find the house in shambles and Frances in a rage. These sudden flares of emotion were usually triggered by Farley or Claire. But this time, the "nightmare" had a different source.

"So far as I can gather, it was the children," Farley wrote to Claire. "So the outpouring of hate and hellery caught them in full tide... But how in the name of the elder Gods can I abandon two soft and pretty helpless human bods to the kind of misery which must be theirs? May the Gods resolve this mess, I can't . . . If only there was some way of ensuring the survival of the boys, there would <u>be</u> no problem. But I can simply not abandon them to the inevitable. Not, at least, until I have reshaped the physical environment a little, and this cannot be done until spring and the emergence of the real-estate men from under their winter logs." Then Frances could look for a smaller and less isolated place.

Feeling powerless, Claire was crushed by Farley's daily reality in a place he didn't want to be, with a wife he no longer loved. She was especially tormented about the boys: "I weep for your miseries in Palgrave. I suspect however that the children's misdemeanours are not entirely responsible for the tidal wave. Some second thoughts as to your whereabouts and then a suspicion to your who-abouts . . . I weep also for Sandy and David, that they have caught the tail end of this hurricane. This is the greatest injustice of all. How I wish I could do something for them to make amends. Could we kidnap them off to St. P. next summer?" Whatever happened, she would love Farley forever: "I know that you love me, and the way that you treat me is splendid beyond all expectations, beautiful and gentle beyond all belief."

Farley told Claire that his war book was in limbo because the situation in Palgrave was more than human flesh could endure, words he immediately regretted putting to paper and quickly took back. After all, how could he whine to her about his situation, when he imagined hers was even worse? The constant lies she had to tell to family and friends about her life in the shadows of Farley's marriage, the inevitability of scandal, her empty job, and a loneliness as dark and deep as the caverns of the moon, always waiting, waiting, waiting.

Again, Farley underestimated the emotional toughness of the woman he loved. No one was better at decoding an sos from Farley than Claire. Brushing aside her own needs, and sensing his growing desperation, she wrote exactly the kind of response he badly needed—saucy, lovestruck, hopeful, and devoted.

"How I want you! Call me a home-wrecker, call me anything you like, but I want you. I will wait for you darling, for I am sure that you cannot spend all your days with F. In all fairness, she has had 13 years of your life to make you happy and, as I see it, has not done that... This is the most important thing... Much more important even than drawing rabbits and owls. I want to make you happy. It is all that I want and I may have to kidnap you in order to do it. To stay in Palgrave indefinitely is sure destruction for both of you. You know, I think the present situation is probably tougher on F. than on any of us. She is the one who daily doubts the continuation of her present existence. Living with this threat is probably harder for her than living alone, although she doesn't realize it."

Claire included some practical advice. Rather than ghosting around the house, waiting for the next explosion from Frances, Farley should spend more time on his writing in the privacy of *Itchy II*. She also advised him to take "leaves of absence" from Palgrave in the name of researching for his writing. "But what terrible suggestions! I feel like a calculating woman writing this down. Better destroy it darling. It would provide grounds for an alienation of affection suit."

Farley was too jubilant about Claire's words to worry about legal consequences. "Such a letter! It is all I can do to refrain from leaping to horse and galloping off in all directions that lead to you. Damn damn damn! How can I write deathless literature when I can't erase you from my galumphing mind for even minutes at a time?"

THEN FRANCES PROVIDED another surprise. In January 1961, when Farley broached the subject of a formal separation, the talk went "frighteningly well." No fireworks, just a calm agreement that separation was the only solution to their predicament. Even more stunning was her apparent acquiescence in obtaining one. But it was only because Frances had the wrong idea of what a separation agreement was, and more importantly, where it would lead. It was a misapprehension that Farley purposely left uncorrected.

"She is clearly deluding herself into the belief that this is a separation for a period, and not a finality. She has spoken in terms of a year or two. I have not, deliberately, disillusioned her. Time will do that."

The couple came to an informal agreement. In broad terms, Frances would have custody of the children and keep the house. Farley would pay support and see the boys whenever he could. Meanwhile, after leaving the matrimonial home, he would stay in the vicinity for some weeks to fix some mechanical problems at the house and find a home for the five sad mallard ducks that were his pets. Jack McClelland offered Farley the use of his family's cabin near the community of MacTier, at Foot's Bay, about a hundred miles north of Palgrave. It was an offer that Farley readily accepted. He told Frances to call a contact, Graham Hazen, if she needed to reach him at the cabin.

When he informed Claire of the latest development, Farley included a report on how the breakup of his marriage was playing in Palgrave. "The attitude is the good old-fashioned one. You are the femme fatale, I am the son-of-a-bitch who wants to eat his cake and have it too."

Happy as he was about his informal separation from Frances, Farley worried that if things broke down, Claire might be drawn into a legal battle. At this point, it was only a possibility, but it was real enough for him to send Claire a stark warning about how bad her life might get if she stayed with him. As he would more than once over the coming bleak months, he effectively offered Claire a dire outlook and an out.

"If you choose it so, you will give up certainty and security (and I am not mocking at these words now) in exchange for what may be many years of voyaging out of sight of those substantial things which, for most people, are a perfectly valid excuse for being. Heavy fog for most of the time. Vague tomorrows. You may not get sea-sick, my love, but you may become soul sick."

In an attempt to keep her from blowing up her life on his account, he cautioned Claire that if she left her job at Simpsons-Sears before summer, she would probably not be able to return to anything commensurate. She might also lose the esteem of her family and many of her friends and acquaintances. "Return to Toronto will only be possible if you crawl, and beg, and abase yourself. You will, quite incidentally, cause pain in Rosedale. The kind of pain that never is forgiven, really."

In most of his letters, no matter how forlorn he might be feeling, Farley tried to include something to make Claire laugh. This time he enclosed a clipping with photos of himself and Marlon Brando. The caption underneath read:

These are two unusual men.
Both have unusual creeds.
Read about them in next week's *Star Weekly*.

After leaving Palgrave according to his agreement with Frances, Farley enjoyed a brief grace period at the McClelland family's cabin. But this interlude came to a swift end with an urgent call from Graham Hazen. Frances had called him in an almost "incoherent" state, demanding that her husband return home at once.

Back in Palgrave, Farley found that everything was in shambles and Frances "had quite gone to pieces." The bottom line? She wanted him to come back. With his wife in major psychological distress, and the boys in need of care, he reluctantly agreed to go back and forth from the cabin to the house until spring. In return, Frances was to try to shed her emotional dependency on him and become an "individual." If she wasn't willing to at least try, he would pack up and leave.

"Awful bloody mess," he wrote to Claire. "This puts the kibosh on any faint hopes I might have had for doing some work this winter." He would have to "mark time" until spring, something he was not sure he could do. "In fact I seem about emptied of emotion. To find myself once more back in the cave after even that short breath of release, is intolerable. The hell with it."

Farley advised Claire to go skiing with friends again that weekend and breathe the "piney" air, even though he could not be there. When this "gone feeling" in the pit of his stomach had abated, he promised he would be with her again. "Meanwhile I am with you in the heart."

Although he was reluctant to say it, Farley felt that he had let Claire down again by returning to Palgrave. Not knowing how nasty the separation might become, he gave Claire some defensive instructions.

All of her letters should henceforth be sent to him care of Graham Hazen in Foot's Bay, MacTier. "Don't write anymore to Palgrave," he wrote. "Documents could be turned against you."

Farley returned to find Frances "suffering a fairly total collapse of spirit." But there was a difference. For the first time, she had called in outside help, and the town doctor and the local Anglican minister were waiting for him. The doctor advised him that the problem wasn't physical; it was Farley. "In fact," Farley wrote to Claire, "he believes that F. needs me absent in order to recover her own emotional stability and self-confidence. He notes, without rancour, that any woman trying to live with me would be attempting the impossible."

Unsurprisingly, the minister viewed the whole thing through the squinty eye of the morality business. He recommended group therapy and psychological help for Frances, with whom he totally sympathized. Farley wrote to Claire that the clergyman had told him that in his opinion she would be better off without him and that "any woman who married you would be crazy."

The minister dealt not just with the sacred issues at stake but also with the profane, hiring a lawyer for Frances to draw up a formal separation agreement. He made clear that he thought Farley should be run out of the family without access to his sons and made to pay. After all, Farley was the villain of the piece, the feckless, philandering male. When the minister later presented Farley with the lawyer's draft agreement, he brandished it like a club. Farley was appalled. He told Claire that the agreement would leave him with "a little skin on my ass but not much more."

But that wasn't what rankled Farley. It was what he saw as an obvious attempt to intimidate him, an attempt Frances never endorsed. "I struck back, and hard. I pointed out that an attempt to blackmail me into accepting a penal contract, in exchange for a divorce, would get them nowhere, but would get me out of the country—and fast. It got quite hot and heavy."

Feisty as he was, the way in which Farley was being portrayed by locals supporting his wife got him down. "I must admit to some depression, particularly in view of this oft repeated theme that I ought to stay out of women's lives."

After many stormy back-and-forths with Frances, Farley made a momentous decision. Given his wife's emotional distress, and considering the vulnerable position of his sons, he agreed to stay in Palgrave until spring. In part, he was inspired by a private talk with Frances. As Farley saw it, Frances was apparently facing reality; their marriage was over, and it would be "death" for both of them to continue living in its empty shell. Frances also agreed that she had been a "succubus" on Farley and that the relationship was destroying them both.

Although Farley could see that his wife was still in turmoil about the situation and still volatile, he saw progress in her outlook and behaviour. She went from being a near-hermit to going out at every opportunity "in search of her sea-legs." She even travelled to Toronto alone, something she had not done in seven years. "It shook the hell out of her," Farley wrote Claire, "but she is persevering." She asked for as much help as possible, and Farley was ready to give it to her, even if it meant a reversal of his immediate plans for a separation.

In a test of his wife's sincerity, Farley told Frances that he had just signed a contract for a book on sea rescues in Newfoundland. It would mean an absence of eighteen months, probably beginning in April. She took the news well, maybe even with a touch of relief, since it was an external obligation, which for the time being took "the necessity of decision" on how to end their marriage out of their hands.

Ironically, one of the reasons Farley was able to deal sympathetically with events in Palgrave was an early February tryst with Claire that restored his own damaged emotional equilibrium. He thanked her in a letter on February 4.

"My darling, What a magical touch you have! I came back through the pale moonshine feeling refreshed and refurbished. You have so much tenderness and you are so very gentle with me; gentle and loving... Without you I should have been unresponsive and dour, and would have turned my back."

Despite her reflexive support under any circumstances, Farley knew that Claire would have reservations about this new arrangement. It was hard to see it as anything but a setback in their plans to be together. Farley argued the opposite. If he acted with "brutality" and simply walked away, the situation would "fester" for all three of them. In the long term, it would benefit their own relationship if Farley left Frances after restoring her self-confidence and self-reliance—especially since she seemed to understand that there could be no recovery of a past that never really existed.

He wrote to Claire, "To leave her in a state of dissolution would inevitably saddle us with shadows and I am desperately anxious that there be no shadows over our life together... I think the risk is worth it. The prospect of beginning a life with you sans ghosts, is worth a hell of a lot. I am susceptible to ghosts."

Farley knew that his decisions would make the next few months difficult for Claire, but he assured her that his "decision to leave here, and to make a life with you—if you will have me—is unalterable and unshaken. It is simply that I would rather go with a good conscience, than go with spectres. And I think you would rather have it this way too."

Farley asked Claire about the possibility of spending the weekend of February 18 together at a cottage. "Excellent snowshoeing, so I hear. Oh Claire, thank God for you! I have just now again re-read your two letters of this week, and I don't have any heart left—just a warm and soppy gob of something in my chest dissolved by love."

On Sunday, February 5, Claire's birthday, Farley sent her a love poem and his wish for the future. "All of my love to you, my love, and may this be the last birthday you spend beardless."

5 | Mistress, Wife, Spinster?

CLAIRE SPENT HER TWENTY-EIGHTH BIRTHDAY cross-country skiing with friends in Georgian Bay. The day was glorious—bracing air, snow soft and dazzling, and a hint of authority in the sun. But her heart was heavy. She was counting the hours until Wednesday, when she would see Farley again. It seemed she was always counting the hours.

By making no legal moves based on Farley's admitted adultery and asserting her official position as his wife, Frances occupied the formidable Alamo of her marriage to make her last stand, hoping the fire might go out between the lovers. She had persuaded Farley to stay in Palgrave until spring, multiplying his family duties and leaving him less time to see Claire.

When Farley and Claire met that Wednesday in February, Claire's world brightened, as it almost always did when they were together. Their meeting was a badly needed tonic for Farley, who had been depressed and unable to sleep. He praised Claire for her healing touch in typically hyperbolic terms. "I am free of my brain tumour, for the first day in eight, and I slept fiendishly well last night."

But Claire had another rival besides Frances that would keep them apart—Farley's new book, a project driven by commerce more than inspiration. It told the story of the incredible sea rescue of the war-built Liberty ship *Leicester,* disabled during a hurricane in the North-west Atlantic and saved by the deep-sea tug *Foundation Josephine* out of Newfoundland. Claire loved the subject matter and thought it might be the first book in a series they could do together on other remote places, like the Falkland Islands.

To meet the terms of the contract for what would become *The Serpent's Coil*, Farley faced a punishing writing schedule. The publication date would leave him two months to produce ninety thousand words by June. If he could do it, he would have $3,000 on deposit in a London bank by autumn, money all three of them needed. As he wrote to Claire, "Unless I am free to write steadily, and uninterrupted by eruptions, it just can't be done." That meant "walking softly" while still in Palgrave in order to provide "gold" for their great escape.

Farley planned to leave Palgrave for St. John's in early May to do some library research with Mike Donovan's help. (Farley's father, Angus, a librarian himself, had recommended that Mike study library services, which turned out to be sage advice.) Farley would also get a chance to check on his boat in Saint-Pierre. But he would be absent from Claire's life for weeks, maybe months, except for the increasingly unsatisfying simulacrum of words.

To lessen the blow of his absence, Farley told Claire that during bad sailing weather in June they could take the coastal boats to explore the south coast, spend July mostly in Saint-Pierre, and August on *Itchy* returning to the south coast of Newfoundland.

After a couple of months in St. John's, they would head to England and Wales to work on a new book and live on the money from the advance for *The Serpent's Coil*. Claire would be kept busy taking notes and transcribing. There would also be ample scope for her accomplished drawings to illustrate the next book. "Fame has come to me," he wrote to her mockingly. "I enclose it. All of it. Eureka."

Included in the letter was a *Wilson Library Bulletin* biography of Farley based on an interview. "Asked if there were misstatements about himself which should be corrected, Farley replied, 'Yes, damn it. People insist on calling me Canada's angry young man. I am middle-aged. I am benevolent and loving towards all mankind. Mostly.'"

In the biography, the *New York Herald Tribune* described Farley as "an inspired nature writer." And *The Desperate People*—Farley's 1959 sequel to *People of the Deer*—won praise for its "poetic prose." Asked if he had any organization or club memberships, he replied, "My god, no!" Soon his picture would appear in *Chatelaine* magazine, elevating him to the status of matinee idol, according to Claire.

With just two months to go before he left for Newfoundland, Farley and Claire tried to steal as much time together as possible. That was easier said than done, given the amount of writing and travelling Farley had in front of him, including an anti-nuclear protest in Regina, where he spoke alongside the premier of Saskatchewan, the legendary Tommy Douglas.

The march in Regina was invigorating. Some eight hundred people from all over the Prairies showed up. A piper led them to the legislature, where they were greeted by Premier Douglas himself. Farley spoke for half an hour and was "scared stiff." Douglas, a spellbinding orator, spoke for an hour.

To the roaring approval of the crowd, Douglas said Canada should get out of NORAD and NATO, and the hell with being a U.S. satellite. Most important, he told the marchers that he was implacably opposed to nuclear weapons. Farley found the premier's words terrific, and could scarcely believe they were coming from an establishment figure. He had the feeling that not a word of Premier Douglas's daring and dramatic comments would get through to the staid Eastern Canadian press.

Farley was also impressed by the jubilation after the premier's speech. He was carried off to a student party, where there was much singing and drinking. But the merriment made him miss Claire even more. "I always do when something exciting, or fun, is happening, because better than half the pleasure is in sharing it with you."

Although it was sweet to return from travelling, and to Claire, it also meant returning to voluntary house arrest in Palgrave. When he was there, all Frances had to do to keep the lovers apart was leave the homestead—and the boys—to Farley. There was nothing he could do but tend to the children while his wife went off in search of her "independence," a quest Farley could hardly begrudge, since he himself had asked her to undertake it. Even worse, at times when Farley was free, Claire was not. He attributed that to her "liaison with that unspeakable fellow, Mr. Simpsons-Sears."

On one occasion when Frances left for a few days, Farley decided to drive to Port Hope with the children to visit his parents for the weekend. Along the way, he picked up another passenger. Just past Bowmanville, Farley caught a glimpse of something on the shoulder of the highway. He jammed on Lulu's brakes and walked back to find an injured saw-whet owl settled morosely on the roadside. The creature, which had come from the Arctic and had no fear of humans, was not much bigger than a sparrow.

Farley cupped the owl in his hands and carried it back to the jeep, where he put it in an empty boot belonging to Sandy and took it along with them to Port Hope. To Claire he wrote, "It is a lovely little beast. Sick, sad, and hopeless, but lovely, and I am nursing it. I think it may live. I think it, and you, and I, are one. Owls seem to be our beasts." He asked Claire if she could keep "Minerva" in her bedroom. "A very little, timorous, and love-needing little owl? If not I shall release it when I think, and trust, it may survive."

They were unable to see each other on Valentine's Day, but Claire sent him a letter answering his question about Minerva, whom she longed to meet. "I have a great deal of love and sympathy for lonely, displaced and innocent owls." The words reverberated with her own situation. She didn't know if her mother would welcome a bird into their household, although they had often nurtured stray dogs, cats, and people. Claire included a humorous Valentine card with her letter. "If you feel about me, like I feel about you . . . Shame on you!!"

To make up for their lonely Valentine's Day, Farley arranged a cottage retreat in Bancroft for the weekend of February 17 to 19. Although the Mowat men were famously healthy and hardy, Farley confessed to being weary. He longed "for a few days of blankness of mind, sloth and quietness." None of which, he stressed, would be any good without Claire.

He also had a book he wanted to read to her: *Daphnis and Chloe*, a sixteenth-century version of the ancient Greek novel by Longus. Set on the island of Lesbos, it tells the story of star-crossed lovers, both abandoned at birth, who overcome immense obstacles to find each other and finally be together. Farley's intention was clear. Life imitated art, including their life, and he hoped that this tale of desire in lonely times might buoy Claire's flagging spirits.

The weekend was full of "snuggling," plans, good food, and wine. When Claire returned home, her parents asked the usual question: "How was the skiing?" The "skiing" was superb, Claire reported. The "skiing" was also sublime for Farley, as he made clear in a bawdy limerick he sent Claire after returning to Palgrave. Farley was in the habit of assigning a name to everything, including their private parts. He christened his "Georgie" and hers "Georgiana," though the spelling would occasionally change, depending on the metric requirements of the poet.

> I think that I have never seen a
> Poem as lovely as Georgiana!
> Her curly hair, and tender lips,
> The heaven hides, where Georgie slips,
> To leave his small sub-pina.

Farley never missed an opportunity to remind Claire that the task she had undertaken by falling in love with him was next to impossible, and only she could do it. "To make a morose, cantankerous, irascible, choleric, contentious, disputatious, querulous and churlish fellow such as I am, happy? Hercules never faced a task like this! But, you child of my own heart, you <u>do</u> make me happy, as no one else has ever done. And if you wish to kidnap me in order to have more time to work on it, I am eminently kidnapable."

Given his wife's passive resistance to a divorce, Farley and Claire decided to consult a lawyer about their situation. Under the circumstances, he told them, there wasn't much they could do about it if Frances, knowing all, didn't want to sue him for divorce. Claire was crestfallen but grateful for his frankness. A divorce in Canada was simply not possible. "There is a reassuring solidity about cold, hard facts, however devastating they may be," she wrote.

As she so often did, Claire tried to make the best of it. Looking ahead to long stretches apart, she wrote, "I don't expect an easy road ... Of course there will be black times. Perhaps a lot of them. But is this not life? Would I not much rather have my black times with you than with anyone else? When I take on this job it will be in its entirety, as has been our relationship all along."

Despite the bravado, Claire was only human. The day Farley called her about his decision to go back to Palgrave to resuscitate Frances, she spent the rest of the afternoon pretending that he did not exist—a defence mechanism that caused her great sorrow. "What an empty thing it is without you," she wrote to him. "I can imagine my life without you, but I hope that I never have to live it." Because her parents were disturbed by her late-night typing, she finished her letter by hand. Tears fell on the white field of her words as she folded the letter and slipped it into an envelope.

Claire knew that "woe-is-me" letters were not Farley's favourites, so she tried to write of other things—a bus ride home from Muskoka, a boring day at Simpsons-Sears, even a visit to the home of a girlfriend from summer camp, where Claire had been a lifeguard. Her childhood companion was now the mother of two, trapped in a Hamilton subdivision. After the visit, Claire vowed she would never have children— more of a judgment on suburbia than motherhood.

But there was a heavier matter on her mind. She couldn't help expressing her belief to Farley that as much as she wanted it, she now believed that they would never be married. "I love you and want you Farley. I had hopes that it might someday be legal, but now I rather think not. F. will fight us to the end . . . I know that life is very black for you right now my love. Forgive me for adding more misery to it. I'm off to bed now and I'll dream of you. My only and precious love, come back soon."

Claire was struggling with the big question that the "other woman" must inevitably face. Would she succeed Frances as Farley's wife or forever remain a dalliance? As it became more difficult for her to live from encounter to encounter with Farley, in a never-ending cycle of ecstasy followed by the agony of loneliness, she couldn't help pouring out her feelings to the man who had taken her life by storm.

"No plans, no promises. What happened to our motto? We failed to live by it. Or rather it was I who failed to live by it. But a woman in love always has hope. How could I dare to think that you would desert that which you held dear, only to cleave to the side of another, who probably wouldn't make a very good wife anyway. Perhaps you have the right idea. I might make an excellent mistress. The position of the mistress in today's society has been vastly underrated. No one ever writes a column for the Ladies Home Journal on the essential qualities of a good mistress. It is all so foreign to me Farley and I know you understand why the idea of it is so abhorrent. I grope for security in love as those caught by The Depression have groped for financial security."

Farley was devastated by Claire's description of herself as his "mistress." It gave his dead marriage a legitimacy he no longer recognized and misconstrued what in his mind was their true status: epic lovers. "The concept of you as a mistress did not occur to me. Such a fearfully conventional and crudely interpreted tag is the antithesis of what I felt for us, and hoped for us. As confining, savage and intolerable as the concept implicit in the word 'marriage'."

Still tangled in an unworkable and unhappy marriage, he tried to make Claire see it from a man's point of view, acknowledging that women might see it differently.

"Perhaps the dry-bone certitudes that remain after love dies, in marriage, are sufficient compensation for a woman, who must always and inevitably, be of less certainty than man—perhaps."

In deep distress about his predicament, Farley sank into an annihilating despondency, as he occasionally did. Horses were his metaphor for the attached and unattached male, both of which shared the same fate: "One is a free and wild-born stallion. The other is a cut gelding. The stallion may well gallop over a cliff and vanish in bloody chaos. The other will die, blind and ancient, in its stall. Both die. Both pass. Love dies and is forgotten."

That is not how Claire saw it, however. She offered a defence of the institution Farley often maligned, using the example of Frances herself to show the importance of marriage to a woman.

"Despite all the unpleasant things there are to be said against marriage, it does protect and preserve the family in times of invasion such as this. F. has this as her weapon and her defense. She has her status symbol, her security symbol. For love she has her children and perhaps this is enough for her. She does not at least, have to face curious friends and snickering teenagers who wondered why no one ever married her... A whole life time as a mistress. Never to be a wife, never a mother. Can you understand all that this implies my darling?"

CLAIRE HAD A WAY of putting Farley on the spot with her disarming honesty. He and Claire told a lot of lies at this stage of their lives, all of them to conceal their secret love. But they never lied to each other. Farley had made no secret of his reluctance to marry again.

The reason he had married Frances in the first place was that he thought that she was pregnant—that, and to escape an intolerable loneliness he felt as a twenty-seven-year-old. So he arranged a hasty marriage with the girl he had met in Botany 2A at university. When it turned out that Frances wasn't pregnant, he decided to go ahead and marry her anyway. That was in December 1947. Robert (Sandy) was born on April 4, 1954, and David was adopted in October 1958 at the age of fourteen months. He had been in five foster homes and was a troubled child.

After many years of unhappiness and a solid decade of misery, Farley realized the magnitude of his mistake. Understanding Claire's need, he wrote a long letter designed to give her comfort, but not by lying to her.

"You see, it is just that I no longer trust the concept. It has nothing to do with trusting, or with loving you. The compulsion to throw myself upon your heart with perfect giving, without restraint, is almost unbearable; and probably our commingling will not be complete until I do just this... I think it most probable that you and I can, and will go on together until there is an end to us... Your life is infinitely more terrible than mine: your vulnerability is greater, your loneliness more fearsome. If those horrors can only be alleviated in marriage, then they will be so... I want you to have as great a need of me as can be borne, and therefore to become as much a part of me as can be brought to pass. I want you to live within me, being secure there, and at ease... I would rather lose you, than lie to you, for by lying to you I <u>would</u> lose you... But, darling, when it is possible, and if you wish—then I will

be happy to go through the motions of marriage. I talk too much ...
Do I love you? I am afraid to think how much, and how much more I
can and shall." Farley told Claire that he believed the coming summer
would set him free for her.

There was nothing Claire wanted more than that. But she had to
face reality and consider a darker possibility. What if things didn't work
out? What if she ended up alone? After all, Farley himself had talked
about his inability to act on the fact that his marriage was over.

"You see, darling, I can be cruel enough by default, as you are witness, but I can only do it by design, under the most terrible stimuli.
My marriage is at an end. It is inexorably drifting now to total dissolution. I believe this completely. And I cannot find it in me to become
an axeman at this juncture. It may be a foolish delusion, but I believe
that time will work for me now, as it worked against me in the past.
In concrete terms, I do not want to put my foot in Sandy's face when
there is no sufficient reason for such action in terms of my own escape.
Which makes it sound like a trial of affection between you and him—
but that, as you well know, is nonsense. To be brutal toward him so that
we might be able instanter to display the flags of victory in terms of
conventional acceptance would inevitably breed brutality in our own
future. I hope that he and I will be friends for a time, at least. I hope no
more than that. Inevitably I shall lose him, and he will lose me, but I
cannot hasten the process by overt actions on my own part."

Mindful of Farley's psychic paralysis, and unhappy with her role as
the "scarlet woman," Claire wrote to him about the plight of the "Old
Maid" in our society. "We have no real place," she said. The spinster sister used to go to live with nieces and nephews to help look after them.
"Now we hide ourselves in A Career, the dull, grey flannel world of the
business man, and with it we bear the stigma that nobody ever wanted
us for keeps."

Like Farley, Claire was quick to feel remorse when she said something she knew would bring her lover more stress than he was already
under. She quickly wrote to ask forgiveness for the self-pitying letter
she had sent the day before: "The last thing you want is 2 whining

women to succour." She was full of fight and courage again, which Farley always loved.

"My fierce and fearsome love," he wrote. "I wriggle with delight as I read your fighting letter. Mind you, you are a scheming wench, and should be punished. Preferably in bed . . . That lovely little chin of yours has never lived up to its promise before. Why? The all too-civilizing influence of Havergal and Douglas Drive? I am filled with joy that you have dropped the pose of a Toronto person, and are breathing fire and brimstone."

If Farley appreciated Claire's feistiness, he also revelled in her inventive sense of humour. In the same letter, she thanked him for taking part in a fictitious survey of Canadian creative artists and their families. The imaginary report she made up and quoted from concluded that none had more than seven wives, while not more than twelve of the remaining eighty-four percent interviewed had reported more than three wives at any given time. She attached a coloured art clipping to her letter, labelled the "The Perfect beauty." Farley knew those breasts. Small and high, they could have been Claire's.

Farley responded with some levity of his own on the subject of domesticity. He assured Claire that the idea of it did not bother him, if what she meant was "the peace and gentleness of sitting quietly beside you." He joked that he could envisage with "rare delight" the domestic image of Claire mending his mukluks by the light of a blubber lamp while he polished the harpoon for tomorrow's hunt. Or the rattle of crockery from the kitchen while he sat at ease listening to Wagnerian overtures. Domesticity suited him just fine, provided it was with Claire—and the door behind him wasn't locked and barred.

And here he made clear that domesticity didn't necessarily mean marriage. In fact, marriage itself might lead inexorably to infidelity. "Really, my love, an unlocked door is a far more secure barrier against the roving instincts of the male than is any amount of leg-irons and other fetters." It was only when the married male feels trapped by an arbitrary and cunning trick that "he becomes restive and bays the moon. Remember this. It is a truth."

DESPITE THEIR ATTEMPTS to cheer each other up, by early March Farley was beginning to worry about Claire. After a meeting where she seemed uncharacteristically distant, he wrote, "There is a fragile quality about you these days... As if you might vanish on a breath of some cold wind... I am damned worried about you—and don't brush this off too casually. The lamp burned low last night and it has always been such a strong lamp, with such a radiance, (at least it has always been this, in my experience of it) and it both wrings my heart and frightens me to see it flicker. If I'm the one who has applied the snuffer to the flame, then bad cess to me, and it were better that you snuffed me out... Mainly, I suppose, I feel guilty and don't want to face it. In the event I offer you so little—you who need so much and deserve so much."

There was plenty for Farley to worry about. Life in Palgrave had been hellish. Frances was screaming at the children these days, leaving Farley to restore order while trying to work on the new book. "[Frances] has lost all control of them, it seems. Don't know what the blazes I'm expected to do about it." He ended his letter to Claire, "Gently, love of mine, gently. We shall survive. And shall know joy. I am in love with you."

On Wednesday, March 5, 1961, Farley was supposed to see Claire but had to cancel. Frances had agreed to seek professional help in her journey back to selfhood, and Farley had to drive her to Toronto for her first appointment with a female psychologist. The Palgrave house would soon be littered with books about personality, sex, Freud, Jung, and "God knows what else." Although Farley was tentatively hopeful that the sessions might improve things, it was once again Claire who paid the price of his marital quagmire and all that it brought with it.

After a subsequent session for Frances, Farley spent two hours with her psychologist himself. He concluded that the world needed more women like her. "Oddly, the Lady Doc did more to restoring me some real equilibrium than she had any right to do. After all, I'm not the patient. But it was very good to hear some detached and uncommitted observer so forthrightly tell me what I know to be the truth—that to linger in Palgrave is to die in Palgrave, quickly. (Lady Doc wanted to know if you and I were good in bed.) She grunted with immense satisfaction when I assured her that she need have no worries on <u>that</u> score... Damn it, if I can't make you happy, who can?... I love you excessively, my small thing, and shall tickle your tummy steadily until Friday when I shall progress to greater things."

Farley may not have been the patient, but he could have been, so great was the distress of feeling trapped by bonds both palpable and nebulous that he could not escape. Held by the iron chains of marriage, he slipped on the golden glove of conscience, all the better to punish himself. Farley confessed to Claire that their situation had triggered a self-interrogation that led to "a deepening gloom that merges almost imperceptibly into a state of resignation and thence into the heart's winter, negation, silence and the hibernation of the soul—or what passes for a soul, the spirit." Claire's phrase "'The Other Woman' hurts and makes my conscience writhe. My moment for self-pity: thinking that I have now involved two of you in an intolerable situation, wound three of us into a gordian knot which I have neither the courage nor the skill to unravel without agony for one; knowing only how to sever it with a sharp blade shuddering from the stroke. Yesterday I sat staring out my cabin window at the ice glazing the bent trees and wished that you would turn upon me, eschew the misery I bring you, and send me packing."

And he offered a confession: "I have never told you this, but this purgatory in which we have been dragging out our hours, effects me in <u>all</u> ways, and that includes my capacity to love you in the way I want to love."

Farley's dark eloquence dissolved into self-pity. Time lost to Frances was one thing. But when Claire suggested she no longer believed they would ever be married, part of him knew it might be true. "I know you feel it is true, and words won't alter your convictions... Damn it, I must stop this or I'll be weeping over <u>my</u> unpolished plywood desk."

Farley struggled to speak of their future, telling Claire that he had just received a letter from Saint-Pierre informing him that *Itchy* had sunk at dockside in a gale. The good news? She had already been refloated and the shipyard men were working on her. Even better, the new diesel engine had arrived. "I love you, my darling, and shall while there is me," he wrote to her. "I don't know what you will do, but whatever it may be, I pray there is happiness in it for us."

As the winter dragged on and staggered into a ragged spring, Farley saw less and less of Claire. He was finding guilt on two fronts overwhelming. His prayer that he and Claire might know happiness went unanswered for the moment. And things remained miserable for Frances as well. As for Farley himself, he was as close to despair as he could come without shattering. "I begin to actively hate myself instead of simply passively despising myself with a kind of amused tolerance," he wrote to Claire. "And you have had to bear all this, without much explanation and that was cruel... Goddam words. All pitiful, useless, impotent words. So I shall make you a small prayer. Don't, beloved, don't let that flame grow small within you. It is not you that I fear for most, it is myself, for if your flame flickers out then indeed shall I go howling into darkness."

Claire never doubted their love, just their future. She wondered and worried what would happen to them. Would she ever be back in their love bunk on *Itchy* with the sound of waves lapping gently against their floating sanctuary? And could Farley ever give up his life in Palgrave? "It is your little homestead; and you made it; and there are two children who bear your name. When I think of this, I am more than sad, for this is all that I would have wanted. Yes, I would have buried dreams of St. Pierre and the Falkland Islands for this... Sometimes I think that nothing in my life has ever existed and it has all been made of my own imagination."

Claire wrote that maybe Farley should go to Cuba for two weeks away from both women. She even suggested that it might be time for them to take a break from each other, a proposal she quickly retracted because it would put even more strain on the less frequent encounters they did have. She still wondered, though, if he might be able to work better on the new book with fewer distractions.

Without Farley, Claire's doubts and depression were magnified—especially when it came to what she saw as her meaningless occupation behind the frosted glass and solid oak desks at Simpsons-Sears.

"Sometimes I want to run screaming out of here. But where shall I run? Down the street to more frosted glass?"

And after work there was the evening meal with the despairing and resigned members of her family, an evening at the movies with an insipid young man, empty chit-chat with a girlfriend, the loneliness of her bedroom. "Perhaps the pit ponies are happiest who never leave the mine. But you and I have left the mine, if only on our day off," she wrote.

Claire's mood darkened one day as she ate lunch by herself in the employee dining room at Simpsons-Sears, "thinking of all the other times I have eaten there, thinking the same thoughts. My little dream is gone. Yesterday you were mine today you are not... we live in our little coffins, with a glass roof to see what is happening around us, and sometimes we pretend that we will leap out... Oh god Farley how am I going to learn to live without you?"

It didn't help that she was housebound with the flu and a deep fatigue that her parents blamed on "too many late nights." She was coming to the conclusion that they suspected she was having an affair. Claire found her mother snooping in her car one day on the pretense of cleaning it. She made a mental note to hide the pâté and Polish sausage she and Farley liked so much.

Being sick at home also reminded Claire that she needed to escape Douglas Drive and her Toronto life, just as Farley needed to flee Palgrave, as a matter of survival. Her father, whose nickname for her was Nuisance, had become suspicious. Twice in the last week, he had suggested that the reason Claire talked so much about Saint-Pierre was that she had surely had a romance there. Nor could she be sure that no one was listening when she and Farley spoke on the telephone.

Before Farley burst into her life, Claire had had two boyfriends. "I was not looking for love then, for I knew too well the improbabilities of it. I was looking for a husband and a place in the sun. Then there was you, my darling and my love. From the time I have known you, nothing has mattered but that I might see you again and love you... Here I am a lonely woman of 28, and where am I going? Nowhere, nowhere, nowhere."

6 | Love at the Precipice

THEIR LIVES HAD BECOME SO ENTANGLED, fraught with so many unresolved issues and unanswered questions, that even making plans for a reunion in Saint-Pierre was difficult. Claire had to make a decision about her job. Should it be a month's summer holiday and then a return to Douglas Drive and Toronto, which Farley called "the city of the living dead"? Or, after Saint-Pierre, would it be on to England or Cuba together, never to go back to the ashes of their former lives? And what if Farley had to return to Frances and Palgrave for the sake of the boys?

Claire also knew that quitting her job would put a financial burden on Farley. She had a horror of becoming an encumbrance to him. Although she pined for him, she knew that "another winter like this would be the finish of us." Claire believed it was easier to leave a wife and rush off to join a cause like Castro's Cuba or the Inuit, because a wife at least retained her status and security, her home and children. What did a girlfriend have?

In a May letter to Claire, addressed to his "Golden Love," Farley painted a characteristically bleak picture of life in Palgrave: he was barely able to stagger to the typewriter, but he would try to scrawl a few words before they carted him off feet-first. "Bottle clutched in my pathetic little paw. Empty bottle. A ragged smile upon my ragged little face."

Palgrave had become a lunatic villa struck by the plague. Everybody was ill, including Kippy the dog and the family hens. At least most of the hens. Farley playfully wrote that there was one "beady-eyed old harridan of a Rhode Island Red" who seemed to bear him a grievance. She roosted malignantly on the doorstep and "cabled doom" at him every time he appeared. He had taken to pacing the night woods for hours, his only companions the occasional rabbit, skunk, woodcock, or unseen flock of mallards taking flight.

Everyone was so sick that Farley had to hire a practical nurse to run things. He was increasingly desperate about work and was now convinced he would not be able to complete *The Serpent's Coil* on time, which meant that if the project wasn't cancelled, it would drag on through most of the summer and "screw my rough plans for the Newfoundland book." He imagined he would be stuck in Saint-Pierre for six weeks finishing it. "It seems self evident that I can't write <u>anything</u> ontarioway, anymore. The total distractions are more than I can handle."

Claire's continued sadness about her situation confounded Farley. He couldn't think of anything to say to cheer her up that he hadn't already said. So he tried to disabuse her of the idea that he was the answer to her unhappy life at home and work. "This is a terrifyingly dangerous concept. No one can do it. We, each of us, fly alone you know. All that we can ever do for one another is to touch wing tips in flight; to fly close to one another." Otherwise, both come to earth, usually in a swamp. Farley was well aware that this was not what Claire wanted to hear. But he had seen how his wife's total dependence on him had turned into a train wreck for both of them. The last thing he wanted was to jump the tracks with Claire.

He tried to soften his message by telling her he had no doubt that together they could fly pretty close to the sun. But her wings had to be strong too. "I cannot carry you, nor you me." The only real defeat for anyone, he said, was self-defeat. To give your whole being into another's keeping and fold your wings was to "assure yourself of defeat at your own hands." Maybe this was fulfillment for a woman, but not for him.

Farley was insistent. If, however, she thought he was wrong, then Claire should "think coldly and realistically of a practical solution." She should put him aside and look for a wingless bird with broad shoulders.

He had no doubt she could find one. His words were a U-turn into tough love, but he thought there was no other way to make her grasp the need for an inner decision, as opposed to an outer action. The time to decide was drawing rapidly closer, "and you remain terribly uncertain—waiting for me to provide the certainty." There was a benefit to shifting the burden of a decision to Claire; it relieved Farley of making one about leaving Palgrave.

Farley sensed that Claire wanted him to insist that she fly the coop, which he wouldn't do, any more than Claire would demand that he leave his family. In the emotional shadow-boxing of indecision, they both turned out to be counterpunchers.

Claire sensed that Farley's enthusiasm for starting a new life with her was ebbing. She mulled over the reality that her life was how she was now living it, not how she might someday live it with Farley. She relayed to him a conversation she had had with herself. "You're a damn fool Claire," she had told herself. "This is your life, make the best of it and stop dreaming of running away with some other woman's husband." Above all, she had to stop drifting, "but I am drifting on the edge of a precipice and I may fall over, never to be seen again."

Farley remained adamant that it was better to live in the moment than to be trapped by believing in a future that was mostly invented. He admonished Claire to look around her office, at the single ones and the married ones, at the young ones and the old ones, and tell him if they were living "or if they are simply trudging blindly forward through the narcosis of their own private dreams of the future-which-will-never-be."

Then he lowered the boom. "The predicted future is delusion, pure and simple. The future built out of the present hours, laid slowly one upon the other, is the only one that ever can be real. At any rate, this is the only kind of future that I know, or will accept . . . So, live for this day though it be as short as the flicker of an eye, or as long as the road to heaven."

And if life resisted? Farley had an answer: "FORCE yourself on life! Why not? What's the alternative? In the garret rooms of the doll's house, the mummified grey shadows of men and women turn to dust— to bitter dust."

Farley observed that most people preferred pretty fictions and lies to the truth. "Not callous lies, but that worse kind, the insouciant, sticky matrix of impossible commitments in which we can trap ourselves and lie blind and dying like some insensate worm caught in a spiders web. The future that so much of the human race sells its freedom and its soul to strive towards, is just a lie we have contrived."

But all was not totally bleak. What he could promise was faithfulness in mutual flight. "I can only tell you that, if you fly with me, it will not be a lonely flight, and I will not abandon you. But <u>you must do your own flying</u>, with your own wings." He didn't like the way she cast herself as a prospective spinster surrounded by snickering schoolgirls. That was not only untrue, it was masochistic. The simple fact was that her present loneliness was the result of her relationship with him.

"If I was not on the scene, the iconoclast and shit-disturber, you would find that it would not be difficult to find community with the people who fill the swarming hive around you. Loneliness, of this sort, is the price you pay for loving me. It was a price that Fran couldn't pay. I'm not sure any woman can, or would, pay it very long. You must consider this fact." Claire was being offered the Mowat version of the old clichés: "What you see is what you get . . . take it or leave it."

But Farley also knew there was deep posturing in shifting the decision about their future to Claire and absolving himself of responsibility. In fact, he believed he had behaved badly to her on many occasions, unforgivably badly. But the "worst thing" he ever did was to encourage her to believe that someday they would have a different basis for their relationship than "no plans, no promises." It was a *cri de cœur* in defence of the status quo, and to Farley, it had the benefit of at least being clear-cut. Either they would remain together in full knowledge of the implications or they would part. In allowing Claire to believe that wasn't necessarily so, "I committed the unforgivable offense upon you," he wrote.

In his next letter to Claire in mid-May, Farley performed the usual about-face, winding up in familiar territory—he was the "son-of-a-bitch" at the base of everyone's misery. However bad things were, or he might be, he loved her totally; "the small spark of vitality which still burns, low, in this emaciated frame, burns for thee." He hoped that they would meet on some distant planet. And soon.

Farley's emotional whiplash originated in the usual place—Palgrave. He had gone through a terrible counselling session with Frances and her therapist. Afterwards, he called the therapist to arrange an interview with her so that she "might conceivably elaborate on the truth about myself, but I'm not sure I could, or would take it. I now feel like a bloody bastard toward you as well as toward F. and the kids et al. Maybe both, all four of you, ought to be wise before the event (and after) and instruct me to, in the memorable phraseology of the Sgt. Major, 'fuck off at the high port'."

Farley had sunk to his lowest depths in his relationship with Claire. He told her she would be a fool if she came to Saint-Pierre. "I hope you will be a fool—my God how I hope you will but if you are wise as you must be, I am afraid . . . I shan't come back here ever. If the choice of death remains open, then I shall take the cleaner one, the purely physical. I haven't the guts to stand the slow attrition, the piecemeal decay."

There was a matchbox in front of him, he wrote to Claire, bearing a quote from Theodore Roosevelt: "When you get to the end of your rope, tie a knot and hang on." Farley paraphrased Roosevelt's words to suit his dark mood: "When you get to the end of your rope, tie a knot, and hang." This, he said, was much closer to the truth. "Sorry, darling. But if I can't talk to you, I have only the wind to hear me." Claire's sardonic response: "If you hang yourself, I'll never speak to you again."

IN THE MIDST OF THEIR STORMY PASSAGE to an unknown destination, Claire injected a new complication in early June: she was "reasonably sure" she was pregnant. Delivering the news with her trademark droll humour, she asked if his insurance covered extramarital pregnancies. Given the situation they were in, Farley's reaction was unusual—euphoric relief.

"If you are pregnant, I will be delighted. Then I won't have to react from thought, but can react from my beautiful Old Presbyterian background. Chest out, head high, Duty calls! And the Mowats, God rot their souls, seem to be unduly dutiful. It is their Achilles heel and their undoing. But in this case, it would be my <u>doing</u> and my salvation, maybe. Something to equate against the status quo of old responsibilities—new ones, and therefore newly vital ones."

A note from Claire followed. She was not pregnant: "RELAX DARLING, JE NE SUIS PAS PLEINE!"

With those words, Farley lamented that "Monsieur le petit 'plein'" had turned a hard eye on them. Since he would not be making any decisions for them, Claire remained where she had been for some time—in purgatory with a Hamlet paralyzed by guilt, unable to act.

On May 12, 1961, Farley's fortieth birthday, Claire sent him a handsome black sweater and a card signed "From your Femme Fatale... happy birthday love!" His call that day had rekindled her spirits, and she concluded her note with "40 magnums of love." Farley told her she was wrong to insist that she was a "negative" character. It was her circumstances that were gloomy, not her. But his sense of family obligations in Palgrave prevented him from doing much about it.

Farley's son David had just started school. Farley wanted the boys to have a good and happy month before he left for the East Coast, perhaps never to return. He was also doing innumerable neglected chores around the property to smooth the way for his departure. "It isn't easy to keep up a state of interest, when my heart is away with you," he wrote Claire. "But it is good self-discipline."

The original plan was for Farley to leave Palgrave between June 1 and June 4, depending on when the Langlade or Miquelon boat came into Halifax or North Sydney. No one seemed to know when or where the boats were due to arrive. If Claire decided to come to Saint-Pierre, Farley would have a place ready for her. Beyond that, he was still thinking they might both like Cuba, and maybe they could even get some work done there. Both of them longed to escape, but it was hard to come up with a definite plan.

Instead, Farley took time off from his work on *The Serpent's Coil* to spend a day planting the vegetable gardens at Palgrave with the boys, who remained serene "throughout the damnedest hurricanes." His wife's "perennial depression" returned with a vengeance, making home life next to unbearable. Despite that, he told Claire that he could not despise Frances, explaining "what a frightful thing it would be if I were to hide my own guilt under a cape of hate. And I do feel very guilty sometimes, knowing as I do, how impossible a beast I be."

Farley was beginning to believe that the damage he inflicted on others could never be undone by a conscious effort. For some things, there is no forgiveness. The kindest thing would be to sever all connections to the past. And it was clear he wasn't thinking only about Frances. "I wonder, sometimes, how badly I shall damage you," he wrote Claire. "Maybe I shall have learned a thing or two, out of the past decade of horror, and maybe I won't be quite so heavy-footed in the future. At least, my love, you know the risks entailed in loving me."

For one of the first times in his life, just at the moment he most needed to produce, Farley didn't feel like writing. After a month of work, he had only a few thousand words, and they needed the money badly. If his wife's depression persisted, he would not be able to see Claire. Although he had to be there to feed the children and pack them off to school, when they were away, all he wanted to do was sit in the woods, clad in the black sweater Claire had given him, and think about her.

Jack McClelland had called to say that unless Farley could complete the manuscript of the sea-rescue book in time for publication that year, the deal would fall through. He doggedly went to work on *The Serpent's Coil*, and, as if by magic, it began to come together.

But his attempt to escape his marriage did not. Frances told Farley flatly that she could not remain in Palgrave alone. She would not stay unless she could believe that someday he would come back with his tail between his legs and hang his vagabond knapsack on a nail once and for all. If he wouldn't give her that assurance, Frances would have no choice but to leave their home with no idea of where she and the boys would go.

Again Farley wobbled. Although he firmly believed that Frances should stay in Palgrave, at least in the summers, if only for the children's sake, he was less than frank with her. Contrary to what he had told Claire about possibly never returning to Palgrave after Saint-Pierre, he told Frances that he would return "home" before departing for England. At that time, she could decide whether to sell the Palgrave property and move to a city or a town. Farley believed that much depended on how Frances reacted to his absence over the coming summer. He hoped that the three-month break would give her time to make a plan for living on her own.

Farley also believed that if Frances felt there was no hope of his returning after he left for Saint-Pierre, she would relapse into apathy and decay. His absence, and its bit-by-bit extension, might turn the trick. It was a dubious proposition, but his wife's psychologist thought it just might work. The alternative was chaos. If Frances fell apart, Farley would have no choice but to return to care for the children. As he wrote to Claire, "It is a prospect that makes me feel as if the bottom of my gut had dropped clean out—but it is a possibility."

Once again, resolving all doubts in favour of the status quo, rather than in Claire's favour, inspired delayed self-laceration. Farley invited Claire to take a long, hard look at him, the way some of his detractors saw him. "I don't really believe that I am quite as self-centered, thoughtless, and pig-blind as all that, but I do recognize some pretty desperate limitations when it comes to treating with other human beings. Make sure you don't delude yourself about me—not too much, at any rate."

If Claire decided to come east that summer and it turned out that Farley had to return to Palgrave, she must not put a burden on him that he could not shoulder. He assured Claire that if he had to go back, it would not be permanent, perhaps just a few weeks. There would not be a re-establishment of his little tribe. But if he had to return at intervals to "straighten out tangles," Claire would be alone for a period but not abandoned. Farley the emotional acrobat continued to straddle two worlds.

Farley again reminded Claire that if it was true that she could not stand living in Toronto any longer, then she had to change the situation herself. Claire must leave her "bad" cave because she had to, not because she was going to a "better" one. "Do you want the world?" he asked. "Then go for it. I'll be there. I go with the world and you get me (if you want me) as a bonus (or a liability), but it is the world you have to go for in the first place. That's your problem."

Claire deftly parried Farley's thrust with his own words. She said that Farley had asked her not to run away with him "but to leave because I can no longer live a happy life in my present situation. I ask you not to run away with me, but to leave because you can no longer live with your wife. I will be waiting for you. You will be waiting for me."

Worried that his words might have been misconstrued, Farley offered a clarification. He wasn't saying that he didn't want her, just that he didn't want her to be warped out of her own orbit by his gravitational pull. "I want you more than I have ever wanted any other human entity—but I want you to <u>remain</u> an entity, and no shadow at my back. I do not want you to give yourself to me in all totality. One woman shattered and pulverized in this particular mill of mine, is quite enough. I'd rather lose you now, than destroy you in the end. Much rather... But I <u>do</u> hold out my hand—<u>after</u>—your decision has been made." He would support her decision, even if it was against his desire. "I love you, you see?"

Claire's response was flawlessly supple and supportive. "Your letter rouses a very real sympathy, for I am all too aware of your ordeal. Lord knows it is a soul-searching business to leave one's wife, even if she was abhorrent to you, which she is not, really. At times you must feel torn in two... The hell of it is that the turmoil and threatened dissolution throughout this past winter has probably in itself provided a bond of sorts, in your marriage. Before this invasion, apathy ruled supreme and a sudden termination would not have seemed so out-of-order. But now, after even professional attempts at patching-up, and Fran's awareness all along of the Other Woman, termination becomes a grim anti-climax. If you do have a change of heart Farley, for any reason, you know that you can tell me. Painful it will be, but there will be no bitterness... slow attrition is not for you. Come fly with me, I will love you to extinction."

As Farley's departure for Newfoundland drew ever closer, arranging rendezvous was becoming difficult. Both felt that they were under surveillance. Claire's lies to her parents and others continued to bother

her. She said it was lucky she was not a Roman Catholic or she would surely be at confession every night. When Farley replied, he included a sheet of paper with six samples of his hair taped to it.

If, with clues, she could identify them all, she would qualify as an intimate companion. He joked that while he was away, he planned to hire the Pinkerton detective agency to keep an eye on her. Their instructions would be to assassinate any man who got a second glance "from those eyes of which I love." The humour was a mask for what he was really feeling, "detached and distant from all the world."

Farley knew that it was going to be painful to be far away from Claire for an extended time. There would be no more leaping into Lulu and driving hell-bent from Palgrave to Toronto and into her arms. But summer would come and Claire would appear in Saint-Pierre "and never go." Somehow his marriage would dissolve on its own, and they would be together. Frances would find herself and thrive. He walked around talking to himself, "C'mon Mo, give yourself to life."

Oddly enough, the pep-talk monologues made him feel better, and he urged Claire to try them. He also asked her if she had thought about what might happen at their first meeting after a month apart. "Ah, but what a glorious way to die . . . A thousand years hence the St. Pierrais will remember us with awe." He had another ten pages to write that night. "God, I am become nothing but a machine. Georgie sends his deepest, and he means it, and most penetrating affections. And I say, likewise. Goodnight my darling love."

Whenever Farley strayed into gloomy thoughts about their situation, he wondered why he seemed unable to make anyone happy. Invariably, he succumbed to the same proclivity: self-loathing. "Why is it that I am a lover of life and a hater of self? So damned silly. Do you know Conrad? Do you recall Marlow saying: 'And I say to you young man, if you cannot give yourself to life' . . . I have been Chary with the giving, and large with the taking these many seasons. Be patient with me now. For I love you dearly." In deference to Joseph Conrad, he asked Claire to make him a little card with the motto "GIVE YOURSELF TO LIFE" to pin up in front of him wherever he might be.

In the meantime, he still couldn't bring himself to ease her passage from Rosedale to a life of roaming with him. But this time, he didn't pretend his advice was wisdom, but put it down to cowardice, as his third-person confession made clear. "As of now, the blind and bull-headed rat, does not want to say to you, 'come with me, as my responsibility, and mine alone.' He wants you to say it, which is not only cowardly, but down-right despicable. He is a despicable rat. He does not seem able to appreciate the truth of things—the undeniable truth that he has led a lousy life for some years past, and that if he fails to take advantage of this golden moment of the Gods, he will go on leading an increasingly lousier life for aeons to come. He wants—oh Lord, how he wants—to seize his moment. But there is in him now a fatal lethargy, a small dying, a time of nothingness."

"The rat" believes Claire will come with him, "but who knows if it is true? If you know the truth of it, then you can make your decision about this rat. If you do not know either, then we can wait and see ... Supposing I was you, I think I should get a tin of rat poison, and not wait at all. It is the best way to deal with indecisive rodents. You are scared about the future? I am not. I do not admit to a future, which is really a sneaky way to avoid being afraid of it." Farley ended his four-page letter by writing, "The bloody birds still sing. It is time to stop this drivel."

It is always painful for true lovers to be apart, but the hardest time is in the earth-rebounding spring, when everything is pushing up, putting on leaf, breaking out. It made Claire sad that as May blossomed and June shimmered just ahead, they could not be together for any length of time before Farley left Ontario. They had just had a weekend together, and she missed him greatly in her bed. "No loving, no snuggling, no one to laugh with ..." But she did have a lasting reminder of their weekend and a certain picnic—poison ivy on her stomach and one elbow.

Farley facetiously asked Claire how in the name of Hermes she got poison ivy in such an incriminating area. He told her not to scratch but to drink brandy, eat cloves, and stay away from hot baths and amorous males. If she did all that, she would be cured. And how had Farley escaped poison ivy? "Rats have thick skins," he explained.

Claire had decided to join Farley on Saint-Pierre, at least for a holiday, but made clear that a month in paradise would merely amount to a brief vacation from the purgatory of their apparently insoluble problem. "Summer is not enough. I love you Farley. I want us to build something together. I could not endure an existence of stolen weekends and holidays. We both know this, but we must also work for it. Neither of us can continue as we are. Sometimes I think another day of it will kill me. It is certain that my situation, both at home and at work will worsen."

Claire often criticized herself for her inclination to complain. After spending a delightful weekend at Jack's house in Toronto, she concluded that the McClellands were the closest thing to the proverbial happy family that she had ever seen. She had forgotten that other people lived their lives without turbulence, leading her to wonder, "Why do I live in a state of unrest and gnawing discontent so much of the time. Perhaps I am the greedy, ungrateful whelp that my father always said I was. If I could only learn to be content with what I have."

She was bursting to return to Saint-Pierre. Apart from loving Farley, the first thing she wanted to do was take a long walk on the Dune, the large sand dune connecting the islands of Miquelon and Langlade, which was their favourite spot. There was so much for them to talk about, including their predicament. Although she reasserted her view that marriage itself was at the bottom of their dilemma, she hinted that she could live without marriage, but not without Farley. "I think the whole trouble with our society is that we take marriage too seriously. I take it too seriously... You take it too seriously. You feel guilt at walking out of it and guilt for not giving it to me. And so we both suffer."

IF THERE WAS ONE BRIGHT SPOT at that moment, it was Farley's extraordinary progress on *The Serpent's Coil*. Claire was delighted that he was writing again and encouraged him in every way. Despite everything going on around him, Farley was now working fifteen to eighteen hours a day on the book. Although he said he would rather go pearl diving in the River Styx than work at that pace, the result was something of a miracle. Farley had written an astonishing one hundred and forty pages in just eight days. At that pace, he would have a sheaf of the manuscript ready for retyping by his aunt Fran, a professional typist, in just a few days.

Better yet, by hitting three thousand words a day, he would have a draft of the entire manuscript ready for Jack in just twenty days, only a few weeks beyond a deadline he had once considered impossible to meet. And by handing the manuscript over in mid-June, his trip east would be unencumbered by unfinished literary business. The long storm would be over. Best of all, at the end of the rainbow would be his Golden Girl.

When Farley returned home each night from his writing cabin, if Frances was still awake, she would greet him amiably enough. Trying to keep her promise to Farley to begin finding her own way in the world again, she had been going to parties, where she jitterbugged the night away. And there was more good news. Farley had received a $2,000 cheque for *Ordeal by Ice*, a compilation of non-fiction stories about northern explorers, which had been published in 1960. All of this put him in an optimistic mood, which he tried to pass on to Claire.

"Be brave, my little lover, and be of good faith. I know that the gods love us, and they will not be evil to us. They never are, to those who really love." He reminded her that the ferry from Fortune in Newfoundland to Saint-Pierre started running June 1. There was a boat every day. He was sure they would find the right path forward once they were back together again. "Here there are just too damned many impingements on both of us to allow of any rational decisions."

Claire sent him a letter about a vision she'd had: "you and I hard at work, hard at play, hard at love ... yes hard at that too." She was delighted that he had asked her to do the endpaper charts for the book. Sadly, her poison ivy was still rampant, and she was beginning to look like a mummy wrapped in gauze. Claire promised that when they finally got together, she would never issue edicts like a wife, but said she might take on the job of adviser from time to time. Where should they go—Cuba, the West of Ireland, England?

On one of her many lonely nights at home, Claire created a filing system for all of Farley's love letters to her. "This of course will enable my parents to read them in proper sequence would they ever come across them. Actually it is for posterity—to speed up the work of my biographer and not keep the public waiting. Seriously, I am a well organized soul and in time you should find that I am indispensable."

Claire made another observation that may have surprised Farley, given how empathetic she had been toward Frances. Although she told Farley that he must never lose contact with Sandy, she was no longer deferring to Frances as Farley's wife.

"You know, it is a curious thought, but I think that if I were to see you with Frances I would probably be irate. I actually forget that you do have a wife. I have come to think of you as mine and would be very jealous if I were to see you with, what to me would be, another woman. Sound pretty cocky don't I?"

Claire's feistiness was clouded by the old insecurities. Even though Farley had lectured her about putting all her eggs in his basket, she offered an explanation of her situation that cleverly incorporated his insistence that everyone controlled their own happiness.

"For once I am scared about the future. Largely because it all hinges on one thing—you. I don't say that it depends on you. It doesn't. No one's future can ever depend on anything but themselves. But my every chance for happiness and fulfillment does depend on you. I know this and it frightens me."

Without him, she would lead the life of an old maid, "the stultifying and irritating days in an air-conditioned prison, a home life surrounded by aging and senile parents or a lonely little apartment all by myself." The matter was simple for him: he could leave his wife and come with her, or stay with his wife and make peace with Frances as best he could. Once more, the frustrated couple bumped hearts.

Every time he stole precious moments with Claire, Farley experienced an overwhelming sense of pending loss, the suspicion that time was somehow against him. He grew concerned that all they could do was write sad and depressing letters to each other, and it was mostly his fault. Whereas he adopted "the ostrich position" to avoid doing anything about their untenable situation, Claire faced the facts as they were.

After Farley had read her last letter three times, he replied, "There is so much truth in you that I hardly know where to start, or even, if there is much use in my starting. There seems to be too little truth in me these days. Too little something, anyhow. I remind myself of a rat in a trap—a live trap with all the amenities—who knows (or hopes he knows) that the door will spring open on a given day. Sooo, until that day, he shuts his eyes, stoppers his ears, and becomes a very cut-off rat. He may make noises, but they are probably largely meaningless."

He even wondered if his psychological problems were congenital. "Maybe I was born miserable, and this is the built-in goad to keep me writing. Not Grumpy Mo. Miserable Mo. That's him—the one with the sunburned you-know-what. You do? Of course you do! My God, I have to get away from here. I hope I can stick it . . . There are times when I have an insane desire to run screaming through the fields, thereby terrifying the poor rabbits all to hell. And getting thorns in my feet. Very difficult for a sane man who wants to <u>be</u> insane. You have to work at it so hard it takes all the joy out of it."

Faced with his impending departure for Newfoundland and Saint-Pierre, Farley felt the first pinpricks of panic. Oddly enough, he did not feel a great sense of pleasure at the prospect of being in God's country again. "I have a hunch that emotionally, we're both run down. Maybe the joy of the land will come back to me when I'm on its rocky bones again." True to form, he tried to laugh it off by telling Claire that by the time she arrived, he would be "a floating blob of greenish weed at the bottom of St. Pierre harbour." But at the sight of her, Lazarus-like, he would rise from the dead "somewhat smelly but still vital."

Sensing his guilt about some of the things he had said to her, Claire reassured Farley not to worry about anything he had ever written to her, no matter what his mood might have been at the time. "You must not have regrets for letters you have sent me my love. If they have been sent in times of anger, despair or boredom I could probably sense it anyway. You must know that you always may speak your mind with me. I loved your bittersweet letter, as I love all your letters."

Farley and Claire spent the night before his departure at Jack's house. Farley said that it was inexcusable to keep her up so late, "but it was very hard to let you go." There had not been enough tenderness on his part, but on that last night, "I felt a terrible and overwhelming tenderness for you."

Jack had been in a drinking mood after Claire left. "Oddly, I wasn't. I simply wanted to sit and moon, and hug the memory of you, and the feeling of your head on my chest." So he sat until dawn, nibbling on a bottle of brandy. "I think I must have eaten it, bottle and cork and all, from the way I feel this morning."

On June 29, 1961, a little after midnight, Claire listened to Farley's plane, one of Trans-Canada Air Lines' new Vanguards, take off from Malton Airport northwest of Toronto. It was bound for Sydney, Nova Scotia, en route to St. John's, Newfoundland. She would not see Farley for a month. In a letter written that night, she conjured up some of the pearls they had strung on the short thread of their romance.

"I have so many little visions of you and I: October days in *Itchy II*, loving on a snowy hilltop, watching ballet in Montreal, a stolen lunch-hour at Cherry Beach, snowshoeing at Lake Joseph, walking home through St. Pierre streets in the middle of the night. My God I hope I never have to suffer the discipline of trying to forget all this. No I cannot and will not forget even though I might have to remember with pain . . . Surely no one could ever love you as much as I do Farley. Remember that; remember me."

7 | Flying Solo

WHEN FARLEY LANDED at Torbay Airport just outside St. John's, Mike Donovan was there to pick him up. They drove back to Mike's house, where his wife, Jessie, and their innumerable children greeted Farley exuberantly. Someone produced a bottle of rum, the cue for Farley's old friend Harold Horwood to arrive out of the bush, half a fresh salmon bulging under his shirt.

Harold had exciting news: the capelin were "rollin'" on Middle Cove Beach. It was one of the planet's wonders, the frenzied spawning of enormous masses of small silver fish, hurling themselves onto the beach. The sea breaking on the shingle was not water but liquid capelin, all lusting mightily.

A few hundred feet offshore, sudden swirls of green water showed where cod and other predators were feasting on the capelin. So were the Newfoundlanders on the beach, men, women, and children in rubber boots, dipping their buckets into the roiling mass of fish and coming away with a bumper catch at every scoop. Farley recorded that he and Harold drove to Middle Cove to observe as scientists "the greatest exhibit of mass-fucking in recorded history. Fifty billion lecherous capelins throwing themselves on the beach in a perfect paroxysm of unbridled lust. We became so carried away that we stripped off and joined them."

Farley may have been swimming with the capelin, but on that beach he was thinking about Claire. He wrote, "There wasn't a bum there that could even dim your image momentarily. I love your little bum to distraction. I pine for it, nor will I be solaced by any proffered substitutes . . . Oh darling of my heart, bring me my bum—and soon!" If she didn't, he warned, "you will find nothing left but a Sclerosis liver and a faint memory of me."

After a few brief days in St. John's, Farley prepared to return to the place where he had met the love of his life. The night before he left, he attended a Newfoundland shindig where his head was almost knocked off when he paid a compliment in French to the fiancée of the second-toughest man in Newfoundland. "Crusher" apparently didn't like anyone sweet-talking his woman—in any language. Farley finally fell into bed, wondering what was driving him to keep such a frenetic pace. He concluded it was solitude. As he told Claire: "I seem to bear some resemblance to an engine minus its governor, in your absence."

The next morning, Farley was unable to reach the airlines to book his passage to Saint-Pierre, so he sat morosely with Mike and Harold on the Donovans' front steps, drinking rum and tea. Giving up on the telephone, they finally drove to the airport and parked at the edge of the runway, waiting for a plane going the right way.

It was a barren return. Without Claire, their fabled island seemed dour and gloomy. Adding to his misery, *Itchy* was in terrible shape. She was on a dock, painted and repaired outside but a mess inside. Engine parts were missing, and things were in such a muddle that with so much work to do he would have no time for self-pity.

And there were other disasters. His host, Theo Detcheverry, had fallen off a roof and broken both arms and several ribs. It was to be a lonely convalescence. Theo's extramarital largesse had finally prompted his wife to leave him. But he still offered to let Farley and Claire have his house for the month of August. Everyone asked after Claire. They all wanted Farley's assurance that she was really coming.

It was difficult to write, since Farley's old typewriter with its French keyboard had broken down. Without it, his brain and hand couldn't synchronize. His first letter to Claire from Saint-Pierre, written in longhand, made clear to her that the trouble with being in paradise alone is that it turns into hell. "It is shattering to find how much a part of me you have become. I could quite easily just sit me down and die. But your first letter which I await with incredible eagerness, may restore me somewhat."

He told Claire that the rowdy Canadians had already shown up at the French school. He joked that he would send Theo, the island Romeo, to Palgrave, "where he will have scope for his undoubted talents."

When Claire's first letter arrived, dated July 2, her words fell like tears on Farley's heart. She told him that a deadly hush had fallen over Douglas Drive, and it was raining. "No people, no children, no dogs . . . Surely the world is stricken by the separation of the god and goddess of love." She had been invited to spend the Dominion Day holiday weekend with a married friend in Sudbury, but had declined. She would be poor company, unable to feign good spirits when she was so utterly miserable.

She had been rereading Farley's letters, especially the one in which he told her that she had "dragons to slay"—a reference to getting out from under her father's patriarchal thumb. For years, the man who had served in both world wars had bullied and belittled her emotionally. Farley told her it had to stop. After carefully considering his words, she wrote, "I know that it is painfully true."

Claire had been dependent on her father until she was twenty-three, when she finished her education. He bombarded her with the message "that his bounteous mercy and generosity was providing this idyllic life for me." One of his nicknames for her was "Useless," because he thought she provided nothing to the family circle. Claire didn't know why he tormented her, but wondered if it had something to do with the fact that she was the first person on either side of her family to go to college. "Perhaps he resented the intrusion on what he considered his intellectual domain, and his undisputed authority over the family in all matters."

Her period of dependency had ended five years earlier, but she had been unable "to slay the dragon." She continued to fear her father and hoped that matrimony might free her from his tyranny. "Probably I am not very brave. 23 years of vitriolic outbursts of temper have had their effect. I was afraid. Just as afraid as a little girl is afraid of incurring the wrath of her omnipotent father."

Despite the painful memories, she was now at least able to defend her mother against him. He was too old to rage now, so he had developed a new weapon: laughing at her. "Curiously enough, my mother has never been submerged by him. She has succumbed many times for the sake of peace, but she is always ready to fight and has managed to keep her head above water. So it was that my early days were spent in a constant state of war."

Claire observed that her father had an uncanny knack for spotting the weakness in those around him and exploiting it mercilessly. She suspected the reason she had not married was the iron grip he had over the women in his household. "Perhaps, inwardly I am afraid of being subjected to masculine domination once again."

Claire also considered that she might be exaggerating his faults, fanning the embers of mere foibles into the flame of mortal sins. In any case, she knew that she should not make her father the fountainhead of her problems.

Claire told Farley that she still didn't want her parents to know about their affair. She could tell them to mind their own business. "But they still have the normal hopes that one has for a daughter—to marry well and happily. If you had a daughter you would hope this too . . . To state openly that I am in love with, and having an affair with a married man who cannot marry me, would only bring them sorrow. Unfortunately it brings me sorrow too, and I would have no defence against them. Don't expose me Farley. Let me find another way to kick him in the ass, but not this one."

She was reading *Owls in the Family* and thought it was the book that would make Farley Mowat a household name. "Seriously, I love it. It really has something. I am just kicking myself that I did not insist on drawing the owls for it." She had his love poem and cherished it. "I shiver a bit as I read it, and I read it every day." She sent her fondest wishes to poor Theo.

Farley had looked forward to leaving his problems behind when he left Ontario but couldn't get Claire off his mind. Four days after arriving in Saint-Pierre, he wrote that if he did not have her close to him soon, he would cut his throat, beard and all. *Itchy* was still a mess, but the new bunks were turning out splendidly, tailor-made for love-making. As he'd suspected before he fled Palgrave, the separation proved to Farley that he could not exist, let alone take pleasure in life, without her. There was so much to talk about, so much life to live together. Words and weekends were not enough.

The only cure for all his ills was Claire. "It's what's always been wrong," he wrote to her, "even long before we met. I've been yearning for you through a decade, and now that I have you, I can't muster the common guts to take you for myself. I equivocate and fuck around like a pig in a poke... I love you. Christ, <u>that's</u> my talisman. And my need of you is so engrossing that I cannot, and maybe dare not, admit it fully to myself. I'm also getting pretty scared. My general ineffectiveness and impotence (all right, all right, impotence of the <u>spirit</u>) shows no signs of diminishing but, in fact, grows steadily worse."

Farley mused that he might emulate a dog he had seen chasing its tail in circles with its eyes closed, under the influence of a small bitch in heat on the boatyard slip. As a matter of fact, if he weren't so naturally lethargic, he might even have a go at being mad. Except that in Saint-Pierre, no one would even notice.

For Claire, Farley's surrender to the power of love was morning mist over a drooping rose: "I am overcome with desire for you," she wrote to him. "What ever will I do?" The gods were smiting her for her self-pity and tears the night before he had left. But "thoughts of you are the next best thing to having you."

It seemed ages since he had gone, but it had been only six days. She daydreamed about where he was and pictured him roaming about their island paradise, "greeting old friends, patting *Itchy* on the rump, sniffing the fog and generally becoming Farley Mowat again." She was not thinking about the future, only the here and now and the fact that she would soon be with him. "Dream of me, I am the golden girl who loves you... Just you stay away from that fish-plant. Be patient, hang on, I'm coming."

One night, Claire had a drink with a stockbroker friend at the Toronto Cricket Club, an upper-middle-class knock-off of the tonier Granite Club. Dozens of Toronto's bright young professionals were there, comfortably surrounded by one another, and, as described by Claire, their dull, well-bred wives spent the evening nodding, smiling, and adding nothing to the conversation.

When she told Farley about the gathering, he was quick to reply. "I see them. Huddled in fear and desperation, born blind, self-blinded by their fear. Eschewing love, and life itself, so that they may not have to know that man is born alone, lives lonely, dies in loneliness . . . I say, they do not live at all. What in god's name is the point of contentment? Cows have it."

Claire was acting as the Toronto contact for Farley, and in her next letter she enclosed some business matters sent by his friends Rose and Martin Kastner. Had he arranged to have his mail forwarded from Palgrave? When Claire spoke to Rose on the telephone, the conversation turned to Farley, and, Claire reported, Rose "just loves your lean loins." She cautioned Farley not to get a swelled head because two women in Toronto were discussing his loins.

WHEN HE WAS IN PALGRAVE and she was in Toronto, Farley had never been able to understand Claire's misery. But ten days of being separated by almost twelve hundred miles changed that. Now he too knew what it felt like to be living in suspended animation. Without her, things were out of joint, the loneliness absolute. "It is a kind of passive despair, a nullity, a frenetic scrambling in a void . . . Can't think, can't work, don't want to do any damn thing. Don't even want to die. Only thing I want is you. Bloody zombie, that's what I am. Nuts. I shall re-read your letters over a small noggin of cognac and dream some dreams of loveliness. Some splendid dreams. Oh woman, woman, woman, I love you so."

It was even difficult to write to Claire and impossible to write to anyone else, including his beloved Sandy. Farley asked Claire to phone Jack McClelland and tell him that he had not received the edited manuscript of *The Serpent's Coil* yet. He also wanted her to let Jack know that the boat was in shambles and would not be ready until mid-July. As it turned out, Jack would not be coming, for his wife, Elizabeth, was in the final weeks of pregnancy.

Farley's lifeline and torment was the mail—heavenly when it arrived, hellish when it did not. The postmaster on Saint-Pierre beamed as he handed Farley two letters from Claire that had come in on the Miquelon boat; it took from four days to two weeks for their letters to reach each other. Farley celebrated by having a small orgy alone, featuring Claire's words and a bottle of Izarra, "which I should not drink since it makes me extremely lecherous."

After reading Claire's letters, Farley was struck by the depth of her wisdom. "The quiet youth I so rarely meet in the flesh, but seem only to know through letters, is surely the daughter of the calm-browed Goddess whose name, they say, is Minerva." He yearned for the time "when we become as intimate and as much at one within the spirit as we are in the flesh. It will come—with long days sans strains, growing into one another, slowly."

Farley firmly believed that talking about her relationship with her father would greatly help Claire to "to banish the old tiger to his lair." Childhood demons would be exorcised with truth, insight, and love. Farley was close to tears at the thought that as a girl Claire had been afraid of her father. He reminded her that she had since grown up. "You are a woman. Not a child hiding in a woman's flesh. You are the mostest woman of all. I know. Take my word for it. The old expert. I may be a wee bit biased of course, loving you to distraction as I do."

The errant sixteen-year-old was long gone, he assured her. So down with self-pity, self-laceration, self-hate, and self-doubt, he said. "I love you as I have never loved another human entity. I have known a few score too. There is, in you, so much beauty, so much compassion, so much loving tenderness that it spills out all over."

That day on Saint-Pierre, Farley notched a small victory. *Itchy* was launched and managed not to sink. "I am beginning to think that wooden women are more trouble than they are worth. I don't have to clean your bilges out, varnish your spars, paint your decks, grease your stays etc etc. All I need to do with you is give you a loving look. Doesn't work with *Itchy*. She is the demanding kind."

Farley reported a small disaster at dockside. He had awakened early one morning, in good spirits and eager to get to work, only to find the boat half-full of water. The inlet tap for the engine cooling system had been left on, and *Itchy* had flooded. Did he walk in his sleep, he wondered, or was this just *Itchy's* natural penchant for becoming a submarine?

Farley had a lot to do on the boat and not much time to do it. He mused that he would probably be dead before Claire got there. "Still, I do yearn to be aboard her, to have my own small home that I can prepare for my love's arrival. A place where I can sit and dream of her, alone with her."

Farley had found out that the first and last chapters of *The Serpent's Coil* had been sent to St. John's and would not reach him for a "dog's age." He asked Claire to call Jack and ask him to airmail copies to Saint-Pierre. His friend Henri Morazé, owner of a shipyard business in Saint-Pierre, had agreed to fly their mail in on his small airplane.

It was amazing what her letters did for his spirits. He was no longer cut off, alone, forgotten, and drifting. "I am in love, and my love sustains me . . . I believe that I need you even more than you need me . . . Write often, write long, write of love and hope."

In the dead zones of Toronto, Claire savoured Farley's letters, reading them slowly, and then rereading them. She was thrilled that Newfoundland had opened its heart to Farley when he stopped there. "But there is nowhere on earth that would not open its heart to you. All the world loves a lover and you are that . . . the world's lover. And also, I am led to believe, a capelin lover. There won't be time for that when I arrive."

She wondered how their reunion would go, and which Farley would show up. "Will you be drunk and disorderly as you were at Footes Bay? Or quietly repressed and a little guilty as you were another time at Footes Bay," she teased.

He replied in deadly earnest. "Your curiosity as to how I shall greet you—dead drunk and disorderly, or guiltily withdrawn, rouses more than guilt—moral awareness. There are occasions when I am totally convinced the race is run and done, and never won. What is so nau-seating as the spectacle of an old nag continuing to canter around the deserted track when the race is over. It wasn't age per se, but decrepi-tude of will, a shortage of essence, a withdrawal from mine own self." There is rust in his throat, he says, because Claire is the only person to whom he can speak truly about himself.

Back in Toronto, Claire had dinner with Farley's aunt Fran, who was retyping Farley's manuscript. She and Fran were kindred spirits. It made her sad that Fran was old and alone and had nothing more to look back on than thirty-four years with the same company, and noth-ing more to look forward to than her dance lessons at Arthur Murray Studios—Claire's nightmare. The two women discussed Farley and his relationship with Claire. Aunt Fran said it was a very great pity that Farley had not met Claire first.

In Saint-Pierre, Theo had become a wharf boss for Henri Morazé and was now in charge of eighty men. Farley wrote to Claire that a des-perate cow brought from Sydney for slaughter had made a mad dash for freedom by jumping into the harbour and attempting to swim out to sea. The poor beast was finally lassoed and hauled back to keep its grim date with the butcher. Farley vowed to eat no part of the doomed but heroic animal.

The carpenters had almost finished *Itchy's* cabin, and Farley was delighted. "Ah, those new bunks! We shall make the most ferocious and memorable love upon them, and we shall sometime just lie qui-etly upon them, in each others arms, and drift into the peace of love." Claire offered her congratulations. "I shall look upon it as my honey-moon cottage, my nuptial bed, my place of true love, our first home."

Farley had painted the masts a buff colour. The hull was now a rakish, piratical black, and the cabin trunk would eventually be a buff colour too. Farley reported that work on Claire's pissoir was underway, but they needed some information. "How high off the ground is your little ass? What is the circumference?" She replied that she was quite prepared to use the facilities at the stern of the boat, provided she didn't have to do so under the eyes of the entire crew of a Spanish trawler.

In a few days, Farley would finish painting the cabin. For once, the weather was gorgeous—clear, bright, and cool. For the first time since returning to Saint-Pierre, Farley walked up into the hills. In mid-channel, he could see a small Spanish side-trawler waiting for her sister ship to slip her lines from the dock. They always fished in pairs.

Farley was getting to know Saint-Pierre as a resident rather than a tourist. He had visited the shoemaker and knew the best butcher and most of the other shopkeepers. He had credit at the local bank. Farley and the gendarmes formally saluted one another when they crossed paths. He was also meeting a lot of people—not entirely a good thing. He was obliged to acknowledge so many acquaintances walking down the street on errands that he suffered from *"bonjour"* fatigue by the time he reached his destination. And the harbour was still full of dead cats and sleek outboards.

The more he thought of Claire, the more he realized that his feelings toward her had undergone a sea change. His overwhelming emotion was not one of physical passion, though that side of him sizzled in almost every letter. This new feeling was of tenderness, a desire to be gentle to Claire. It puzzled him. "What does this mean? That I am growing old before my time? Or that I am not eating enough grass."

Farley toyed with the idea of taking her on a ten-day sail to Baie d'Espoir on the south coast of Newfoundland. "It would be magnificent to be totally alone with you . . . You would learn to hate me, though. Dirty finger nails, whistling under my breath, etc. Will you hate me some day? I do not think so. You do not hate at all, as far as I can tell. No more do I. A sullen waste of time. Loving is better. Loving you is best of all. I am busy loving you right now. I am tickling the warm soft flesh of your thighs. I am nibbling your nipples too. I'm a devil . . . Lie down Georgie. DOWN Boy! Down." And then: "Now to bed, with *Lord Jim*. I hold your round, brown bum in both my hands, and love all of you to distraction."

Claire was distressed about Theo's terrible fall and felt even worse that his wife had left him because of his relentless philandering. She told Farley she had no objection to staying at Theo's house, but that he might well have an issue with her cooking. As for Farley's gloomy thoughts about death, she scattered them as best she could. "Do not harbour thoughts of sitting down and dying. I shall be furious . . . Ernest Hemingway shot himself—probably because he had not discovered St. Pierre and love. Count your blessings darling. Your love is on the way."

Hemingway had committed suicide on July 2, and it had become a subject of conversation at Douglas Drive. Claire's mother asked if her "friend" Farley Mowat had known Hemingway. She said she didn't think so. "Well, why not?" her mother insisted. "They were both writers."

AS THE DAYS APART dragged on at a glacial pace, they both lived for comforting replies to their letters. Except for that, all they could do was count the days until they were together again, reread old letters, and bask in the ersatz glory of memories. At night, before falling asleep, Claire thought of snuggling in Farley's beard.

"There never has been anyone else," she wrote to him on July 8. "No one who even came close to being the things you are." She suggested that if their love story had been a nineteenth-century novel, one of them would die of consumption, he would be killed in war, or she would die in childbirth. Only today do love stories have happy endings. She was going to Muskoka with her parents and planned to read and sunbathe, then go to sleep and dream of him. "I want you to need me. I need you and love you, terribly." She enclosed a photo from their time on Saint-Pierre.

Farley put in time working on the boat and the edited manuscript as the chapters arrived. With so many things going wrong with *Itchy*, he began to think it was a local conspiracy to keep the shipyard busy in the off-season. He spent two twelve-hour days on the cabin over one weekend, thinking of Claire with each ticked-off item on his to-do list. He thought the boat looked quite attractive, very clean, and homey. "Your home. My home. Our home."

Some missing parts had arrived by air, and the next day, with the help of the cargo ship *Miquelon*'s boom, the shipyard workers hoped to swing the new engine aboard and close up the gaping hole in the stern deck. At first, the engine did not fit the available space. Finally, after several beers had been drunk, it miraculously slipped into place. Farley shunned socializing, the better to apply himself to the tasks at hand. Early to bed, early to rise. "No bars, no dances, no parties. They wait until you come," he wrote to her.

There were, however, a few exceptions.

A certain Mme Versailles was madly in love with Farley, as he reported to Claire. She wheedled him into taking her to a dance. "Poor thing. She does not know that I have taken vows. Vows to love one Golden Girl into practical extinction." He advised that Georgie had become morose and hopeless. Would Claire still love them if Georgie became atrophied?

Farley also joined in Bastille Day celebrations—but not before putting the final touches on *Itchy*. He rose with the sun streaming in his window, wolfed down a *petit pain,* gulped a cup of coffee, and then hurried off to the quay. He painted steadily from 8 a.m. to 4 p.m., sharing a bottle of Napoleon brandy with his friend Paulo, the shipyard foreman, who was helping him complete the decks and the cabin.

After Farley finished, Theo cajoled him into going to the Bastille Day festival on the quad. It was a scene of merriment and mayhem: firecrackers, fights, much drunkenness, and confetti thick as snow. Farley made his way back to Theo's house, which had clearly been the scene of celebrations of its own. "The Place littered knee deep in popcorn boxes, old safes, exploded firecrackers, dead bodies (semi, in fact they were only moribund Newfoundlanders)." He then crawled off to his lonely bed, thinking of Claire. "With one person, or in a crowd," he wrote, "I am alone if you are not with me."

Farley told Claire that he was walking more than he had in the army—twenty miles every day, usually on small tasks and errands, sometimes just exploring. During these solitary treks, he marvelled at the turn his thoughts had taken. He was shocked to discover in himself the truth of an old cliché, the one about the effect of forced absence on love.

"Despite my disinclination to envisage a future, I find myself more and more thinking in terms of the frightening prospect of a future without you. It is a terrifying and ghastly prospect. Absence has not diminished my love for you, nor my need of you, but has intensified both to an astonishing degree. Astonishing to me, because I had not believed myself still capable of such longings in the inner heart."

But the old doubts, primarily about himself, crept in. "Claire I need you so bloody badly that I can't admit the magnitude of the need." He was obsessed with his own inadequacy. He feared "that I have damn all to give ... If I go back to Palgrave and all that is entailed ... one more zombie joins the walking dead ... I wish to hell sometimes that I had never been awakened, never come to life, and had remained in the ranks of my compeers in death ... Half dead without you, and the other half more sick with longing."

Perhaps, he told her, the old gods would be moved to pity if they made love magnificently. Putting his amorousness on a biblical scale, he declared he would do so for forty days and forty nights. *"Aprés moi, le déluge."* With that in mind, he instructed her to bring "rubber protection" when she came, because it was not obtainable on Saint-Pierre. Claire demurred. "It's just something that nice girls from Rosedale don't go and buy for themselves." Farley said he would write Jack and ask him to be their condom courier if he came to Saint-Pierre. And if he didn't? "Then we shall simply have to be prepared for a *baptême*."

A glowing piece about Saint-Pierre had appeared in the Toronto magazine *Star Weekly* on July 1, 1961, extolling its many charms, including its marvellous weather. The piece had attracted so many visitors that accommodation was almost impossible to find. Surrounded by tourists who moved like ghosts though the constant rain and fog that had descended, Farley lowered the bombastic boom on the author of the piece. "The bastard who wrote for the *Star Weekly* should be castrated. Sunshine? Lard Jesus! Rain, rain, rain. I am saturated, boat is saturated, St. Pierre is saturated." The bastard who had written the piece was one Farley Mowat.

Alternating between hope and despair, Farley entertained the idea of flying to Toronto to see Claire. His depressions were worsening, affected perhaps by Hemingway's suicide. He told Claire that she must know that someday he would take his little boat, in reality or figuratively, and sail east single-handed "for no port on any chart ... The most dreadful thing a man can ever have to bear is quietude within himself."

Cessation would be the only answer. "When the lines were slipped I do not want to see you standing on the shore crying after me, 'you were false.'"

Although he possessed the boundless creative energy that would see him through forty-two books and put him in the vanguard of all the great causes of his time, Farley had a bent for nihilism that pulled him off course like a riptide and sucked him down like an undertow.

"Claire, my Claire, my love—the wheels have stopped! The only thing which saves me from becoming one rusting chunk of amorphous tissue is your love. Tissue can't rust. But did you ever see one of the Peruvian mummies taken from the dry and arid plateaus of the high Andes? They too have the semblance of life. The dry winds have blown through me for too many years, I think."

And then he wrote of a strange dream he had, a dark vision of his death that somehow bestowed great peace.

"We lie together not having made physical love, but consumed by a magnificently ecstatic intercourse beyond the flesh; we lie in the aftermath and you take my head and gently bring it to your breasts, holding it, and me, tenderly and with such sweet silence that I voluntarily open the last, small door at the end of the corridor, and pass through it into nullity. There is nothing grim about it. *Au contraire*, it is an almost perfect moment—imperfect only in that it is a dream."

Desperate as it sounded, Farley was not speaking of their love, which still sustained him. "In that, I live and have my being, but it is a small being now, I am afraid it is too small for you. I fear that you will think so too. Fear is not the right word. Without your love the bateau would have sailed and perhaps that is what I want. No. Not 'want' for I am no longer a wanting-man. To make an end: not because of a compulsion, but from total lack of all compulsion. Oh my god I wish you were here."

With the walls already closing in, it didn't help that Farley was still having difficulty finding suitable accommodation. They might be able to rent a room at l'Escale, but for now it was overrun with "loud-mouthed" tourists. The few places that were available were demanding a year's rent. Theo's house was overcrowded with his children and rowdy boarders from the French school and their broods, who were "wreaking havoc."

But staying at Theo's had its advantages. They would have a guest room for visitors and a real bathroom, though the kitchen aboard *Itchy* was better, with its new propane stove. Farley asked Claire to decide if she wanted to be domestic and do the cooking. If she didn't want to stay at Theo's, he would build her a house himself. "St. Pierre without you is the afterworld, the wrong side of the Styx. And I am damn well going to end this epic in self-pity and go and get quietly, and decently, drunk. Alone. I am very much alone."

Claire assured him Theo's place would do just fine. In any case, their real nest would be on board the newly gussied-up *Itchy*. She had already reserved a room in Sydney for the night of Saturday, July 29, and was delighted that, weather permitting, Farley would meet her CNR train there. In the last month, Saint-Pierre had had only two days of pallid sunshine. The rest of the time, the island lay shrouded in fog. Claire also worried that the inn she had booked was run by a "puritanical old couple" and Farley's appearance "might raise a few eyebrows." So she registered as Mrs. Claire Wheeler, just in case she had a bedfellow for the night.

"Oh how I need you, and peace. What do you say we spend the first two days in bed? We will just make love and then rest. And then we will make love and rest again." She enclosed a picture of herself sitting on a rock, Farley's Little Mermaid. Claire thanked Farley for arranging her travel between Sydney and Saint-Pierre, booked as a student of the French school in Saint-Pierre. Farley had sent a telegram to her home in Rosedale with the arrangements, signed "Georgie."

Farley was growing desperate. "Oh Jesus, I hope you get here soon. And I hope, as I have never hoped for anything that you can work the miracle, that you'll want to work it ... I do not have the sustaining satisfaction of being self-engrossed. I'm simply un-engrossed. Engross me Claire, kick my ass, pull my beard, beat me with lobster pots, be drastic!"

Although Claire didn't mention it, she was terrified of making the trip. The last time she had travelled east, it had taken forty-eight hours to get from Montreal to Sydney, two days of misery caused by weather delays. A strike was looming at Trans-Canada Air Lines, so this time she decided to take the train from Montreal to Sydney. She worried that she might be on the verge of a nervous breakdown and felt that she would crack if she didn't get out of Toronto soon. She had been stressing about a job she couldn't bear and what seemed to be her permanent state of loneliness. And it was eighty-eight degrees Fahrenheit and raining. As one of her professors had remarked, cities were made for winter; summers in them were merely to be endured.

Farley told her that he had arranged a week in Langlade, the island connected to Miquelon by the tombolo called the Dune. She loved the idea. It would clear away all the cobwebs in their weary souls. Claire received another telegram on July 27, informing her that *Itchy* would be ready for her arrival. Best of all, Georgie would be flying to Sydney to meet her on Saturday, July 29, after all. The telegram concluded, "ORDEAL ALMOST ENDED HAPPINESS AHEAD BE FORTE."

On Friday morning, with only ten minutes' notice from the airport, Farley flew from Saint-Pierre to Sydney in Henri Morazé's small plane. Claire's train from Montreal was due in at 10:50 p.m., by which time he had already walked from the inn to the station three times. At the stroke of midnight, the magic coach pulled into the station, and off stepped Cinderella.

They unabashedly clung to each other, oblivious to their very public surroundings. Then they retreated to their room, where they read poems, drank brandy, and contemplated having a hot bath to relax. The water grew cold while they talked. It was a lovely summer night, and the moon made a fire-path across the harbour, pouring through the open window like a silver promise of better days. Claire handed Farley a small present from Jack. Farley smiled. It was their baptism protection.

Farley awoke early on the morning of Sunday, July 30, but let Claire sleep in. After a late-morning breakfast, they ambled through Sydney. Claire loved to visit old graveyards and was delighted with the city. An acquaintance of Farley's from the shipyard docks gave them a gift of wine and dried capelin. They strolled hand in hand along the "aptly named George Street," sniffing the roses. Back at the hotel, they made love in the summer sunlight and fell into a deep, velvety sleep.

Afterwards, they sat on a bench and watched the harbour darken as the day drained away. Then it was back to the room for a feast of capelin toasted over a candle. They sang Newfoundland songs and held philosophical discussions in the bathtub. They went to bed as the moon came up "and bathed my love in beauty," as Farley noted in his diary.

Because of heavy fog, there were no flights to Saint-Pierre, so they had another day in Sydney for doing what lovers do. Although Sydney was a coal-mining town, not known for its beauty, to Farley and Claire, it might as well have been Paris. They went to bed early and read D. H. Lawrence together, feeling like characters in one of his novels.

On Tuesday, August 1, the fog in Saint-Pierre suddenly cleared, and they rushed to the airport to catch a flight before it closed in again. They were the only passengers on board, their only company a few bags of mail. Close to their destination, the pilot, Charlie, gave them a spectacular aerial tour of the south coast of Newfoundland, taking them down to just three hundred feet.

Over the Grand Barachois, basking seals plunged into the ocean at the sound of the plane.

8 | Paradise Regained

THEIR RETURN TO SAINT-PIERRE was Miltonic: paradise regained.

Claire thought it would be easier to hold a picnic in a rugby scrum than to live in the chaos of Theo's house. Although the boat needed some organizing, and the bedrolls were still damp from all the rain, they took up residence aboard *Itchy*. The smaller the space they shared, the better they liked it. Working side by side, they got her shipshape.

Claire loved the way *Itchy* moved gently beneath them, exactly as it had the year before. They fell asleep as night sounds of the harbour softened and faded. Farley woke once to see a beam of moonlight coming through the porthole and shining on Claire's face. There she was, less than an arm's length away. It was an intimacy that could never be found in someone else's house or a hotel bedroom. As Farley wrote in his diary, "We had come home."

The next morning, Thursday, August 3, they sat on deck as the day grew brighter, then continued making the ship ready to sail. A couple of days later, a huge French research ship, the *Thalassa*, arrived in port, and that night there was a dance at the Salle de Dance. The hall was packed with locals, tourists, and burly Portuguese fishermen. The band was loud and the room was smoky and hot. Even though he was no Fred Astaire, Claire convinced Farley to get up and dance: "I need not have worried for in her arms an elephant could dance," he wrote in his journal. "She danced, in fact, magnificently and with such vivacity that she quickly became the cynosure of all eyes, and there were some honestly lustful eyes amongst them." At 3 in the morning, they made their way home.

The first week together passed in a flash. One night, after a 9 p.m. tour of the *Thalassa*, they stopped at l'Escale for a quick drink and navigated home through the fog. Farley was just climbing into his bunk when he heard a resounding splash. He hustled on deck with a flashlight.

There in the dark and oily waters was Claire. She had squatted over the side of the boat to pee and missed the handrail in the dark. She was an excellent swimmer, but with her slacks down around her knees, her legs were useless. There was no question of opening her mouth to scream for help; swallowing any of the harbour's foul water would be dire. Farley fished her out, and they clung together on deck "laughing like mad fiends." He helped her to clean up, and they were soon warm and snug in their bunks against the chilly night.

After a week in Saint-Pierre, they set sail for Fortune, Newfoundland. A light southeast wind held the promise of a fair voyage. Farley exulted in their escape. "Claire and I imbued with a heavenly sense of release. A pale sun warmed our backs as the island drew astern. I, in particular, felt like a free man again after a long month of incarceration in a dirty harbour. We streamed our log and set our course, North 50 East."

Nature saluted them. A pod of pothead whales spouted nearby, and puffins swung overhead. "We were alone and in a new and different world." For the first time in a year, the ship was fully alive and doing what she was built to do. Farley and Claire sat together in the steering well, revelling in the magnificent isolation. "We looked at each other and grinned with the joy of it," he wrote. They had a picnic of crusty bread, pâté, cheese, sausages, and good red wine. "I for one would not have given over my place at the helm of the little vessel for a place in heaven."

After a perfect day on the ocean, they lowered their sail, started the engine, and made their first port, Fortune. Tied up at the wharf after clearing customs, Claire cooked a magnificent stew while Farley "sat and glowed with pleasure in her, in my ship, and even a little, in myself." The fog came in and they crawled into their sleeping bags. "We cuddled close and listened to our own heartbeat on one another's breasts."

Despite grey skies and a strong onshore wind, they left the next morning, bound for Pass Island Passage. Early in the afternoon, the sun broke through and they stripped off their clothes and sailed naked for a while, eating cheese sandwiches and sipping wine. By the time they reached the settlement of Pass Island, at 4 p.m., they had logged thirty sea miles. They decided to set a course for Pushthrough in Great Jervais Bay, a settlement of 250 people. Claire was entranced by the place and couldn't wait to go ashore to explore.

That night, they were fogbound, and Claire joked that "the fog follows Farley." After a dinner of boiled cod, they lay on their bunks and read Lord Byron's epic poem *Don Juan* aloud, sipping rum. It was celebration day—the first anniversary of the day they fell in love on Saint-Pierre.

They spent the night anchored in tiny Clay Hole in Roti Bay. It was a spectacular experience. Farley wrote that "this became one of our most poignant nights together. We were quite alone, as alone as though the world had ended while only we survived. The wind moaned and whinnied more and more loudly from the high hills, our rigging sang a nasal refrain to it. The ship tugged at her chain like a restive horse tugging at its bit. Yet we were secure with womb-like security. I lay, naked, on my berth smoking and fiddling with the radio trying to get a weather report—and succeeding, by damn, in getting one at last but from Moscow... *Itchy* moved under us as if in sympathy with our passion and we were one, my love and I. I slept an almost deathlike sleep, and heard nothing of the night." Outside in the bay it must have been blowing half a gale, and all was black with fog and rain.

The next day, they scrubbed the ship, and by noon the sky had begun to clear, so they rowed ashore in search of fresh water. They climbed up from the beach and found a pool of crystalline water no bigger than a bathtub. They stripped and bathed, "like a maid and centaur." It was a fairy meadow, surrounded by giant ferns and wet moss. "My love was lithe and golden in the dappling sunlight, and more beautiful than all the world." When they reached the beach again, they became children together, digging clams with scallop shells.

Farley's fame occasionally intruded on their anonymity. In one of the small outports, they visited the principal at the local school, who guided them to a berth at the government wharf, and recognized Farley from a photo in *Time* magazine.

One of the highlights of the trip was how Claire took to the Mi'kmaq residents of Conne River. Farley always felt more at home with Indigenous people than with anyone else. "I used to think it was rank sentiment which always made me feel more at home with Indians, but I begin to think it is an honest feeling. There is much goodness in them, no more than a normal amount of evil and, what is more vital, they are not afflicted with the perverse pettiness that mars so many of us."

Although a novice, Claire proved to be a brave and competent sailor and could handle the tiller or the engine. Farley was impressed. "One would have thought she had been born in a fisherman's dory." They moored in Gaultois, a small village on Long Island, on Newfoundland's Coast of Bays. A small boy got them cod tongues from the fish plant, which they ate with blanched asparagus and mayonnaise, homemade bread, and a bottle of Sauternes.

"There is nothing more pleasant than lying in safe port after a hard, or an exciting passage," Farley wrote in his journal. "I think the one thing which occupied our thoughts most, was the feeling of unity which such a passage engenders and which goes beyond sex into the realms of perfect companionship and trust. I felt that I would be prepared and ready, to go anywhere with the golden one by my side; and though she may have had some reservations about doing likewise with me . . . she did not indicate it in any way."

Claire was fascinated with Gaultois. The children of the tiny settlement had made teeter-totters from planks laid across a concrete wall and were singing in unison as Farley and Claire returned from a hike up the side of a cliff. Farley noted that the children here were imbued with the wild freedom of life and the adults were wise enough to let them live it.

The final stop on their voyage was Hermitage, a community of a few hundred people on the south coast, not far from Harbour Breton. They left *Itchy* there and booked passage for the next day on the

depart at once, before the gale grew worse. He hurried to collect his gear, but by the time he got back, all he could see was the ship rolling and pitching out past the inner harbour light. Then they learned that the DC-3 was planning to make a break for Sydney after all. They managed to get Claire to the airport just in time. It was all over, abruptly and in a rush. As the plane rumbled down the runway and lifted off, Claire gazed down at Farley waving a slow goodbye and cried.

"She was gone," he wrote. "Let there be no more partings as sad as this one."

Claire sat in the Sydney airport numb and disbelieving. "I can't quite realize that I've left you; that I won't be able to snuggle up beside you tonight," she wrote to him. "I'm still warm and glowing with your touch." This time last year, she had been on exactly the same flight, going back to exactly the same place. "One day our time will come I'm sure," she wrote through her tears. "We will go away together and never return."

9 | Farley Adrift

WITH CLAIRE GONE, Farley was dazed and adrift on a sea of loneliness.

His boat was now moored at the head of Baie d'Espoir, Newfoundland, and she needed to be hauled up for the winter before he could head west. But the familiar depression that often afflicted him when he was on his own descended. He walked for hours on the high ground toward Anse à Ravenel, in and out of the mist. He saw the sun slip behind the shrouded hills and watched the waves break on the rocks. The contradictions of his life crashed against his troubled heart, a pounding surf of guilt and longing.

By dawn the next day, he was desperate for Claire and full of dread at the idea of returning to Palgrave. But he couldn't bear another moment of feckless pining and paid a dory man, the estimable father of sixteen children, fifty dollars to set sail for Hermitage in a gale. That was where *Itchy*, again called the *Happy Adventure,* her original name, was moored. Farley felt she had earned the name now. Six and a half hours later, just after dark, they dropped anchor in Fortune. Farley was up at 4 a.m. and sailed off early to rendezvous with Harold Horwood, who was waiting in Hermitage. This was unknown territory for his Saint-Pierre crew, so Farley acted as navigator, using a compass and an Irving road map of Newfoundland. "Still it was probably more than the Vikings had," he noted.

Claire's departure had depressed him so much that he barely cared if they went under in the rough seas. He had to flee the place where he and Claire had experienced brief ecstasy, followed by a parting that felt like an amputation. The *Happy Adventure* was the only sanctuary he had to ease his misery. Then Mother Nature blew him a kiss—a staggeringly beautiful dawn that impressed even the doryman and his crew, who handed one another chunks of bread smeared with butter and pâté, passed the wine bottle, and grinned at each other. A moment of shared perfection.

At Dawson's Cove, Farley paid off his crew and hired a car to take him to Hermitage. As they descended into the hamlet, he could see the spars and trim black hull of his snug little boat. Harold was nowhere to be found. Farley located the dory and rowed out, only to find Claire's ghost on the decks, in the companionway, and especially in the cabin. As he looked at the empty mate's bunk, "there was no tousled little head with its dark eyes half open, peeping up at me," he wrote to Claire. "You haunt me. By day and by night."

He rowed back to shore and eventually found Harold, who had a surprise for him: the new name boards Harold had painted for the boat. After stocking up with supplies, they set sail with only the vaguest of plans. They began their run for Milltown on another achingly beautiful day, stopping at a remote mooring along the way so that Farley could spend some time with the Indigenous people who lived there. He revelled in their company.

He and Harold decided that, depending on the weather, they might go inland to hunt caribou with a Mi'kmaq hunter from Badger. But Farley's thoughts were too focused on Claire to make any definite plans. He was mopey, moony, and in a letter-writing mood. He remembered how, in her earlier letters, Claire had spoken of the necessity of dispensing with "our brief times of glory," since there was so much agony between them. In his darker moods, he still worried that she might walk away, while he stood "rooted, tongueless, unable to call upon you to stop, or even to look back. Are you indeed walking away love? The knife is kinder than the noose, you know. I would rather you use the knife."

But Farley also realized that something profound had happened during their most recent time together, at least for him. "There is a new quality in my love of you," he wrote. "A certitude, a calm and peaceful knowledge that our love is as nearly perfect as human love can be, and an inner assurance that we will be together, for ever and aye, before too long. There is no other love but yours."

A southeast gale was on its way, so Farley and Harold took shelter. It rained or drizzled all day as they awaited the gale in a protected cove. Farley tried to write, but his typewriter wasn't cooperating, and his mind was elsewhere. They had cod for lunch and fried redfish filets with a side of winkles for supper. Farley went to bed early, apprehensive about the coming storm and what awaited him in Palgrave.

The gale struck at night, the wind gusting to fifty knots, accompanied by tearing sheets of rain. At midnight, Farley hauled the dory aboard the *Happy Adventure* to prevent it from being smashed against the boat by the wind. He was haunted by a "mad rat" that had boarded by the rope lines and frantically raced around the decks until dawn, stopping occasionally to peer in at the mariners through the portholes.

CLAIRE'S TORMENTS WERE MORE MUNDANE as she found herself back at her oak desk in the vapid surroundings of Simpsons-Sears. But she was not quite the same person who had set out depressed and uncertain for Saint-Pierre, though all of the old frustrations were still there. She wanted to be with Farley and wasn't. She didn't want to lie anymore but had to. Her job was soul-killing, but she dutifully went to the slaughter. She wanted to tell everyone about their wonderful trip but could not. The atmosphere at Douglas Drive was electric with suspicion.

Nana asked after Farley with a smile. Her sister-in-law, without one, informed her that her parents were highly suspicious that something was going on. "I need my head read for sending that letter from Pushthrough," Claire wrote, referring to a letter she had sent home to prove she hadn't only been on Saint-Pierre. "Perhaps I have a guilt complex with a deep rooted need for confession."

One night, she dreamed she was hiding under a bed, watching Farley and Frances cavort at a party. The vision tormented her. She visited her parents at their cottage and they showed interest in everything she told them, but didn't question her skillful inventions and evasions. She gave them credit for a noble attempt at minding their own business. She had less praise for herself. Her smooth lying made Claire strongly doubt she would ever be eligible for heaven.

But she had been accepted into a journalism course, which she attended on Monday nights. The hunt for an apartment continued, though she wouldn't move until her parents came home from the cottage, so that Nana would not be alone. Claire advised Farley to remain in Newfoundland for a few more weeks and to stay away from Palgrave. "On cold wet nights when you are shivering in your sleeping bag it must appear to be an almightily cosy corner... try to stay with *Itchy*."

Despite the persisting uncertainties, Claire had experienced a boost in her confidence and hopes for the future. Like Farley, she knew that their love had deepened in some way during the magical month together, that something had changed for the better. It was partly why she could consider leaving Douglas Drive and even finding a new job. She thanked Farley for the experience they had shared. "Believe me when I say that no one has ever been so good to me."

Back on Newfoundland's rugged south coast, Farley and Harold were doing the adult version of Tom Sawyer and Huckleberry Finn, untrammelled boy-men following the wind where it took them. They discovered Little River, a fascinating place not even on the charts, and navigated a narrow, rocky channel that led five miles into the mountains. Suddenly, it opened onto a huge lake with "fine forests, a good river, sand beaches, mountains all around, and only the narrow doorway for entry and exit."

They swam naked and then had a shore lunch of fried redfish on the beach. Farley decided that he and Claire should camp there for a week next summer, if there was a next summer. As he sat on the deck writing to her, a school of squid took cover under the shadow of the boat. "They are altogether weird, and clearly do not belong to this world," he noted. In his bad moments, that is how Farley described himself.

As they travelled toward Milltown, Farley collected stories of old times in the fabled bay. Claire's pencil portraits of people on the coast were now famous. Everyone asked about her all along their route, praising her artistry. Farley joked he would never need to work again. Claire could earn their fish, flour, and contraband rum with the flick of her pencil.

Roti Bay appealed to Farley's longing for remote places. Farley and Claire had spent their first day and night there completely alone in the natural world. The only people on Earth. Farley wanted to return there with Claire one day so that they could feast on mussels, scallops, trout, clams, and codfish to their heart's content. They could climb the ridge and "make love as Roti Bay has never known before." He planned to have a small dory built for them that winter so they could explore the beaches and coves next year.

Farley and Harold visited an array of out-of-the way places along the coast. In the past week there had been two full gales, which Farley thought at one point would de-mast the *Happy Adventure*. But he sailed on, explaining to Claire, "I have been under a compulsion to keep moving, despite the weather, as an anodyne for your absence."

Farley was doing his best to lose himself in raw Nature, putting off the inevitable for as long as he could. The interior of the coast was spectacular in September. They picked blueberries, bathed in a mountain stream, and climbed down into Richards Harbour for a scoff of fish soup. Harold cleaned a mess of "conners" for their supper, small white fish with tough skin, but tasty flesh.

Harold followed Farley in his "mad-cap" adventures without a word of complaint or restraint. One day, they planned to walk five miles over a range of mountains to visit Muddy Hole, a remote settlement that would later feature in one of Farley's best-known books, *The Boat Who Wouldn't Float*. "I can't wait to see their faces when two bearded men descend on them, unannounced, from the hills!" Farley told Harold. "They'll probably all take to their boats."

Farley and Harold finally reached Milltown from Richards Harbour, driven by a fresh and fortuitous westerly, which blew them into the bay. On Saturday morning, the wind dropped, and Farley took the dory around to the beach where he and Claire had dug for clams. He couldn't bring himself to dig alone, so he stripped off and went wading. He discovered a bed of huge, blue mussels and collected half a pail of plump winkles. He and Harold ate the mussels for dinner. They were full of pearls, and the two joked that ground pearls in wine were considered an aphrodisiac in India. "I can see why, having looked at a mussel sans shell," Farley wrote. "The damned things bear an unholy resemblance to Georgiana."

On one of their last cruises of the season, a moose came down to the shore at dawn, snorting in surprise at finding the *Happy Adventure* there. Her new nameplates were on, and she sported them "with grace and pride." But a shadow hung over everything. There is a barely perceptible slowing on a Ferris wheel that portends the end of the ride. With Claire, the summer, and his voyaging all gone, that's how Farley felt. The ride was ending.

That meant facing "the self accusation of cruelty on a terrible scale" when he returned to Palgrave, "the prospect of which makes my stomach drop to my knees. There have been ill reports of happenstances in Palgrave, and God knows what tribulations await my arrival. But I know, that love awaits me in the canyons of Toronto... Claire, I do love you so! And I cling desperately to your love of me."

IN ONTARIO, Claire was doing her best to fill in the time. She attended a regatta party with her stockbroker friend, where it was pleasant to sit on the club veranda and sip gin in a cool breeze. But the small talk was unbearable. The one exception was a visitor from the Bahamas who had read *The Grey Seas Under*, Farley's 1958 book about a sea rescue.

Other than that, she found the club members dull and cliché-ridden, pale shadows of the word-wizard she loved, whose mind was always swarming with ideas. Claire decided never to see her friend again. Everything was completely empty without Farley. "I tell myself that surely someday I will have to learn to live without you and so I should practice now. But all I do is long for the sight of you, the touch of you, the smell of you."

She was dreading the thought of living with her parents again and their diligent surveillance of her comings and goings. The search for her own apartment began in earnest. She eventually found one on

St. George Street, which she would share with a friend of a friend. She had even had a job interview with the communications company Maclean-Hunter. Claire had finally mustered the courage to leave what Farley called the family "bathtub" in Rosedale.

Things seemed to be going in the right direction, but Farley still obsessed about losing her. "Bad night last night," he wrote. "Ship was uneasy in a groundswell, and I could not sleep well. I dreamed badly— of you. That you had decided to wash me out of your hair. Woke in a sweat and drank some rum . . . You are so much a vital part of me now, that your loss would be tantamount to death."

Farley missed Claire the way people miss someone they have known for a lifetime. "You have been such, having somehow twisted time itself so that the year with you is all my past. Will be all my future. No matter what befalls. If I lose your presence, I cannot ever lose your essence, for it is one with mine now; and for all years to come. Love? Hell. It's so much more than that—this commingling of me with you. You've raised the dead, you know—now you are the life's breath of me. I love you, dear one. Remember this. Now to the dismal job of dismantling 'our own home'."

Stripping down the *Happy Adventure* for her winter sleep was painful work. Farley found an inscription on the forward deck beams that Claire had written in red ink: "I love you Farley." Farley and Harold took her out for one last sail, using her bull engine, which was about the only thing left on board. They set a course for Conne River. After a lunch of cod steaks, they scrubbed the decks, and Harold, who shared an affinity for graveyards with Claire, went off to look at the local St. Anne's cemetery. After visiting with friends, Farley and Harold sailed home by moonlight.

On Saturday, September 16, Farley walked to the Strickland boatyard to make arrangements to haul the *Happy Adventure* out of the water. The first job was to build a cradle to hold her. Farley hoisted the sails to dry them for winter storage. "Undressing my wooden woman is not (unlike undressing my living woman) a cheerful task."

On the day the *Happy Adventure* was scheduled to come out of the water, it was discovered that the crib was not in water deep enough to catch the morning tide. Farley and Harold used the one-day reprieve to walk the shore to an abandoned cove, where they dove for winkles. Farley told Claire that he got half a bag, and in the process "froze my balls into complete insensitivity."

By the last week in September, the rum was all gone, the food was running low, and Farley and Harold were reduced to eating moose meat and winkles. There was a radio warning about Hurricane Esther, and the *Happy Adventure* was finally hauled ashore. After the damage from last year, Farley hoped the boat would be safe for the winter. It had to be. Even high and dry and covered with snow, it was the one place he and Claire could count on.

It was dark by the time Farley went down to pay a last visit to the *Happy Adventure*, giving her "a farewell slap on her fat buttocks." Then he and Harold went to a friend's house to wait for the coastal boat. The *Bar Haven* arrived at 2:30 the next morning. The lights of the places they saw from the coastal boat reminded Farley of his voyaging with Claire, but there was no pleasure in it. "I badly need her presence in order for anything I see or do to have a savour."

When the coastal boat reached Terrenceville, Newfoundland, Farley and Harold piled into an overloaded taxi—four people in front, five in the back of a standard-size Chevy. A pregnant woman sitting on Farley's lap was car sick. After five and a half hours of agony, they reached St. John's just before dawn. Farley roused Mike and Jessie Donovan, and they all drank rum until it was time for breakfast.

Farley arranged a TCA flight to Toronto and told Claire he hoped she could take the weekend off so that they could be together. "My hunger for you, and need of you grow intense and but for them I believe I would never turn my face westward at all. Nausea strikes me when I think of Palgrave and all that it entails. I wish that I could exorcise this damnable Presbyterian sense of responsibility from my soul—or exorcise my soul *in toto*."

10 | The Steady-Flaming Love

FARLEY ARRIVED IN TORONTO on September 29, 1961, where he resumed riding the elevator between heaven and hell. Three days before he landed, he'd sent Claire a telegram saying how much he was looking forward to a good "visit." His meaning was clear. He signed it "Georgiana."

After a stay of several days, he reluctantly returned to Palgrave, where he would have to navigate through the "sunkers," submerged rocks that lay waiting. The melodrama of his broken marriage picked up where it had left off: fighting with Frances, caring for the boys, and slipping off to see Claire when he could—all the while overdosing on guilt and paralyzed by indecision. He was particularly worried about Sandy. He believed his son, whom Claire longed to meet, would be permanently damaged if Farley left the house for good. Realizing that Sandy could be the perpetual excuse for his never leaving Frances, Claire challenged Farley's logic.

"Sandy will grow up just the same, you know. Well maybe not just exactly the same without your constant influence, but he will grow and thrive. It would be an awful heartbreak to sacrifice yourself, stay with him, and then watch him grow up and turn into a stockbroker. Or worse still, a complete neurotic, shattered by the unending tension between his mother and father."

When Farley told Claire that Sandy was in tears over a recent spelling test, Claire offered an explanation. "It is a by-product of tension and will do him no good. Better that his father is a haven to him somewhere away from it all, than the nasty man who fights with mommy all the time."

During one assignation, Farley told Claire that she looked ten years older, hardly an observation to lift a despairing woman's spirits. What he meant was that she had an aura of sadness when she was in Toronto that he never saw when they were in Nature. Some carry their hearts on their sleeves; Claire carried hers in her eyes. "When your heart is sore, you cannot hide the fact," Farley said.

Much as he loved her, Farley sometimes took the miseries of what he called the "Palgrave Syndrome" out on his Golden Girl. It was a survival tactic. He knew that he was the "taker" and she was the "giver" in their brief encounters. He also knew that he had behaved badly toward her, sometimes out of selfishness. In future visits, he promised not to be the "spoiled and demanding child" he had been. But by mid-October, he was again feeling "wormish" and "despicable" after ruining yet another evening together.

One night, he had had to wait half an hour to see Claire, leaving him upset and peevish. When she finally appeared, Farley played the spoiled, obstreperous brat. Remorse was not far behind. He called himself out in his next letter to her: "I deserve a fat whack in the fanny, and not your loving kindness."

Claire was always gracious about accepting his apologies, but she was beginning to suspect that Farley's antics might mean that he wanted out of their relationship. Never one to mince words, she asked him if he was trying to show her the door.

"I was showing you where the door stood," he equivocated. "Imbued with a kind of fiendish desire for self-chastisement I <u>was</u> making it as easy as possible for you to open the door." He told himself it would be better for Claire to dump him than to allow him to ruin her life. He was still unable to break with Frances, meaning that he had nothing more to give Claire than what was already making her deeply unhappy.

Because of his deep life-weariness at the time, Farley may have half-hoped that Claire would wield the sword he often thought she was fingering. Then he could pull the walls down on himself with his last bit of strength. He was enervated unto death but not permitted to die. "I wish I was in your arms now, but you would have to be a necrophile to take any pleasure from it," he wrote to Claire.

At times, distress made Claire look at life through a dark glass. Farley frequently asked her what was wrong, and Claire's answer in a November 15 letter was casually crushing. "Probably nothing more than creeping paralysis of the soul." A week earlier, she had written that the only good thing about working at Simpsons-Sears was the view of Lake Ontario from the eleventh-floor ladies' washroom. "The Lake is calm and bright and blue and invites me to sail away. Someday I will jump out the window, thinking all the while that I will land in the Lake . . . If there was no Farley how much blacker the picture would be."

Farley often asked Claire why he couldn't help her out of the mire, the way she so often freed him from his frequent depressions. One of the reasons came from his own admission to Claire that he was not "perceptive" when "the worms are eating into your vitals." He could write books, but he couldn't read her.

It was only when her brilliant letters arrived, lucidly describing her emotional state, that he instantly understood and had tremendous empathy with her. He knew his own black outpourings added to the load she carried, but they enabled him to keep afloat. Farley implored Claire to do likewise—share every agony she was experiencing rather than hold things back in the mistaken belief that she was protecting him. "I exist for you to talk to," he wrote.

Apart from Farley's curious claim that he couldn't help Claire because he couldn't tell when she was in need, there was another reason he often left her floundering. While Claire longed to be his wife, Farley didn't believe in marriage. Despite half-hearted hints that they would one day be husband and wife, he made that painfully clear.

"I do not want, ever again, to be the master of any other human being's destiny, or of their being itself. . . Perhaps I am quite wrong, but I feel you want your own destiny to be absolutely and inescapably lost in the hands of another, namely me. Long, long ago before we had come to be so much a part of each other's lives, I tried to impress my attitude upon you when I spoke so vehemently against marriage and any other bonded way of life between two people."

Farley's marriage was the core of his aversion to making a formal commitment again. "Do you understand why I so resolutely eschew the future? For ten years and more the future, conceived, has been only an extension of the present, endured. The trap is iron-bound, I knew, I built it, within, and without myself... I cannot even kill myself, for to do so I would have to be totally enclosed within the body I destroyed, and I am not—I stand off and watch with an unpassioned eye, the self I call my own go down in weakness and decay."

Farley was nearing disintegration. It had been hell back in Palgrave—again. Tears, screams, and desolation. He had been in Toronto recently to see Jack but had been unable to stay with Claire, because he had promised Frances he would babysit the boys so that she could go to her Voice of Women peace-activist meeting. He was exasperated.

Farley saw his only defence as arming himself with hatred and rage, but he was incapable of doing that. The habit of trying to understand someone else's mind was deeply ingrained in him. He could not manage to subdue his sympathy for the enemy within the walls, even though his own life was at stake. "I feel no guilt, in the ordinary sense, but an acute awareness of the hell that haunts the enemy and, with this, an intolerable sense of frustration and futility which leaves me dumb, numb and incapable of self-defence."

As a result, Farley kept resolving all doubts in favour of Frances. Sometimes his actions hurt Claire more deeply than he realized. In early November, she had listened to a two-hour radio show that featured Farley and two other guests.

"I think basically you are a first rate showman, quite apart from the fact you are a first rate author," she wrote. But she noted that references to his "wife" on the program demoted her to the rank of the "Other Woman." In the eyes of the world, she was just a married man's mistress.

"I can't go on much longer. You must get away from both your wives and decide what you want to do. There are times when it seems to be too much to endure. I cannot really have a life of my own, yet I do not have a life with you ... Either leave me in peace to die, or take me away somewhere to live."

Claire immediately apologized, as she almost always did when she knew something she had written might add to Farley's woes. "I suppose I don't believe in the future either. I only see what I am today and it disgusts me . . . Everything I do seems to be a lie. Except loving you, there is so much truth in that."

Farley felt the sting of her words. He knew the situation was becoming absurd. Lovers should not be the instruments of each other's torture. He sensed in Claire the growing conviction that their relationship was untenable because of the agony it brought to both of them. Each feared the other wanted to bolt. But the fault was his, he believed, because he could not give her the certainty she needed. In part, he explained it as emotional exhaustion, the inability of his overloaded soul to carry any more weight.

"You are the only living thing in my dying universe, and I torment you and tear at you like a jackal, driven by my own despair . . . I'm like the Coxswain of a lifeboat whose ears are filled with passionate cries for help from a drowning world, and whose own vessel is implacably filling and sinking." One more pair of hands clutching the gunwale, and everyone would go under.

Perhaps she believed he had altered his beliefs about marriage, and perhaps Farley himself had even given her reason to believe that. But he explained that was just the effect of trying to be what she wanted him to be. Then he brought in the intellectual heavy artillery. To make his point about the need for her to have an independent identity, he quoted the brilliant Simone de Beauvoir from her landmark book *The Second Sex*.

"One day . . . it will be possible for woman to love not in her weakness, but in her strength: not to escape herself, but to find herself; not to abase herself but to assert herself—on that day love will come for her, as for a man, a source of life, and not of mortal danger. In the meantime love represents in its most touching form the curse that lies heavily on women confined in the feminine universe, woman mutilated, insufficient unto herself."

He advised Claire to read the book, which she did and concluded that de Beauvoir was the "wisest woman in the world." Farley also suggested that Claire quit her job and come to England with him. He was asking her to perform a variation on Kierkegaard's famous phrase—a leap of love. They would be together in new places, with new faces, and new ideas. He believed that he could write there and that their doubts and misgivings would scatter like autumn leaves in the fresh winds they would experience. If they did not go away together, "then we will have to give it up."

"For <u>my</u> peace of mind I have to believe that I am not willfully and selfishly exposing you to another blind plunge into the black ocean. I have to feel that, should the worst occur, I have not betrayed you utterly." Farley said he no longer believed in the "absolute validity of dreams and hopes." He remained distrustful of a contrived future made of vows.

Despite her unhappiness, which was not helped by the fact that her period was late, Claire stood her ground. "You are playing the game with an ace up your sleeve my love," she wrote. "The game has been played, the cards are laid on the table, and now you show your last card. I turn it over and it says, I Can't Give You Anything But Love Baby, and so of course you've won. This was the winning card . . . You leave me no choice Farley. I cannot go with you on these terms. My God—one more fling. It would kill me."

Farley quickly regrouped, firing a volley of devotion across her bow. "You are one of the rare ones, the very rare ones, who has the full capacity for love, and therefore of an uninhibited and complete experience of life, for joy is love, and all that is worth knowing in the world takes its roots from love."

Sensing that they might be closer to the end than he had thought, he wrote to reassure Claire that he loved her more than ever. "My sad, sad love. Did the dawn break any brighter for you this morning?" He hoped it had. But instead of helping her when she was depressed, he became depressed too, a trait he put down to a defect in his character. But that was only a minor consideration when seen against the big picture.

"I want you with me. This is the prime fact, and not to be forgotten or overlaid by doubts." But she had to understand the situation. If she went to England with him, she would be without formal status for an unknown length of time. If both of them were extroverts, it would not matter. They could laugh at petty conventionality. But Claire was not an extrovert. Farley couldn't say whether they would end up being miserable together because of Claire's need for security, something he couldn't and wouldn't guarantee.

Farley declared that their real problem was that they were so laden with distress and despair in Ontario that it was impossible to know themselves. "We don't bloody well know what we are doing, in fact." In the summer, they had been freed from the miseries of life, and it had been paradise. Here, they struggled with doubts and difficulties, which brought them to the brink.

Under the current circumstances, Farley thought that neither of them was fit to make any decisions, let alone divine their chances of happiness together. He thought Claire should simply come to England with him "so that we can know ourselves once more . . . I do not ever want to lose you, it is a prospect so bleak and nauseous that I cannot even face it."

He reminded her that they had been happy in Baie d'Espoir, and they could be happy again elsewhere. "For the love of all the gods, let us see things calmly and well, and let us not kill each other." To reinforce the truth of what he was saying, he began sending Claire installments from his diary about their glorious time in Newfoundland. Claire was deeply moved. Those days spent aboard their little boat had been the happiest time in her life.

As for her recurring fear that he was looking for a means of escape from her, Farley was clear: "I'm only telling you the risk you run—not telling you to run—that you must run . . . You are now more vital to my content and hopes than at any time since I have known you, and I believe I am as vital to your well being. But NOT as a savior, as an escape for all the world . . . Will you choose to be, not a 'woman', but a liberated being? A soul free to suffer and to know joy in honesty, and not in lies? Or will you choose to immolate yourself, your 'self'. Forever." It was a plea for Claire to release herself from the myth of marriage. The words were spoken by Farley, but Simone de Beauvoir was the ventriloquist.

Farley framed their dilemma in the usual way; the choice was Claire's. If she wished him to give up going to England, he would. Being there meant little to him without her presence in his life. If she wanted him to go, he would go and make an end of it. But if she wished to go with him in hopes of freedom, "then I will be happy." Farley wanted her desperately but would not contribute to what he conceived of as her losing herself if marriage remained her be-all and end-all.

"I do not wish to end our love. God knows, the thought is unendurable. But I will not, and cannot promise ineffable and eternal joy, particularly when this is predicated on your giving yourself unconditionally to me, losing yourself in me, forcing both of us into the age-old morass of the myth. And make no mistake, I am not rejecting you, nor your powers of giving... No promises, No plans. A silly phrase if interpreted literally, but in essence, this is what I believe must be the basis for our mutual, shared, but never wholly intermingled lives."

Farley knew how hard those words would sound to Claire, so he tried to assuage her fears of succumbing to a free relationship with him and a fresh start in England. He told her that what he had by way of material possessions would be as much hers as his if she came with him. They wouldn't "starve," and she would not have to work unless she wanted to. Jack was even thinking of opening a literary agency in which Claire would be involved. Until she resolved the question of their future, Farley suggested that they keep apart.

"I am afraid that many more evenings like the last two, will wound us both so deeply, and cripple us so badly, that we may die of it." He would stand by while she weighed everything on the scales of her heart, and he promised to come right away if she called him.

LOVING FARLEY WAS IN SOME WAYS like living with a brilliant but impish child. Claire listened intently to everything he said but remained draped in a heavy melancholy. She wrote to him that she hoped he and Frances would be able to find some peace between them. Frances, after all, held the winning card—a marriage licence. Claire also updated Farley on her period. "I am not pregnant, the knowledge of which both saddens and gladdens me. I still love you and I always will, the knowledge of which both saddens and gladdens me."

Later the same day, Claire wrote to say she was feeling better. Suddenly, it looked as though Farley, Simone de Beauvoir, and love might win out after all. She informed Farley that she had the apartment on St. George Street all to herself for the weekend. No printed invitation was required. He rushed into her arms on Sunday, and on Monday, back in Palgrave, he wandered around in a state of idiot joy, thinking of their magical hours together the day before. Farley was learning that true love comes with a thousand unearned permissions.

For the first time, a plan to be together began to coalesce, a rough blueprint that had the blessing of Jack McClelland. Farley had cancelled his booking to sail to England on October 31. Instead, he would go to Newfoundland in mid-November and stay with Harold Horwood at Beachy Cove until just before Christmas. Then he would return to Palgrave for Christmas and depart for England with Claire on December 27. Farley demonstrated that these were not mere words by announcing publicly during an interview on the Toronto radio station CFRB that he was leaving Canada and heading for England to write.

Farley theorized that by saying he was coming back for Christmas, Frances would be more relaxed, making it possible for him to hang on in Palgrave for another two or three weeks. But he would be guided by Claire. He proposed that perhaps he should sail from St. John's to England before Christmas and not come back to Ontario at all. The point was that he was going abroad, and Claire would join him there to begin a life of their own.

It was beginning to feel real to Claire. Just an hour after leaving Farley's arms, she wrote him an ecstatic note. She had loved having breakfast with him. "Oh lover, lover, let's get out of here. Let's get out of Toronto and Palgrave and preserve this precious thing we have before it withers on the vine and dies. I am dying. Dying a slow and tedious death."

Late in the afternoon of Thursday, November 16, 1961, Farley flew to Montreal and checked in to his Mount Royal hotel. The next day was a flurry of publicity for his books *The Serpent's Coil* and *Owls in the Family*, with television, radio, and newspaper interviews. He also did an interview about nuclear disarmament on a radio show called *Sounding Board*.

Farley picked Claire up at the train station at 10:30 p.m., and they went back to a party featuring various artistic and literary figures that Farley had been attending. They rose at 10 the next morning and took breakfast in their room. They idled the day away with cuddling and conversation and then went to dinner. "Claire extremely lovely and loving this day," Farley wrote in his journal.

Sunday, November 19, was their last day together for an unknown period of time, but they were jubilant. The next phase was finally starting. They luxuriated in their room and "made ecstatic love." Afterwards, they went for a walk on the mountain, and then had dinner in the Kon Tiki Room.

Farley took Claire to the station. It was all he could do to turn and walk away from the train, leaving the "slim, small, and very brave" figure behind him. He wanted to stay and give her back some of the comfort and assurance she had given him. The night she left, he wrote her a letter. "You are more beautiful to me than all that I have ever known of beauty. You are all lovely things that I can ever wish to know. You are my sustaining and steady-flaming love. Know this—I love you as I would love life; and loving you love life again, and for all time that there may be."

It was now near midnight, and her train was rumbling westward through the darkness. But this time, he did not feel that it was taking her away from him. "I do not think that anything save Death himself can take you from me now." He was filled with a calm certitude about their love, and no dark, fleeting thoughts could spoil his mood. "Your beloved presence secures me against all shadows and your love guards me from everything except the fates themselves."

The ghosts had been exorcised by love.

11 | An Untrammelled Love

WHEN FARLEY ARRIVED IN HALIFAX en route to Newfoundland and then England, he indulged in some media naughtiness. He got through two radio shows in the morning by playing the familiar role of famous author. But during an afternoon television interview about *Owls in the Family*, when the subject of pets came up, he decided to introduce his new pet, the cockroach he and Claire had found in their hotel room in Montreal.

He had transferred "Clotilde" ("Clotty" for short) into an empty condom box, which he now displayed to the television audience. Someone from the station later called him to say that there was a $500 fine for advertising prophylactics on television, which the close-up of Clotty might inadvertently have done. "Damn it, I was advertising cockroaches," Farley complained to Claire, "not cockcovers." Claire joked that they would have to live on uninhabited Simmonds Barasway—a small, shallow saltwater bay on the south coast of Newfoundland—to escape the dreadful scandal. "You mad bad, bad mad, mad bad poet," she wrote.

Farley had asked Harold Horwood to arrange passage to England for him, adding that it didn't matter what type of vessel was available. Harold wired back: "CANOE BEING PREPARED FOR OCEAN PASSAGE PRESS AND TV ALERTED FOR YOUR DEPARTURE." After thanking Harold for his help, he replied that Clotty had informed him that she would not cross the Atlantic in a canoe. "She is a difficult cockroach," he explained.

The real arrangements would have Farley sailing for England on December 4, only four days after he reached St. John's. The

Newfoundland was a combination passenger ship and freighter, with just over twenty spots for travellers. She was due in Liverpool on the tenth of December. In the first of several attempts to entice her to join him, Farley told Claire that if she escaped from Toronto now, they could make the journey together. "There is no living at all without you," he wrote. Claire was relieved at the idea of a December sailing for Farley. Terrified of flying herself, she had begged him not to risk a plane crash. "If I lost you now in the fathoms of the Atlantic, there would be nothing for me to do but join you."

Claire was tempted to follow Farley's suggestion and confess all to her parents. Sometimes she thought they would understand; more often she feared they would be reflexively judgmental. When she had recently visited her parents, they had proudly shown her the *Globe and Mail* book-review page, featuring a favourable assessment of her "friend" Farley Mowat's new book. In the end, she decided to keep their secret a little longer. She was worried about burning bridges behind her in case she ever had to return to Douglas Drive.

Because of heavy seas, the ss *Baccalieu* was running a day late, and Farley's public was impatiently awaiting him in St. John's. A telegram arrived urging him to get to town for a press conference. "Not bloody likely! Where the hell do they think they are? Ontario? Anyhow, there's a gale warning for a westerly due tonight," he wrote. "Balls to them."

Despite the dirty weather, passage on the ss *Baccalieu* was a pivotal experience for Farley. The ship was just off Burin, meaning that they had sailed almost the length of the south coast. He was now five days distant from Palgrave. As that distance grew, so did his certainty about Claire. Part of it was an almost physical sense of the fetters that had constrained him falling away. The regeneration came "with a rising passion for existence, and with a consuming desire for you." He felt a new-found appreciation of small things and, much more than that, a sense of peace.

"One of the strange manifestations of this rebirth is a slackening of the masochistic, pulling-wings-off-flies, attitude of self-analysis which has so blackly plagued me for so long," he wrote to Claire. "I am becoming more and more content to let myself live, unquestioned by myself, uncriticized, unjudged. Oh lover, how I yearn for you!" But now it was without the despair and horror of the July interlude. "Truly we will be the world's lovers—the world's great lovers and whatever else befalls us, this intermingling of we two will be the salvation for us."

If the voyage scattered his fears about commitment and the future, it also brought home how much he owed Claire. He was appalled by the ordeal he had put her through the past summer. "Gentle and enduring against the multitude of rebuffs and hurtful things I said and did to you, you persevered in loving me even in those times when I must have made love very nearly impossible." She had often talked about her desire to bring him happiness. Then, her declarations were only words in his ears, "but now they live and I understand them, and so begin to understand myself again." Claire had done no less than dispel the shadow of death creeping over Farley Mowat.

Claire had written many times that she would be good to him. Now, he wrote that "we will be very good to each other... with a depth and strength, and with a tenderness that surpasses every emotion I have known throughout my forty years... The thing is, darling heart, that I trust my love of you now, and therefore trust myself, and therefore am trustworthy for your love of me." There might still be old habits to be thrown overboard, and some rough water ahead, but through it all, they would "grow together into one sentient whole."

FARLEY WASN'T THE ONLY ONE who was lovesick. Claire realized that he wouldn't be coming in from Palgrave for an evening together anymore. She also worried about the bleak moments he might have in England before she arrived. And she knew she might well have some of her own. Profound change was coming. It meant moving out of her apartment, quitting her job, perhaps confessing to her parents that she was running away with a married man, booking passage, packing, and leaving. She took the first step of her plan, making a reservation on the *Empress of Britain* leaving for England on January 6, 1962.

"I am afraid sometimes," she wrote to Farley. "It seems that we have not said enough, it all happened so fast. Are you really leaving your wife? Such a cold, hard question, but somehow I cannot believe that you really are. I too, will have my black times, between now and the time I see a funny bearded face looking for me in the crowd." She was leaving the apartment on December 15 and asked Farley to send his letters care of Jack or Elizabeth McClelland at their home address.

Farley understood completely. "To give up family, career, home and the certainty of habit, in exchange for nothing more certain than my love. But do not be afraid. I know beyond all doubts that we shall be together and grow young together until we've had our full measure of time on this earth. I shan't leave you, nor will I let you leave me."

As for Claire's "cold, hard question," Farley was unequivocal. "Have I left my legal wife? Yes, darling, I have left, and now have no wife but you. I have passed the point of no return. There is only you ahead of me, and if you are not there, then there is nothing."

Farley grudgingly accepted the fact that Claire had to stay in Toronto until January, but not without noting, "this time it was you who must be sure . . . I am sure! Sure of our love. No more time is needed. I am resolved, and irrevocably, that we shall live one life together. What I am trying to say. . . is that if it is a doubt as to my certainty which is holding you away from me and prolonging the period of our separation, you should throw that doubt out the window of 206 St. George St. and let the street cleaners take it away and bury it." Farley emphasized his message by describing for Claire the "manner in which my love of you, freed now of all incumbrance, is swelling within me like a quintuple pregnancy."

When the ss *Baccalieu* sailed across Placentia Bay, headed for port, Farley knew that it was the end of a part of the journey "away from hell, and into paradise." He still fantasized that Claire might meet him when his taxi from Placentia arrived in St. John's. The course by the North Star, he told her, was east, half-east. "Time now to wrap this up and say goodnight to you whom I hold most dear of all that is and ever will be, in my life. Good night, my love."

St. John's was his last Canadian stop. With just days before his departure for England, Farley and his father, Angus, who had accompanied him from Sydney, bunked in at Harold Horwood's house in Beachy Cove. Drinking in the salt air, Farley sat on a stone fence in the sun, reading the five letters from Claire that were waiting for him. Her words thrilled him, and Farley replied on December 1:

"How wonderfully strong our love is become—yours was always strong, but now mine equals it and then a bit, perhaps, for now I am a veritable Samson of love for you." He told her that he could withstand this absence from her without the pain and despair that had filled him on previous occasions. "The time of doubts and questioning is over... Oh how I want to hold you close again, and gentle you, and caress you quietly, and love you into peace. And, sometimes—not more than four or five times a day—love you like a leopard too."

Angus, who was supposed to be looking after Farley, suddenly became the one who needed short-term care. He had received just a single letter from his own love, Barbara Hutchinson. Farley and Harold spent three days with a manic-depressive septuagenarian on their hands, snatching him back from the edge of cliffs and out of the path of speeding automobiles.

Eventually, Farley telephoned Barbara so that she could personally reassure Angus that Cupid hadn't fled the scene. Angus relished the phone call and returned to good spirits. "All Mowats are children," Farley noted. He joked to Claire that she had it easy with him, compared with what Barbara had to deal with. "Hell, I'm an amiable, well adjusted little lambie pie compared to the grizzled old badger."

When his ship docked, Farley planned to go straight to London and visit the only person he knew in the city—expatriate Canadian playwright Ted Allan. He would stay with Ted for a few days until he decided how he would pass the time until Claire arrived. Farley also arranged to send Claire $500 for her passage. But there were strings attached. "If you spend it all on brandy for the handsome young officers of the Queen Mary, I'll bite your little tits." She allayed his fears. Five hundred dollars was far more than she needed for her passage, so she would save the rest to buy groceries in England.

The most precious thing Farley Mowat had ever received arrived in the form of a special-delivery letter from Claire, including a photograph. "The little picture of the funny face was heart stopping," Farley replied in a letter postmarked 4 p.m. December 3, the day before he embarked. "Your eyes looked into mine as they used to in those first days when you would come down the steps of *Itchy* in St. Pierre harbour. Straight eyes, naked and unashamed... and unafraid. I have not shown you much tenderness in the past, but I'll make up for that, tenfold... for now I want, more than anything else, to be as vitally important to you as you are to me. God, but I love you so!"

Farley finally wrote to Frances to say he now planned to sail east on a trawler for the Faroe Islands. It was not true, but he thought his wife would understand his meaning. The phrasing, he believed, would allow her to save face for the moment and permit the boys to have a good Christmas. He would administer the final *coup de grâce* after Claire joined him in England.

To her surprise, Claire received another love letter from a Mowat, but it wasn't Farley. "What a wondrous experience! To be loved by two Mowats!" Angus wrote to her. "Did I spell that right? M-O-N-S-T-E-R-S? But no! Nonsense! You can't make monsters out of 5' 6½" lengths." Angus had learned a lot about her, and his mind was now at peace for Farley. He knew his son feared daring to love again but that Claire had somehow worn away that distrust not only of love but of life. For that, the senior Mowat was mightily grateful to her.

On Sunday, Farley wrote his last letter before sailing. "It is not a departure letter, for this is not a departure but a beginning." When the ship thrust her bow into the North Atlantic, it would be carrying both of them to a life together. "I know that it holds one sure thing—a growing and expanding love for one another—an untrammeled love." It did not matter that the physical distance between them was increasing. "Your funny face, wistful, and a little sad, but infinitely loving, is clear before me now and it shall always be this clear and comforting... It is the face of love—the face of my love... Think of me at sea, for I shall think only of you."

On the day of Farley's departure, Angus, Mike Donovan, Harold Horwood, and his girlfriend, Marguerite, saw Farley off. Angus had to lead him aboard the ship, and even then his son had doubts. "Farley seemed to go, shrink miserably within his beard till I couldn't stand it any longer and took him ashore and we walked up and down in the rain trying to talk, trying not to talk, being Mowaty, till I had to leave for the plane," Angus wrote to Claire. "But one thing did come out dear, 'Tell her that I am more nearly myself than I have been for years. And the next few weeks will pass,' and I felt certain that it is true Claire." Angus believed that Claire had the responsibility to "bring him back to writing as he can write. Do it dear. It's worth doing."

12 | Lady in Waiting

WHILE THE NORTH ATLANTIC was battering Farley, life was buffeting Claire in Toronto. Her old Scottish nanny, Adda, whom she loved, died. On a single Saturday, Claire went to Adda's funeral, a friend's wedding, and the hospital to visit her ailing father; then she went back to her empty apartment to pack. "A weary depressed girl who needs you very much sends you her heart," she wrote.

Using a packing case as a desk for her typewriter, she poured out her feelings to the man who was steaming steadily farther and farther away from her. Claire had seen news reports of storms and tidal waves off Newfoundland and worried that fate had put Farley on those very waters. She told him that Adda's funeral was a pitiful affair—just twelve mourners. Claire said she knew Nanny would have loved Farley. As for her father, he was in Mount Sinai Hospital, where he had undergone twenty-six blood tests. It looked like it might be leukemia.

If indeed her father had to undergo debilitating cancer treatment, Claire was full of sympathy for her long-suffering mother. Still, she had to make her escape from Toronto with the minimum of fuss, meaning it would be better to go before her father was diagnosed. She again reminded Farley of how important that letter of a job offer was; career advancement was a baked-in family value and the prime motive in life at the Wheeler house.

After pondering her situation, Claire decided that deception would be preferable to shocking her parents with the truth—that she was quitting her job to run off to Europe with a married man. If they could be offered concrete hope for a divorce, they might give their blessing, "but this may be years away or maybe never, and this they just couldn't understand," she wrote. Still, she was troubled by the web of deceit she and Farley had been spinning from their first embrace.

As a charm to keep him safe, Claire tried to imagine what the weather would be like when Farley finally arrived in England. She guessed that it would be cold and drizzly, as it was in Toronto. In the meantime, it would be stormy seas for her love. She was concerned that he would become lonely and homesick, especially with Christmas looming. She hoped he would use this unencumbered time to sort things out for himself. But she also knew better than anyone how terrible it sometimes was to be alone.

When her own spirits drooped, Claire reached into her handbag, where she kept the poem Farley had written after their perfect summer day on the Dune at Langlade. She especially loved the last stanza of the eighteen-line homage to her.

> Close to the foam, where the surf-birds race,
> We strive in each other's blind embrace,
> Till the rising flood of my ecstasy
> Climbs like the surge of the sounding sea,
> And sweeps me down to the peace that lies
> In the heaven between her golden thighs.

After work the next day, Claire was too sad, too enervated, to write. Instead, she reread Farley's account of the trip on the coastal boat in Newfoundland, laughing as she relived every moment with him. "Oh my love, I just hate to think of what I would do without you . . . Oh Farley, don't leave me, you are all the sunshine in my life."

It didn't help her spirits when a friend she had confided in pointed out the perils of joining Farley abroad. The friend said it all sounded wonderful, but surely Claire realized she could never have children under the circumstances. And what if she met someone else when she was living "common law"? Claire shared her assessment of this advice with Farley:

"Vapid, conventional, selfish thoughts, from a thoughtless girl who did, I suppose, mean well." Claire regretted calling her. She told Farley not to worry about her, that she would reread his letters and then go to sleep "and dream that a red beard is tickling my nose." The apartment was nearly bare now, and she was nestled in her sleeping bag, wishing he was in it with her. "Goodnight my only darling. I love you beyond all reason."

AS CLAIRE SLEPT, the *Newfoundland* was fighting a gale 250 miles northeast of St. John's. Her hold contained mail, salt cod from St. John's, and apples from the Annapolis Valley to brighten the Christmas of English children. On board, it was known that a famous writer of sea stories was in Cabin A-10. Farley, one of just three first-class passengers, felt as if he had chartered a personal passenger-liner. "Rockefeller has nothing on me," he quipped.

When weather permitted, Farley jogged around the deck in shirt sleeves. But it was such a stormy passage that he spent much of the time alone in his cabin, reading Boswell's *London Journal,* composing letters, and thinking of Claire. He begrudged losing a single hour from the twenty or thirty years of ardent passion that he hoped awaited them. He even began writing an epic poem about their summer on the south coast of Newfoundland. But mostly, he pondered the wonder of his love for Claire and wrote her incessantly about the profound changes he was experiencing.

"The quality of <u>my</u> love for you has undergone a sea-change since the day I began my voyage toward the east. My love for you is no longer compounded largely of despair and demand, as it was in July of last summer. I am no longer greedily and blindly sucking at your compassion, as a simple antidote for my misery. I am no longer hiding my black devils behind your skirt. The devils are vanquished, and I am free—free to want to give to you, rather than to take . . . And, oh my golden love, I want to give myself to you with a passion that I have never known. I shall cherish you in many ways, and from the cherishing my love will grow as ceaselessly as the winds blow. . . Come to me and I will do for you what you have done for me. I will banish fear, and solitude, and all uncertainties, and you will be secure within my arms, and all dark shadows will have fled."

With forty-five-foot seas and winds gusting up to hurricane force in one of several storms the *Newfoundland* rode out on the way to England, Farley made a joke based on his book *The Grey Seas Under*, saying that his next book would be called *The Grey Seas Over* or *Which End of the Boat Is Down*. He was spellbound by the terrible fury of the sea. He was also trying to work on the outline of a Newfoundland book, a collection of photographs underpinned by an essay, which he planned to co-author with Harold. But when he gazed at Claire's photographs arrayed before him on his desk, a question plagued him. How could someone as lovely as her choose someone like him?

"I do not speak very often of your beauty, and do you know why? It is because I am afraid that too great an awareness of it on your part will find me bereft of you completely. You would no longer care to have a bunje nose, protruding from a face-full of rusty steel wool by your side. But my darling, you <u>are</u> lovely beyond compare, and I cannot keep silent about it."

Much as he mythologized her, Farley also relished using bawdy humour to make her laugh. Why did he go unshaven? "I wear a beard so that I can tangle delightfully with Georgiana and titillate with my wiry caress. Oh how I wish I could titillate you right now... I lay my wooly face between your breasts, and bless the hour that the Gods turned their faces toward us, and smiled and gave us leave to live."

In his obsession with Claire, Farley shunned physical contact with other women, many of whom found him attractive. He told her "there is not one soul upon this vessel with whom I can make even a brief alleviation of loneliness—not because <u>they</u> are not willing, but because <u>I</u> am not willing... I can only look inward, down the lengthening corridor that leads to you—or leads away from you. The touch of your hand, the softness of your breath against my chest, a word from you, one long, loving look would help."

Sex with Claire and his own virility were never far from Farley's thoughts. He had become friends with the ship's doctor, who was caring for a dying woman on board who was beyond his help. In their rambling, eclectic talks, Dr. Mackay mentioned that men of forty were subject to atrophy of the penis. Harold Horwood once told Farley that was what had happened to Newfoundland's first premier, Joey Smallwood. As a result, he had to build that "monolithic phallus he calls a Confederation Building in compensation." It came complete with a fountain that shot a jet of water two hundred feet into the air.

Farley thought about lovemaking with Claire to the exclusion of almost everything else. He told her they must make it one of their foremost pursuits and worried that the fire might go out. "God help us if it is overlaid with the dust of habit." Did she feel during the end of his last time in Palgrave "that some of the spark was dying out of us"? Farley thought so. "I think probably our loving had to suffer, for we two were suffering, and the tensions were growing unbearable for both of us. The overlay was faint, but it was there."

Writing to Claire was his salvation. After stuffing a twenty-page missive to her into an envelope, he thought he had done with letter-writing for a time. But when he sealed the letter, it was as if he had been cut off from the woman who was "the fountainhead of my existence." So he started a new letter, elaborating on his hopes, transformations, and fears.

"I find myself talking constantly of you as my wife, and thinking of you, concretely, in that context. Do you suppose the old iconoclast is weakening? Damn it, the times don't matter. Wife in reality as opposed to wife in name, is no longer a thing of fear to me. But the word still means lover and friend, for this is what you are and always shall be if the Gods are willing. I really have no conviction any more against marriage, so long as we are married <u>friends</u> and <u>lovers</u>—and in this phrase, the meaningful words are the last two. I still dread the possibility of finding ourselves left only with the marriage part. That would be unbearable for me now, or later. I've had that one."

Fresh from his readings of D. H. Lawrence, Farley found his already powerful eroticism was supercharged. In each other's bodies, he wrote, he and Claire would find solace, forgetfulness, ineffable joy, ecstasy, and humour too. But he acknowledged that fleshly delights were different for men and women. "We must possess each other, physically, in complete totality... The desire for loving comes almost instantly to man (this man at any rate) and I am always, except when asleep or dead, ready to make love to you."

Passion came upon Claire unexpectedly, and at intervals. "There cannot be anything so artificial as modesty, or shame, between us— ever... We must discover love in every way within the scope of our senses and perceptions."

Farley joked that he would not work on the new book until Claire brought him Georgiana. He told her that he wished he could "hibernate" until then. Couldn't she fly instead of sail? And he worried she might think he was talking too much. He apologized for the barrage of words that he fired her way each day. Was he too repetitive or clumsy in his language? To make up for it, he promised not to say a word for a month after she arrived, though he would not be idle.

"Do you know what I will do first of all? I shall kiss every inch of you—nay every square centimeter, long, hard, and searchingly. (That last bit was Georgie's interjection on—long, hard and searching!) and after that—after that, well I shall, not to mince words, proceed to fuck both of us into a coma. And I won't say a single word."

Apart from the emotional storms raging in Farley, yet another Atlantic storm was about to envelop the *Newfoundland*. Farley told Claire that he was beginning to think that he and the ship were cursed, doomed to spend an eternity on a boiling sea, never to see land or her again. At 22:00, with the wind outside screaming "like a madman's memory," he felt compelled to write to her. He begged Claire to spend Christmas with him. After all, she had already given twenty-seven of her Christmases to her parents and none to him.

He was feeling morose after attending a farewell dinner as the *Newfoundland* drew near the end of her voyage. It was served to four people in a salon built to accommodate fifty. Despite the twelve appetizers, three soups, and three fish courses, the evening was dismal. The other diners kept asking where he was going to spend Christmas. Farley had to tell them that he didn't know. Since he could not spend it with Claire, perhaps he should have planned to spend it with Sandy and David? But this was self-pity talking, and Farley had had his ration for the day.

He left the dinner deeply depressed, writing to Claire that it was "reminiscent of the end of the world... Claire, you are now more to me than my own life. I could not say this easily before, since it inevitably sounds trite. But I know it is true now, and therefore I need have no hesitation in saying it. In you lies all love—and all love of men and women for me; and without you there is no love, and therefore no life."

At night, he tucked himself into his bunk and reread her letters. They were his one refuge, and they offered some comfort. But the old darkness closed in. He worried that some handsome first officer on her ship would sweep her off her feet. He even contemplated what he would do if Claire decided not to come to England.

"It is a black thought, a haunting one. God damn it to hell! You are my catalyst—my contact and perhaps my being too. If I was to lose you, there would be no effort left, to make another search—and no will. Well, you are very far from me this night, and I cannot reach you even by telephone. Come soon, come soon. Oh darling heart, come soon, come soon."

It was the twentieth day of their separation, and Farley wondered if it was really necessary to endure thirty more. He was beginning to think that Claire's decision to come by ship involved something more than her fear of flying. A trial by ordeal perchance?

"I think you have made your decision as a species of testing, of you and of me—but must the test become a torture? It is a torture, and not easily endurable ... There is no happiness, in reality, without you—and I am without you now, and feel it fully now." Farley explained that his escape from Palgrave meant nothing if all it amounted to was "exchanging a familiar loneliness for an unfamiliar one ... I shall see whether the red devil can conquer the black devil, and whichever one wins—I lose."

After rereading his own words, he later added that in the end neither devil had won. He poured himself two stiff drinks, stared into space for a while, "then began to grin, and then to chuckle." Whenever Farley fell into the sloth of self-pity, he invariably became ludicrous to himself. He told her he would turn back if he could. "I love you. Love you? Christ, I die without you! The hell with it."

On Sunday, December 10, when the steward brought him his morning tea, Farley could hear the whistling and bustle of the crew outside his cabin. He drowsed, bobbing lightly just beneath the surface of consciousness. Then suddenly Claire's face was next to his. He could feel her soft breath against his beard. "I opened my eyes, startled, and your face remained. You looked into my eyes most lovingly, and kissed me and I <u>felt</u> the kiss and responded to it—and I feel it still." Then she vanished. Farley was a skeptical fellow, as Claire well knew, but he had always responded to his senses. He had no doubt that his sorceress had found a way to come to him.

But visions or hallucinations were no substitute for the real thing. Farley considered taking a plane back to Canada and joining her in just ten hours, instead of suffering through another month without her. His mood evolved into truculent begging. "Enough of this shilly-shallying. You pack up, and come to me at once. I'll make the decisions now—not you. And I'll take the responsibilities for both of us, nor will evade them, and equivocate any more. If you love me—and I believe implicitly that you do—then come. Come now."

On deck, Farley thought he could smell peat in the air off the Irish coast. The sun was shining brightly when Wales loomed to starboard. He would go to London with an empty mind and a sore heart. "And I will know only emptiness, and the slow ache, until you come to me ... My little golden love, your red beard waits for you, and loves you, meanwhile, with excruciating passion."

The *Newfoundland* moored at the first dock in Liverpool. One less passenger disembarked than had started on the storm-tossed journey. The sick woman in Dr. Mackay's care died at sea the day before the voyage ended.

13 | The Last Open Door

AT 11:45 A.M. on Tuesday, December 12, 1961, Farley disembarked in Liverpool. He hit the dock running and by 11 p.m. had made his way to London. His first task was to help three women who had never been there before find an affordable hotel. He then contacted playwright Ted Allan. They met the next day for lunch, but the extent of Allan's help was the suggestion that Farley scan the rental notices in the newspapers for a London flat.

Farley paid a visit to Innes Rose, his European agent. They had never met, and Innes instantly raised Farley's spirits with news that a Bombay publisher was considering translating *People of the Deer* into Hindi. He also advised Farley that only aristocrats and the wealthy could afford flats in London.

Things looked gloomy until Farley landed in the offices of Michael Joseph, his British publisher, where he was rescued by Roland Gant, a junior editor who was about his own age. After taking Farley to a pub for a dark ale, Gant invited him back to his own small flat, which he shared with his Parisian-born wife, Nadia, and their infant son. The couple wholeheartedly embraced Farley.

Gant had read some of Farley's books and kindly suggested that the "bombed out hive" of London was not the kind of place where the author would be happy. "You and your light-of-love might be a damn sight happier close to Mother Nature," he sagely advised. Gant described a sheep farm in Dorset where he and Nadia rented a cottage as their getaway from "the Big Smoke." Another cottage was available nearby. It was rustic, but it was in the heart of some of the most romantic country in the world. If Claire needed to go to art classes, the train to London ran almost every hour.

Farley decided to get out of London. He believed he wouldn't survive Christmas if he stayed. The smog was heavy, and he couldn't shake a bad cough. Was he getting pneumonia? Of London he wrote, "The grey and impersonal rat-barrens are not for me." He would go down to Dorset and look at the cottage that Gant had suggested. If he liked it, he would spend Christmas there.

After attending to business in London, Farley made his way through the fog to Paddington Station and took the train to Dorchester. Allan Percival, the owner of Coombe Farm, picked him up in his beat-up Land Rover and invited him to "come aboard." They drove ten miles west along the seaward side of the South Downs, past "boundless flocks of sheep." The vast expanses of light and colour were like a trip through a Turner landscape.

Coombe Farm was stunning, eighty acres of rolling hills and hollows that had been in the Percival family for seven generations. Before the war, it had supported several tenant farming families. The Percivals now maintained the place by keeping their own expenses low and renting the farm's cottages to vacationers.

Allan offered Farley the cottage for three pounds a week, roughly fifteen dollars. Discovering that he was a writer without a machine, Allan's wife, Liz, lent him a vintage replacement—her 1908 Smith typewriter. Farley took the place for two months, writing to Claire, "Well, we are now landed gentry and gentlewoman." Five days before Christmas, he took possession of Cottage No. 2.

On moving day, Allan picked Farley up in Dorchester. He had a bucket of coal in the back of the Land Rover, the same coal, Farley wrote, "which is rapidly reducing me to the level of a dying pup in a thunderstorm." He moved into his new home by the flickering headlights of the Land Rover "as the worst blizzard in a century swirled across the land."

The cottage was dank and dark. "There was no kindling, no axe, no knife, no hope," Farley wrote in a December 23 letter to Claire. He crouched hopefully in front of the electric fire. A flashlight gave off more heat. He went to the bedroom and discovered that the sheets were damp. He brought a bed downstairs, set it up in the dining room, and closed off the rest of the house. It felt like minus twenty degrees Fahrenheit.

Farley now had a fever. "By dawn I had decided to die, but death was un-cooperative." So he put on every article of clothing he owned and ventured outside, where he found an axe and split some wood. He tried to make a fire, but the wood was wet and wouldn't catch.

"Got raging mad. Drained a litre of gasoline from car and poured over wood. (Viking death-wish again, do, or die) and to my great surprise, got a fire going." Once the gasoline had burned off, it went out again, so he added coal. "Great billowing clouds of coal smoke filled the house . . . Made breakfast (at 12:00 hours) of cornflakes and rum, without many cornflakes. Felt better."

As love nests go, there wasn't much down in Cottage No. 2. The kitchen was barely big enough to swing a dishtowel. A combined living and dining room was heated by an open fireplace. Heat in the upstairs bedroom depended on a hot water bottle and a good companion. In Claire's absence a stray cat Farley adopted filled that role, purring all night as she slept with him. The bathroom had no heat or hot water. If the pipes froze, as they often did, there was no water at all. Farley joked that he couldn't light a cigarette in the cottage; there wasn't enough oxygen. "Concluded we are both mad. Me for being here, you for contemplating joining me."

David Percival, the landlord's son, showed up the next day with a hundredweight of coal loaded into the Land Rover. Farley was delighted. The fireplace did not draw very well, but by evening the place was as comfortable as a cave, although the smoke would have "suffocated an alligator."

Farley sent Claire a photo of the cottage. There were narrow roads inland from the farm leading to several villages with pubs. They could do their shopping in Bridport, a market town about five miles away. Liz knew a woman who could do housework for them for an hour or two a day, freeing them to pursue his writing and Claire's art. "Garth" was the Percival household's working pet, an immense old English sheep-dog, loved by all.

Claire relished getting all the news from Coombe Farm, hearing about the trips across the hills to check the water troughs, riding in the Land Rover, visiting the local pub. She reminded Farley that she could not live without him. "I will never give up. I will love you till eternity. You are mine you hear, as much as anyone of us can belong to another. You will be so happy with me darling. You will never regret asking me to come to you, and I will never regret coming."

Claire wondered if she was acting like a lovesick teenager. "It occurs to me that I am acting like a moon-struck Grade VIII calf," Farley replied. "All I need is pimples . . . I feel idiotically worshipful as any high school Romeo who ever drooled . . . Oh but I drool over the thought of you. Maybe that's second childhood? A drooling old man. Be toothless old man if you don't get here soon. Grinding them to dust . . ."

Farley was beginning to understand the importance of establish-ing a home for them, even if it was only for their first few months together. They would have infinite time to go adventuring in the future. He would have a lot to do, and Claire would be central to every move he made. "Oh lover, lover, lover, come quickly to me, and I shall nur-ture you, and love you fabulously, and we will be inordinately happy . . . You are my true love; I adore you and cannot, will not, choose to exist without you . . . Merry Christmas, my darling . . . I kiss you in many secret places. F."

Farley also advised Claire to get one of those "diaphragmatic machines." He didn't like them either, but if they didn't have a shield against the ways of Nature, they would be "conceiving like fury." He was not going to share her with offspring—"not yet anyway." Rubber socks aren't much fun, Farley told her, and "Georgie has had his fill of being incontinently kicked out of heaven just when heaven is in his grasp. So have I."

Just before Christmas, the Percivals invited Farley to stay overnight in the main house. He quickly grew fond of both Allan and Liz Percival, not least because their path to happiness had been even rockier than his own with Claire. For Liz to get a divorce from her first husband, Allan had to get her pregnant. Their son was born three weeks before they were able to get married. That night, Farley and the Percivals shared each other's photographs, including slides that Farley proudly produced, displaying a very happy and beautiful Claire in Newfoundland.

After exchanging life stories, they sat up until 2 a.m., talking and drinking whisky in front of a glorious fire. Farley thought the story of the Percivals' struggle to be together might lift Claire's spirits. "Makes ours look easy-like," he wrote. Bedtime in the seventeenth-century farmhouse was pure luxury, a four-poster bed boasting three mattresses and a canopy. It was "OUR kind of bed," Farley wrote. He snuggled in with an eiderdown pulled up under his chin, and dreamed of Claire the whole night.

"I shall love you with my hands, with my body, with my voice, with the heart of me, and always, and at all times, be it through the fingertips, or only through the eyes. You must never hesitate to reach out to me, in the most crowded place, and touch me secretly or openly... I am very proud of you and I am fiercely proud of my love of you, and of yours of me... We are not ordinary lovers. Are there two people in the world who have the capacities for love, to equal ours? I don't believe there are... Let us always let the other in, when he, or she, comes bearing love. (And I'm not talking about that scoundrel Georgie at all. He <u>has</u> to be kept under control, or he'd exhaust us both!)"

Farley felt that he had found the right place for them, a spot where they could get off to a good start. Coombe Farm had acres of rolling land on the brow of the downs, sweeping toward a broad valley that ran to the sea three miles away. It was mostly sheep and cattle country. The landscape was enchanting, well-kept fields and copses, and ancient ruins that had slept for centuries. And there was one other attraction that Farley knew would appeal to Claire. "Eureka, so many graveyards that I suppose I'll only see you when it gets too dark to read the inscriptions."

BACK IN TORONTO, the weather wasn't the only thing depressing Claire. Her apprehensions about the voyage were mounting: so few letters from Farley, the petty obligations of Christmas, and always the prospect that Frances would throw a fit and guilt Farley back to Palgrave. And what if everything blew up and her world filled with a chorus of "I told you so"s? She couldn't wait to get word from Farley, but the mails were not their friend.

There was a two-week gap between sending a letter and receiving a reply, sometimes longer. Their moods and thoughts often reversed in those intervals. Just when they most needed to connect, their emotional life was suddenly out of sync. After sending a sad and gloomy letter, Farley tried to make a joke of it. "So. By the time you get this, you will know that all is well. That I am healthy, wealthy (not very), and wise (after the event)."

In keeping with their pledge to always tell each other the truth, Claire shared her state of mind. "Sometimes I fear for both of us. But the thing I dread most is that we may have to come back to the lives we left. I must stop thinking like this."

Despite Farley's desperate requests that she fly to England to shorten their separation, Claire begged him to be patient; she needed to travel by ship. He knew how terrified she was of flying—the only time she wasn't an atheist, she told him.

And being dropped into an unfamiliar environment always struck her like a blow. If she went from Toronto to a new life in England overnight, it could take her weeks to recover. The thought of twelve hours of sleep a night on the voyage and a chance to relax at sea appealed to her. She was physically and emotionally exhausted by the last year and a half of their tumultuous and furtive affair, and now her father was in hospital with suspected leukemia.

"I badly need a rest," she wrote, though she hated to do so because she remembered reading a letter from Frances to Farley the previous summer describing how tired she was. "There and then I decided that I would never write and tell you how tired I was . . . Well anyway, with combined moving, weddings, funerals, shopping, Christmas visits to the hospital and the tension of departure I am ready to collapse . . . I am trying so hard to tell you that I love you and not to worry about me, but it all seems to come out in short gasps."

Farley sensed a hint of reluctance in Claire to break away from her family and the "safe" life of Rosedale, and he tried every trick he knew to bolster what he suspected was her diminishing resolve to join him. The first attempt was an appeal to follow his example in leaving it all behind. He said that the distress, uncertainty, and general hopelessness that had overwhelmed him in the ten days before he broke free of his marriage would have been fatal to him but for the knowledge that she loved him. She had the same advantage.

"Cling to the knowledge that I love you—and that I shall not betray you, and that you are safe with me. Be very strong and brave, because you must be both, for both our sakes. What you are doing now must be done alone—even as I had to break up my old, habitual, safe world in order to be free for you—and for myself."

To emphasize the point, he added a startling confession, designed to show that he truly understood her trepidation in taking such a momentous step. Just a month before he left Palgrave, he too had considered throwing in the towel and staying put. He described his own and Claire's doubts with a striking metaphor.

"The winkle was pulling back into it's shell. Mowat winkle did it often enough. I remember (with a shudder of revulsion) one morning only a month ago that I lay abed and heard Kippy sniffling outside, and the hens coebling, and Sandy & David rampaging in the living room, and smelled bacon cooking, and I pulled back into my shell and said: It's madness to cut all this away. I have only to put my head under the covers and forget love, and things will go on in their comfortable pattern until doomsday."

But Farley knew that the moment he accepted such graceless surrender to mere comfort and the banality of habit, doomsday would be upon him. It would mean betraying the only great emotion he had ever known—his love of Claire. He was not ready to die with that love unfulfilled.

Farley offered her an alternative, but it came with a poison pill. If she chose to remain where she was, he would come back at once—but it would only be to the half-world they had. "That was such a terrible juxtaposition of hell, and brief moments of heaven. And then we will both die; only our love will die first."

Above all, Claire was not to panic, no matter how conflicted or apprehensive she might be feeling. He told her she was creating obstacles that did not really exist. He reminded her that he had performed a more brutal amputation. Claire was not cutting herself off from a husband and children—only her parents. She was not leaving a home she had built, "and a social milieu that was intricately constructed around a family."

True, she was leaving friends, but only in the physical sense. They would remain long-distance friends. She was leaving a career, but for the year and a half he had known her, she had hated her job. She was going to something, "to love, to one who loves you passionately and abidingly... the excitement and adventure of two who are really one."

Next, he painted a picture of how wonderful life together would be if she would only make the jump. "I shall be so very good to you that you'll forget what a hairy old idiot I am. But you will never forget that I love you, for I won't give you a chance. Oh lover, I've never been so desperately in love with anyone, not even you, before. Trust me. Trust me!"

He saved his most effective, and slightly devilish, attempt to sway Claire for last. "I live in terror that, in your absence, some horrid things will occur in Palgrave and, without you to cling to and strengthen me, and to give reality to our dreams, I might succumb and feel impelled to return." He knew that was the last thing in the world that Claire wanted.

Farley had still not levelled with Frances. He had received a friendly cable from her, telling him all was well and that he was still loved. "I have not yet severed the last of her hopes," he told Claire, "though I know I should tell her soon." If he told her now, and there were wild reports of her disintegration, "it would be terribly hard to keep my footing." Unless, of course, Claire was with him.

Farley had also received some gossip about Frances from Toronto friends. She apparently did not expect to see Farley back in Palgrave. "Girl must be prescient!" he wrote to Claire. "I begin to wonder if, maybe, she isn't relieved by the prospect of no me-prospect. Would be, if she had any sense. Thank God <u>you</u> have no sense. You can't have, to come galumphing across an ocean to the arms of such a wooly wild thing as me."

As Farley had promised, a telegram and a letter arrived at Douglas Drive from Ted Allan Productions, offering Claire a job in England. It was a good cover story, written by Farley. Her mother telephoned Claire with the news, astonished that her daughter was looking for a job abroad. Claire thought the telegram was marvellously done, though it did seem presumptuous to be invited to be in *charge* of the publicity department. Her mother told Claire that she thought her ailing father, who still didn't know Claire was going to England, would approve of her career decision.

"I feel a lot better now. I have had a bad time this week, with all sorts of black thoughts going through my brain," she wrote. "But the one thing I do not doubt, is the love we have for each other Farley. There will be lots of obstacles in our life together, but lack of love is not one of them."

Meanwhile, Claire was trying her best to endure the demands of the holiday season, writing cards, wrapping presents, and visiting boring people. She had reluctantly attended the office Christmas party at Simpsons-Sears, telling Farley that she drank as an antidote to the boredom, superficiality, and hideous sense of forced gaiety.

Farley had better company. On Christmas Eve, the Gants arrived from London to spend a few days at their Dorset cottage. Farley joined them on a walk along the shore, followed by a ploughman's lunch at the Crown pub in Puncknowle. On Christmas Day, Farley used a fire-starting device called a "witch" to clear his chimney and was smoke-free for the first time since his arrival. He joked to Claire that he could die and would be "so thoroughly smoked that no self-respecting bacteria would linger in me."

Claire sent Farley a Christmas present—a device that ran along a map and told you how far it was from point A to point B. Turned over, it became a compass, and with another twist, a pencil. He told her he would give her her gift when she arrived, and sent a message: "Merry Christmas to both of us, we <u>are</u> the world's lovers, and <u>nothing</u> can keep us apart. I am gravely chucking Georgiana under her chin, and tickling her just the least little bit. I love you. I love you. I love you."

He told her he hoped she had had a good Christmas, then teasingly changed his mind. He actually hoped she'd had a terrible Christmas and got the collywobbles from too much plum pudding. He could give her "nothing but words, words, words." He was going to drink some rum, hoping it would numb his longing for her. "Somehow I must dull this longing before it reduces me to a whimpering caricature of a man. Oh Claire, love me Claire! For I love you much more than life. Good night, good night, I sleep with you and weep with you, and I'm damn near weeping now."

Farley was invited to the Gants' cottage for Christmas dinner. They feasted on roast duck with mushrooms and artichokes, and drank Algerian red wine chased by single-malt whisky.

Roland was like a dog escaping from a kennel when he exchanged the confines of London for the wide-open spaces of Coombe. The next day, they walked all the way to Eggardon Heath, where they surveyed the old bones of an ancient hill fort. Several hundred sheep milled around the site. According to Roland, this was Thomas Hardy's favourite place as a boy. Like Hardy, they enjoyed the magnificent view over half of the West Country, and up and down the Channel. Two days later, the Gants reluctantly returned to London, leaving Farley by himself.

He tried his hand on Liz's ancient typewriter. To his surprise, it did a fair job, although it could not reproduce accents like his old Olivetti could. Obsessed with thoughts of Claire, Farley had trouble focusing. Unable to work, he tried to be useful by driving the Percival boys, David and Jimmy, to Dorchester in his old car to do some shopping. He had bought the 1936 Pilot from Allan Percival for a hundred pounds. It handled like a tank and looked like a hearse. To make things a little warmer at the cottage, Farley bought himself heavy corduroy trousers, boots, and a thick sweater. He couldn't wait for Claire to join him.

"My heart is beating like a jack-hammer. Georgie is twitching madly in the depths of, and brand new, and immense, pair of corduroy trousers which I bought him as a Christmas present."

Desperate to fill the time, Farley helped Allan check the cement water troughs scattered over the property for the sheep. "This is a spooky place on a foggy day, which is every second day during winter," he wrote. "Nevertheless it was a wonderfully vigorous and exhilarating ramble." Garth the sheepdog came along too, flushing four large hares, a covey of partridges, and flocks of wood pigeons.

Farley was in good spirits until the postman arrived on December 29 to deliver the first letters to his new address. Four of them were from Claire. The first three were full of happiness, humour, and questions—for example, did they have TV dinners in England?

"Well you better lay in a supply because when I arrive my love I do not plan to leave our nuptial bed for at least a week... Maybe raw beef-steak would be better than TV dinners. Better get some... I feel rather like a bride right now, leaving the life of my family and my childhood to follow my heart. I am coming to you completely this time. In fact you will have everything now but the dowry. You'll have to make it legal for that. Am I tempting you?"

The fourth letter took all the pleasure out of the previous three, at least to the man-child Farley sometimes became when things didn't go his way. Claire informed him that her father had been positively diagnosed with leukemia and likely had only a few weeks to live. She hoped that Farley would understand that she had agreed to postpone her January 6 departure. There was a Dutch liner, the ss *Ryndam*, leaving Hoboken, New Jersey, on January 15, and scheduled to arrive in Southampton on January 25. Considering the family situation, there was really no alternative for her at the moment. In any case, it was only a brief delay.

Farley was crushed. He had been hanging on by his fingernails, counting the days until Claire's arrival. One extra day of life without her, let alone ten, seemed like damnation. He immediately dashed off three letters, each one freighted with more self-pity than the last. He then composed a cable, which he took up to the farm to call in to the telegraph office. After reading it, Liz Percival calmly tore it up and threw it in the fire. She told Farley not to be such a bloody fool. For a moment he was stunned.

"Then slowly the ludicrousness of the situation began to penetrate my black fit of self-dramatics, and in a moment all three of us were full of giggles, and then outright laughter with me as the willing butt... Yes, love, I can wait." But Farley warned Claire that if she was delayed again, he would pack up and come back. "I have to have you. I shall have you, and neither God, nor ex-Colonel, nor Simpsons-Sears can stop me." He joked that if she was not there by the new date, he would shave off his beard, have Georgie circumcised, and get a vasectomy.

Farley, Liz, and Allan went to a New Year's Eve party at the nearby Asker Hotel. There was black ice and drifting snow that night, hence a dearth of merrymakers at the party. Only three of thirty tables for dinner were occupied. Despite Farley's best efforts to make an ass of himself, the party was a flop.

The highlight was a tipsy game of musical chairs. Then the revellers sang Christmas carols a little off-key. Farley got over-refreshed, and Liz and Allan whisked him back to Coombe Farm. "I lay there on the floor, weeping bitterly, flat on my face kicking my heels, and having tantrums," Farley wrote. At 2 a.m., he staggered back to his own cottage, got into bed, started giggling, and couldn't stop.

The following morning, he wrote a note of apology to Liz. In a New Year's Day letter to Claire, Farley said he had a head like a barrage balloon and was now convinced that nobody loved him except Claire. "I shall go drown myself in the sheep-dip tank any moment now." He was also expecting to be evicted for his antics the night before. "I think, maybe, I should not drink? You think? Damn it, if you were here to hold my hand, and jog my elbow, these things wouldn't happen. Ah well, no doubt time will cure all. I need a cure all. You are my cure all. Come and cure all."

Despite his promises, it wasn't long before Farley's declaration of patience turned into the usual hopelessness whenever he and Claire were apart. He mused about taking a drink of hemlock. When he went out for walks, he left a sign on the door of Cottage No. 2 saying, "Farewell, cruel world." Although he felt sorry for Claire's father, the best he could offer was a nihilistic blast from his doomsday trumpet. No one played that instrument better than Farley.

"Darling heart, we are all dying." It was madness for her to think that she was deserting a sinking ship. "Your father will die. You will die. We shall all die. But it is necessary first to have lived, in order to accept the reality of death. To make death bearable. You have wanted to live, more desperately than anyone I've ever known, but you were terrified to step out of the living tomb and try the real, rough, inimitable reality."

And there was something else he didn't want her to forget: "Perhaps I am now sounding childish and a little petulant, but damn it to hell, my need of you is immediate, and ten times as vital, as theirs is of you," he wrote. "You do NOT belong to your family. You and I belong to one another, and we must belong to one another totally without reservation if there is to be any future for us. If one of us begins to demand codicils and special considerations in regard to the world, and the people we've left behind, then the other will begin to do the same thing, and that will be the beginning of the end."

A new and disturbing tone crept into Farley's letters, going beyond despondency, self-pity, and doubt to the threshold of morbidity. These days, he was finding himself "stale, dull, aimless, and generally obnoxious." He suggested that Claire stay where she was because he was a poor choice of a mate and probably destined for oblivion.

"I'm tired, darling, very tired, and a lousy bet. The odds are heavily against you, you know. If you wish to cancel out, don't hesitate. In October you said that I held all the cards, complete with joker. It's still true, and it is probably a worthless deck." This wasn't self-pity, he claimed, "it was more like self-realization." She would not be letting the side down if she cancelled. "I'll sleep, that's all, and Hamlet said it beyond any capacity of mine to restate the phrase."

If he could not have Claire, that would be the end for him. "You're more than the woman I love. Much, much more. You are the last open door. I have my shoulder against it, to keep it open. The wind blows hard against it, and my muscles ache with the effort. If it closes? That's the silent slam that no ears will hear. If it opens, and stays open, maybe I'll come through it—if you take my hand... If I'm only trembling before shadows, then cable me at once. You need to say nothing more than to tell me I am a fool." He signed off: "Goodbye love, I live in you, and die without you."

Claire was alarmed at the bleakness of Farley's despair. She tried to pull him out of the tailspin, but she too was frustrated. "How can I tell you how I feel? At one moment bubbling over with anticipation, at another moment full of grave doubts about you. This is surely the way with lovers. My own happiness will always be affected by your unhappiness. I do not doubt your love for me Farley, but I just don't know what to do—your letters are so sad . . . For all I know I may be writing love letters to a man who has already committed suicide. Oh Farley you must be brave. Brave and patient . . . Please be strong for me."

Farley apologized for his depressing letters, then tried to explain. "But, damn it, why do we both feel so guilty when we write each other sad letters? Surely this is the measure of our love . . . I am less than half a man without you, so what sense is there in pretending otherwise? You, I hope, are not a whole woman, without me. But very soon we shall be both whole and happy, for we shall be together . . . We must love each other very much, you know."

BY NOW, CLAIRE'S FAMILY and most of her friends knew that she was going to England. Nana had taken the news of her departure well, even suggesting that a new job meant new faces, and who knew, maybe a new boyfriend. Her father was similarly supportive. That was surprising, because he now knew that his own days were numbered. The doctors had allowed him home for Christmas Day and then readmitted him to the hospital. Claire made him a present of art supplies.

The daughter who had always felt bullied and belittled by her father thought badly of herself for leaving at a time like this. But it helped that the man Farley called "the Colonel," based on Wheeler's rank in World War II, seemed at ease with her decision. Claire readily admitted that her situation was not even close to the one that Farley had faced. "But good or bad, I must be kind to these people right now. It is the nature of me . . . And it was also the way you wanted to leave your family— in good grace and without deliberate cruelty. Please understand lover, please try to be brave. I am coming."

After rereading her letters, Farley spent an entire afternoon walking in the rain. Doubts fell on him like raindrops. Was there more to Claire's delayed plans than affection for her parents? "It may be your own uncertainty about us, and our future," he wrote. He thought he detected an abiding doubt running through all of her letters to him in England. "Oh darling, if you are not sure of it, for the love of God, say so and say so now." He had counted on the date of her arrival and the change "shook the hell" out of him.

It was then that Claire made a touching confession that changed everything. "In truth my love, I was born a timid soul and life has been just one long battle to try and muster the courage to face the awful uncertainties. Some of us are born with a stutter, or a limp or short-sighted, but I was born timid... Don't lose faith in me lover. I badly need someone to have faith in me. This is something my parents never had in me. Not that it matters now, but it has affected me Farley and I am acutely aware when I feel that you are losing faith in me. Maybe sometimes love is not enough. Trust me, trust me."

Farley rejoiced in these heartfelt, disarming words. In one of her letters, Claire had said that she was "floating on a pink cloud" in anticipation of joining him. "Stay on your pink cloud, lover, and let it waft you quickly to me," he wrote. His good humour returned. He joked that he had lied to Claire. She thought he was rich, successful, young, and handsome. Actually, he was poor as a church mouse, dyed his hair, and would be fifty-six come Michaelmas. He hoped she had lots of good books to keep her company on the voyage over. "I refuse, absolutely, to countenance a shipboard romance at this stage. Later, maybe. Not now... Have I mentioned to you that I love you, dearly, deeply, desperately?"

His emotional perspective also surged back. Farley chastised both of them for all the sadness they had caused each other when the only real problem was being so far apart, with letters that passed like ships in the night as their only means of communication. Over the two months of their separation, their words of despair had been "transient nonsense."

"What a silly pair we are. To have exhausted one another emotionally, to such a degree, at such a distance, over such a time. Idiot children.

I hope that there'll never be need again for more than a single letter between us, and not even much need for talk. I am beginning to hate all words, with an abiding passion, which probably isn't a very sound attitude for a writer to take. But they are so inadequate to the real need, always."

His new priority was to get himself in shape for the joys of the matrimonial bed by walking six to eight miles a day. One false spring morning, he set off along the Channel shore westward to Lyme Regis, "a snug little port" where he had been stationed on coastal watch with his regiment in 1942.

He got as far as the tiny village of Swyre before a gale sweeping up the Channel chilled him to the bone. He took cover in the Crown pub at Puncknowle, where three roadmenders playing darts and warming by the fire shared their lunch with him: rabbit pie, Stilton cheese, bread, and onions. After the men went back to work, the publican regaled Farley with tales of great-grandfathers who had gone off fishing to Newfoundland—good material for the book Farley was planning to write.

When lambing season began, Farley helped Allan with the work, grateful for a way to pass the time before Claire's ship docked in Southampton. He spent hours on the downs checking for ewes in difficulty, hauling feed, and taking the occasional animal back to the farm for help. Garth usually accompanied him.

"Every living thing seemed worthy of his care, whether it was a baby rabbit, a hedgehog, or a lamb," Farley noted. There was only one creature Farley wanted to care for, and she would soon be with him, such as he was. "Worn out by longing for you, I shall be only a shadow fellow, all beard and no bone."

CLAIRE FINALLY GATHERED HER COURAGE and informed "Mr. Do-or-Die," her boss, that she was leaving the company for a job in England. He was gobsmacked and told Claire that he didn't know what he would do without her, but would instantly take her back if it didn't work out overseas. He backed up his praise in the written recommendation he gave her: "Miss Wheeler has proved to be a very competent young lady, with a most pleasant personality, which has assisted her in her

Public Relations work... I have no hesitation in recommending her for a position of responsibility and trust." Farley was surprised at how little resistance his old rival had put up to her departure.

Claire had two going-away parties and many fond farewells. The big question on everyone's mind was one she hated being asked: Why was she still unmarried? She couldn't tell them that she was off to be with the man she loved. "The long struggle is almost over, and I do know how hard it must have been for you Farley. I love you unbelievably much and I'm going to make you very happy. I nibble your beard and kiss your funny nose... When I get there I am going straight to bed for a week. Want to come?" She reminded him that she had his offer in writing to light the morning fire and make tea.

Just before she departed, she got a call from the McClellands. Jack's mother had died the day before Christmas, and the mood in the household was sombre. But they had four letters from Farley to give her. There was also a telegram saying "RELAX DARLING, EVERYTHING UNDER CONTROL. MEETING RYNDAM." She read the paragraph about procuring a "mechanical contraceptive devise," but it was too late to get one. Claire hoped she would have better luck with diaphragms than with TV dinners in England. Farley informed her that the latter didn't exist there, but that he would keep a lover's stew on a hot plate by their bed.

On January 10, 1962, after four years and four months of trying to endure the emptiness of it all, Claire left Simpsons-Sears for the last time. It felt like she was getting out of prison. During her time there, she always had the feeling she was "waiting for nothing." She told Farley that if they ever became destitute, she would rather take in laundry than go back to her old job. Claire had crossed an emotional Rubicon, leaving her natural timidity far behind on the other shore. She wrote to Farley about what she believed lay just ahead, provided they stayed true to their love.

"Never never let us destroy the precious thing we have between us. It is a very rare thing you know, our love. Not many people have such a thing, so we must be careful never to let it become damaged. Like beautiful silver we will use it every day and it will become more and more lovely with the passing years."

The long train trip to New York was peaceful but not without worries. Two things bothered Claire most: leaving her dying father, and not knowing what Farley's wife would do when she finally found out that her marriage was over. "Frances will have to know soon what the score is. It is cruel to keep her in suspense," she wrote. Claire was worried that Frances would throw a tantrum or even attempt suicide. As for Claire's father, he was weak and depressed and seemed to have lost the will to live. As she reflected on her parents, she felt loving toward them. "They did the best they could for me, because after all, I was not an easy child for them to understand."

Claire made her way from New York to Hoboken, New Jersey, where she boarded the ss *Ryndam* on January 15. A telegram and a letter from Farley were already waiting for her. The telegram read: "FORGIVE FOOLISH LETTERS RESULT OF DESPERATE IMPATIENCE ARRIVAL YOUR LOVING PRESENCE I ADORE YOU DARLING FARLEY."

The voyage passed like a long ride on a pink cloud. Claire was feeling refreshed, in love, and excited about the new life awaiting her on the other side of the ocean. As the ss *Ryndam* neared the end of the voyage, there was a gala dinner featuring twelve courses, starting with French hors d'oeuvres and ending with Parfait Rothschild. Her table mates signed her menu, which was adorned with a carriage drawn by two white horses and driven by a coachman and two footmen. The way she was feeling, she might as well have been riding inside with Farley. The cloudless night sky was filled with stars.

14 | Love on the Wing

ON JANUARY 25, 1962, a bearded figure arrived in the cold, grey dawn at the docks of the Holland America Line in Southampton. After two months of separation from Claire, Farley wasn't in the mood for waiting.

By 7:30 a.m., he had obtained a boarding pass and was searching for her among the ship's 645 passengers. Then he had a better idea: stake out her quarters. In the dining lounge, Claire was aflutter at the prospect of seeing Farley again. After hurriedly finishing her breakfast, she rushed back to her cabin to get ready and found Farley standing at the door. They shared an exuberant embrace in front of an astonished cabin steward. A more joyful reunion took place inside the cabin. Afterwards, Claire finished packing while Farley drank the remainder of her morning coffee.

After passport checks, baggage claims, goodbyes to friends met on the voyage, and a jovial customs inspection, they loaded Claire's luggage into the Pilot and set off on the two-hour drive to Dorset. Halfway into the journey, they stopped at the World's End pub, where Claire joked that she was probably the first passenger off the *Ryndam* to be sitting in an authentic English pub. The roaring fire delighted her, as did the bread and cheese that came with their pints.

Farley showed off his prowess at driving on the left side of the road and took the scenic route to Dorset along an old Roman road. When they arrived at the cottage, Farley carried his bride over the threshold. They enjoyed a drink by a cozy fire, toasting their luck at finally being together, and spent the rest of the day in bed. After a quick supper, they headed back to bed for their first night together. It was a universe away from their stolen evenings in Toronto—no curfew, no painful parting, no agonizing wait for the next hours together, just the dizzying prospect of a life without goodbyes.

It was also a period of adjustment for both of them, especially Claire. At the best of times, the transition from mistress or lover to wife is difficult. Anyone can look good under the Japanese lantern of romance; the searchlight of marriage is another matter. With hikes into the hills and woods, a shopping junket to Bridport, and simply living side by side in Cottage No. 2, Claire began to ease into her new role. They both gradually began to relax and unwind from the emotional whirlwind of the past eighteen months. Claire only had one complaint: the toadstools growing in the damp, dark corners of their kitchen.

The sense of freedom was intoxicating. There was no longer any need to hide their relationship, at least not in England. Farley revelled in showing off Claire. They had tea with Allan and Liz Percival in the main house, where Claire was an immediate hit. Farley also introduced her to Roland and Nadia Gant, who had just arrived from London to spend time at their cottage. They loved Claire. Roland shared some news: he had resigned as an editor-director of Michael Joseph publishers. The firm had just been purchased by Canadian millionaire Roy Thompson, and Roland refused to work for him. He would soon hang his editorial hat at William Heinemann Ltd. in Mayfair.

Farley and Claire made the rounds of the neighbourhood pubs, where the locals greeted them warmly. They were made as welcome in Dorset as they had been in outport Newfoundland when they showed up aboard the *Happy Adventure*. It was not surprising, since Dorset working people shared the same ancestry as many of those who had crossed the Atlantic as sailors, fishermen, and indentured servants and then had chosen to stay. Both Farley and Claire felt at home.

They spent most afternoons "snuggling" in bed. No work was done in the white heat of reunion. Their pastoral honeymoon was interrupted, however, by a trip to London to preserve the complicated story of Claire's fictitious job, with Ted Allan as her nominal employer. Farley was bothered by the crowds and endless traffic. They had a quick sandwich in the bar of the King's Court Hotel and then saw the stage musical *Irma la Douce* at the Lyric Theatre, which they both thought was pretentious and trivial. After the show, they had a supper of over-priced prawns in a restaurant designed for tourists and wished they were back at their cottage.

The next day, they visited the typewriter repair shop, the bank, and the office of Innes Rose. To break the tedium of workaday chores, they climbed to the top of the dome of St. Paul's Cathedral, marvelling at its splendid view of London. Then it was off to have Claire's mail forwarded to Coombe Farm and a brief but necessary parting.

To maintain the charade of Claire's London job, she took the train to Cambridge by herself. She had to pay an obligatory visit to her Aunt Kitty and Uncle Maurice, who did not know about Farley.

Claire took the train back from Cambridge and arrived in Dorchester at 1 p.m. on February 5, her twenty-ninth birthday. Farley picked her up at the station, in a state of excitement about the dinner he had planned for the occasion. As a gift, he gave her an antique silver brooch.

But a birthday bash wasn't the only thing waiting for Claire. A letter arrived from her mother, telling her that her father was dying. Joy and grief crowded into her heart, making for an unusual birthday. It was "an evening of much feasting, drinking, and emotion," Farley wrote in his journal. "Strange combinations of laughter, tears, love-making, drunkenness and decisions."

Between the laughter and tears, they also agreed that now was the time to write Claire's parents about their true history and plans to marry. Both of them sent letters to her dying father.

Claire composed hers in front of the fire on a frosty February evening. "It seems that I have some good news for you. At long last your wandering spinster daughter is destined to become somebody's wife. I am going to be married, eventually, to Farley Mowat."

This meant waiting for "the long, slow legal process of divorce... I don't need to tell you much about him really. He is a grand fellow and

I love him and I know that you would like him too. He is an immensely interesting man and we are very happy together." Claire said she was hoping to do the illustrations for some of Farley's future books.

And she offered her father another comfort: "I have met Farley's parents who are extremely friendly and who seem very pleased that I am going to be one of the family. Farley and I decided that we were in love from our first meeting in St Pierre but since both of us have had some unfortunate experiences in love, we wanted to be absolutely sure. Over a year ago we decided that we wanted to get married, but for obvious reasons it was best not to announce it then." She knew this would come as something of a surprise to her father, if not a shock, "but I know you will be very happy that I have at last found happiness."

Farley began his letter with an apology for not speaking to Claire's father personally. "As Claire has told you, she and I are very much in love, and have been for nearly two years now. We intend to marry as soon as I can obtain my divorce from my first wife. To this I want to add my personal assurance to you, that I shall do everything possible to expedite the time when we can be married."

Farley explained that he was anxious to protect his two sons in the wake of all that was happening. His first wife had tentatively agreed to a divorce, but any premature public discussion of the matter might derail the process.

"I want very much to assure you that my love for Claire is the most important element in my existence. She has given me more happiness than I have ever known, and without sounding melodramatic, I hope it is not far fetched to say that she is completely vital to me. Both my work and my personal happiness now depend heavily upon her and there is nothing I would not do to return to her some of the happiness and delight which she had brought into my life." Farley told Louis Wheeler that he would meet him when he and Claire returned to Canada in the spring. "I hope you will find it possible to accept me as Claire's husband."

WHILE AWAITING THE RESPONSE from Rosedale, Farley attempted some work on his elusive novel. The well remained dry. Claire put the cottage in order and tried to draw, but most days it was too cold to work. So they decided to help Allan with the lambing and then hit the road. They drove to Cerne Abbas to see the 180-foot Cerne Giant, a full-frontal male nude carved into the west-facing hillside above the town. The figure is clutching a huge club and has a prominent erection. From there, they travelled to Dorchester and climbed to the top of Maiden Castle, an Iron Age hill fort.

Farley was deeply moved by what he had seen. "The truth was that I was becoming more and more affected even by the brief glimpses we did have of places like Stonehenge, Eggerton Heath, Maiden Castle, and the Giant of Cerne Abbas, that somebody a long, long time ago had carved into the chalk slopes of the South Downs. All these spoke for themselves—but in alien tongues for which there seemed to be no interpreter. Perhaps I could have a go at becoming one?"

They decided to visit Jersey, in the Channel Islands, where Farley thought the museum library might have information about early trade connections between Jersey and Newfoundland. His hunch paid off.

The librarian, Patricia Webb, was intrigued by Farley's project and eagerly dug out information about the islanders and their early voyages across the Western Ocean—the North Atlantic. After gathering the research, Farley and Claire rented an Austin and set out to explore the island. Claire was anxious to see the famous Jersey cows, but sadly most of them had been eaten during the German occupation of the island during World War II.

Back at Coombe cottage, the Percivals dropped by for a drink. Liz expressed mock horror at the nude figure Claire had drawn on the wall above the fireplace, using Farley as a model.

Allan had some advice for Farley's research. They should explore the West Country if they wanted to trace the people who had gone to fish off Newfoundland. Thousands of people from Cornwall, Devon, Somerset, and Dorset had made that journey. Coincidentally, Claire's mother, Winifred, came from Torquay, on the Devon coast, not far from Coombe Farm.

Luckily, Farley took Allan's advice. In a Plymouth museum, he and Claire found the journal of a seventeenth-century ancestor of one of the city's oldest families, James Yonge, who had made several trips to Newfoundland as a ship's doctor on fishing vessels. It was one of the few surviving first-person accounts of the voyage during that era.

According to Farley, as the winter dragged on, life at the cottage was becoming "a little tense." He was uneasy about his work and their future. Some magazine pieces he had laboured over for months hadn't panned out. He decided to abandon his novel. Even the outline for the book on Newfoundland's early history had stalled. Farley had done superb research but couldn't find the narrative thread that would bring it to life. He told Claire that if he didn't get another advance from Jack McClelland soon, "both my families are going to run out of money." Claire suggested that he put aside the Newfoundland book and try something else. "You're probably trying too hard," she said.

In the meantime, there had been no response to their letters revealing their love affair and planned marriage. Would they be embraced or spurned? They needn't have worried. When a letter finally arrived from Claire's mother, they couldn't have hoped for a better reply.

The family was delighted with the news, and they all thought that Farley was an "intellectual giant." Claire's father had been happy to see the March issue of his favourite magazine, the *Atlantic Monthly*, which featured excerpts from *The Serpent's Coil* on the cover. Winifred had read the book aloud to her husband and Nana over four days. They all agreed it was "the most fascinating saga of the seas" they had ever read. Concerned about how cold the English cottage was, Claire's father had sent a clipping about an electric fan heater he had noticed and told Claire to take it to Harrods and order something similar.

Claire was happy and relieved. "I am glad that you were both pleased with the news," she wrote, "and I know that you will like Farley when you meet him." He was busy doing research on a book about the early history of Newfoundland, she said, and "the only thing Farley is worried about is upsetting the apple-cart with his wife, who is, at best, a temperamental woman."

Claire asked her mother to put aside a copy of the *Atlantic Monthly* for her. Farley added a note thanking Winifred for her letter, and saying that he looked forward to meeting her husband. "I still firmly expect to see him in the Spring. Do give him my best wishes, won't you? Claire is quite right. You do flatter me outrageously and, of course, I love it."

The news on the medical front steadily worsened. As his cancer advanced, Claire's father had moved from Mount Sinai Hospital back to Douglas Drive. He had gone from 165 pounds down to 114, the same weight Farley had been when he was rejected by the Air Force while trying to enlist in World War II; recruits had to weigh at least 120 pounds.

The Colonel had lost interest in food, and his mind had begun to wander in and out of focus. He was full of strange questions and chilling vacancies. Winifred apologized for bringing Claire such bad news, but she knew her daughter was woman enough to face the truth of a desperate situation. "Thank goodness you have a real good boyfriend in Farley to lean on psychologically now, am sure he will be a tower of strength to you, at this particular time." Winifred hoped the good Lord would spare her husband long enough to meet Farley in person, "for nothing right now could give him greater pleasure . . . next to seeing <u>you</u> again dear."

Winifred spared her daughter the details of how difficult her husband had been since he had returned home and moved into Nana's quarters. Winifred slept on a chesterfield in the apartment and catered to her husband's every need. Although he had no specific pain, he was dreadfully uncomfortable. Claire received a letter from her sister-in-law, who gave a blunt description of the reality that faced both her mother and Nana as caregivers: "He treats them like he would the army regiment . . . He makes me want to hit him, he is so nasty."

WHILE CLAIRE WAS GETTING BAD NEWS about her father, Farley received some of his own. He had instructed his lawyer, Robert Burgess, to get the name of the lawyer Frances was using so that they could proceed toward a divorce. The reply Burgess received from Frances was discouraging: "Received your letter of March 15th re solicitor acting for me in regard to separation agreement and divorce action. I intend to do nothing at the moment and have no lawyer to act for me and do not intend to engage one. Sincerely, Frances Mowat."

According to Burgess, there was no way that Frances could be compelled to bring a divorce action or even enter into a formal separation agreement. Since Farley was already making provision for her and the children, he had no leverage. All they could do was wait. Burgess later advised there was no reason that Claire could not use Farley's surname, pointing out that a person can use any name they wish, provided it is not for fraudulent purposes. She could open a bank account in the name of Claire Mowat and probably be safe using that name on her driver's licence.

Beset with problems on multiple fronts, Farley kept turning over in his mind Claire's advice about a change of scenery and perhaps of projects. "She could be right," he wrote in an unfinished manuscript. "Maybe I'm chasing an over-loaded bus when it's really the individuals aboard that matter . . . Individual voices from antiquity telling us how it was away back when."

Late one night, after Claire had gone to sleep, Farley considered advice that Angus had given him when he learned that he and Claire were going to Britain. "He told me of the post-war journeys he had made in Britain—not to the southerly but to the most northern parts where he had fleetingly encountered the spoor of human beings who were old long before the Flood.

"Northern Britain, he had told me, and especially Caithness Shire and the islands of Orkney and Shetland—was a world of 'first-footers'— mysterious folk who had apparently been the first human kind to settle that region after the last ice age slackened its hold on land and sea, and who had found a future for themselves in a world being reborn."

It suddenly sounded like an intriguing destination to Farley, not least because Caithness was "reputedly the Mowat ancestral home." Angus "had gone there seeking ancestors and found a remarkable degree of acceptance. Perhaps, he said, I should write a book about it."

The next morning, Farley broached the idea to Claire of travelling six hundred miles north of Coombe Farm to a wild place, full of ruins so old that nobody knew who had built them, when, or why. If they left now, they could welcome spring while exploring a whole new world. It was not exactly the warmer climes she had suggested to him, but she nodded in agreement. "How soon would you like to go?" Claire asked. Less than a week later, they were saying goodbye to Liz and Allan Percival, Garth the dog, Zoom the cat, and the West Country, where they had begun their new life together.

Their eventual destination was the northernmost tip of Scotland. They crossed the great Severn Estuary aboard an open-deck ferry that landed them in the southeast corner of Wales. The Cambrian Mountains were still capped with snow. Pushing ahead, they reached Birkenhead, on the shores of the Irish Sea. Then they fled the wastelands and coal smoke of the Midlands and drove to the Lake District. It was so enchanting that they took a detour to see if they could find the château where Farley had spent his first wartime leave in the spring of 1943.

Built by a wealthy Englishman as a summer place, the château had been used as a leave-hotel for officers of the Allied forces. At that time, only six officers were staying at the hotel. The place had been run by the owner's staff, and the butler offered exquisite food, including venison, salmon, grouse, and real butter—luxuries to people used to bully beef, fish-oil margarine, and powdered eggs. The officers had the run of the wine cellar, and sat at a mahogany table, set with real silver and bone china. In the evening, they danced to jazz records played on a wind-up gramophone.

Back then, it had been a treat for the officers, who got four days of leave there. But when Farley and Claire found the former oasis of elegance, it had become a gaudy tourist trap, with commercial signs and a kiosk that sold cheap souvenirs and Coca-Cola. Farley wanted to drive on, but Claire was exhausted, so they stopped for the night. It was a decision that ended in tears and trauma.

A violent storm came up that night. Farley wrote that Claire slept, "but for me, the wind raging through the chateau's cluster of chimneys, it became the paralyzing scream of German rockets plunging down. Lightning flared blood red in my shuttered eyes, and accompanying thunderclaps shook the walls and became salvos shells bursting over and around the slit trench in which I cowered—until I wakened trembling to find myself drenched in sweat.

"I had to get out of there but as I fumbled for my clothes in the flickering light of the receding storm, Claire woke and anxiously asked what was the matter. I hardly heard her—and could not really answer. 'Bats in my belfry,' I muttered, stumbling through the doorway and down the dim-lit hall. Once I was outside the demons let go of me. The storm passed and the valley echoed to the crystalline music of a hundred newly born waterfalls cascading into the loch; and to the sibilance of bird-song welcoming me back to a living world."

When he returned to their room, he found Claire slumped on the edge of the bed weeping. "I thought you changed your mind . . . about us . . . I thought you'd gone for good . . . were never coming back." Farley tried to soothe her, but he could not find the words to explain his reaction to the old demons of war released by the storm. "We were a divided, almost silent couple as we resumed our journey northward."

To break the ice, Farley adopted the role of tour guide as they drove through the narrow streets of Carlisle, once the western anchor of Hadrian's Wall, built to keep the wild Picts out of Roman Britain. They stopped at Castle Douglas. According to Farley's grandfather, Robert McGill Mowat, "Black Douglas," a highland chieftain who supported Robert the Bruce, king of Scots, may have been a relative.

The stark ruin was, according to Farley, "a particularly grim looking stone tower." A sleet storm had started, and Claire was shivering in the car. They drove on. At dusk, they reached the small town of Stow. An unassuming Royal Inn welcomed them as if they were long-lost relatives. A birthday party had been in progress for a day and a night, and they were plied with food, drink, and casual affection until long after midnight.

They stumbled upstairs to a snug little room and slept in until noon the next day, when they were wakened by the innkeeper's wife. She was standing by their bed with a tray of hot buttered scones, oatcakes, honey, and a huge pot of tea laced with single malt Scotch. "If this is what the Scots are really like," Claire said, "I may never leave."

Early the next morning, they took a car ferry across the Firth of Forth estuary and headed toward the market town of Crieff, the home of Ian Mackay, the doctor who had become Farley's friend on the trip to England aboard the ss *Newfoundland*. He volunteered to be their tour guide for the next few days.

Continuing to be concerned about her father's condition, Claire wrote regularly to her mother during their trip through Scotland, staying connected through their friends from London, Roland and Nadia Gant, and Farley's British agent, Innes Rose. She made sure that her family had the cable address in case of an emergency.

Claire wrote to Winifred that Farley's mother had been in England and that they had had several get-togethers. "She is quite a charming lady and lives at Port Hope, Ontario. She will be going back to Canada this week on the Empress of Britain... She is quite fond of me (amazing!) and says she is so glad that Farley has found someone suitable at last... Give my love to Pop. I know he is being very valiant at this tragic time and he's not one to give up easily."

Winifred enjoyed Claire's vivid descriptions of their travels through northern Scotland. She wondered if it was a combination pleasure and business trip or "just plain gallivanting with friend Farley." And then she found the words not easily shared between mother and daughter.

"Well dear, I don't know whether you will receive this letter in time to do any good or not, but if you wish to see Dad alive once more before he leaves this Vale of Tears, I suggest you take the next plane home... I sometimes wonder if he isn't determinatively hanging on in the hope of seeing you and Farley in person, not that he has ever uttered a word in this direction, but I just have a hunch about this."

Claire replied that she and Farley had talked things over, and in light of her father's condition, they had decided to return to Canada as soon as possible. They would likely find a freighter or small vessel sailing from the Clyde to Canada and planned to be home at the beginning of May.

Claire's father died on Thursday, April 19. Innes Rose sent a telegram to Farley in Glasgow with the news. The funeral would be held on April 23. It would come and go with Farley and Claire an ocean away.

FACING, TOP: Students from the French school on Saint-Pierre, August 10, 1960. This was the day Farley and Claire met, while Farley was painting his boat, and Claire was sketching in the harbour. Farley and Claire are in the centre. © Claire and Farley Mowat

FACING, BOTTOM: Claire Wheeler with George Detcheverry at the helm of *Itchy* on August 13, 1960, on their way to Miquelon with friends. © Claire and Farley Mowat

ABOVE, LEFT: Farley Mowat unrigging his boat *Itchy* on August 21, 1960. © Claire and Farley Mowat

ABOVE, RIGHT: Farley Mowat's schooner sailing in Bay d'Espoir, 1961. Harold Horwood is at the helm. Photo courtesy of Andrew Horwood.

FACING, TOP: Smelt vendors, Piccadilly, Newfoundland, 1961. Kids with Farley Mowat. Photo courtesy of Andrew Horwood.

FACING, BOTTOM LEFT: Portrait of Farley Mowat by Harold Horwood, circa 1961. Photo courtesy of Andrew Horwood.

FACING, BOTTOM RIGHT: Farley and Claire exploring an abandoned outport on the south coast of Newfoundland and Labrador. © Claire and Farley Mowat

ABOVE, LEFT: Farley looking at Toltec Warriors at Aztec site, Tula, Mexico, 1965. Photo courtesy of Andrew Horwood.

ABOVE, RIGHT: Claire with cacti in Mexico, 1965. Photo courtesy of Andrew Horwood.

FACING: Wedding day in Corsicana, Texas, on March 29, 1965. © Claire and Farley Mowat

ABOVE, LEFT: Sailing on the *Happy Adventure* while they lived in Burgeo. © Claire and Farley Mowat

ABOVE, RIGHT: Farley signing books at Eaton's in Victoria, BC, November 1970. © Claire and Farley Mowat

LEFT: Raspberry-picking at Brick Point in Cape Breton, August 2002. © Claire and Farley Mowat

15 | Burgeo

WHEN FARLEY AND CLAIRE returned to Canada, they were embraced by both the Mowats and the Wheelers. They spent a few weeks relaxing in Ontario before heading for Newfoundland. When they reached St. John's, they stayed with Harold Horwood for six weeks in Beachy Cove, waiting for good sailing weather. When at last it arrived, they departed for the south coast and enjoyed a supper of cold pancakes, marmalade, and rum the first night.

The next day, they boarded the *Bar Haven* in Fortune. "We both notice that it feels like coming home," Claire wrote in her journal on July 20, 1962. There was an eleven-year-old boy on board who loved Farley's work and quoted whole passages from *The Dog Who Wouldn't Be*. Deck cargo included a horse bound for the coastal town of Burgeo who refused to eat, and a dog in a crate who howled all night.

On July 24, they docked in Milltown, where the *Happy Adventure* lay in winter storage. Mildewed in her cradle, she looked forlorn and abandoned. They rolled up their sleeves and set to work cleaning and painting. Two days later, the vessel was shipshape and ready to launch. After their first night on board, they awoke in great spirits for the usual reason. "A morning of great loving as a prelude to this busy day," Claire exclaimed. They took on fuel and water and loaded their gear, and Farley rigged the sails.

That summer, they sailed the south coast, revisiting old haunts and discovering new ones. After the *Happy Adventure* developed mechanical problems, they made for Burgeo to get a part. It was a stroke of serendipity. While there, adjacent to the village, they spotted a house under construction in Messieurs Cove. After seeing it once for only twenty minutes, they bought the unfinished property for $4,000, which Jack McClelland advanced to Farley. Their first home on terra firma.

The couple returned briefly to Ontario to pick up books and papers, and on November 2, 1962, they arrived back in Burgeo on board the *Bar Haven* from Port aux Basques. The house was not nearly ready, and jammed to the rafters with crates and packages that had arrived on the *Swivel* from Halifax. The place still lacked the basics: plumbing, heating, and water.

They stayed as guests at a house in town while they made the transition from Ontario, with its superhighways, to a Newfoundland outport with fifteen hundred people and no road in. They painted and hammered and, with the help of locals, dug a well and a drain, and closed in the cellar, which Farley would use as his writing room. Later, they added a Franklin stove. Meanwhile, the *Happy Adventure* was moored in a pool behind the fish plant. The boat had to be pumped out every ten days. "The one thing we have an abundance of in Burgeo is the weather," Farley quipped.

By late December, they were ready to begin their creative work, but Christmas and a Newfoundland tradition, mummering, intervened. Neighbours would dress up in disguise and go from house to house in groups, where people would offer treats and try to guess their identity. Friends brought the couple fish, caribou, and partridge, quickly filling up their larder. Mummers, two of them wearing Santa suits, visited their home. Harold Horwood arrived on New Year's Day and stayed for a week.

After Harold left for literary business in Toronto, Farley went back to work on two books, including *Never Cry Wolf*. Although he had written the first four chapters before Christmas, he had an astonishing creative burst in January and finished the first draft in just three weeks. "I am wedded to this damned book until the last wolf howls," he joked. He was also reading proofs for the U.S. edition of *The Black Joke,* a classic sea tale set off the coast of Newfoundland in the 1930s.

Claire had more work to do in Burgeo than Mr. Do-or-Die ever gave her at Simpsons-Sears. She did the cooking and washing, baked bread, answered Farley's fan mail, socialized with locals, kept her journal, and even accepted an invitation to give an art class at the local high school. Even in howling nor'easters, Claire ventured out to teach her still-life class, clutching wine bottles and old slippers for the students to draw.

They both revelled in the isolation and bad weather and the chance these gave them to work in a place of their own. Claire typed a draft of *Never Cry Wolf,* a great boon to Farley; he was a search-and-peck man at the keyboard, she, a touch typist.

One of their regular chores was to collect the bags of mail and packages from the post office. Judging by the volume, Farley was now a genuine celebrity. On one trip, the postmaster took Claire aside and told her that a select group in town had decided she was the prettiest girl in Burgeo.

Farley and Claire socialized with everyone, including the local RCMP constable, Don MacDonald, and his wife, Mary; the local doctors Ann and Mike Caulder; and the owners of Burgeo's fish plant, Spencer Lake and his second wife, Margaret. The Lakes came to dinner one night, and Margaret complained that her husband didn't appreciate her intellectual qualities. She said that what Spencer really needed was three women: a mother, a mistress, and a child-bearing wife. She was expecting her fourth child that spring.

Spencer told Farley that he was pessimistic about the future of the fishery. Five years earlier, government officials had warned plant owners like him that if they persisted in processing small haddock, there would soon be no haddock fishery at all. They persisted, and the stock, as predicted, collapsed.

The Lake plant was now sometimes forced to buy fish from Iceland to fulfill its commitments to the U.S. market. Even the Russians, who kept everything they caught, were abandoning the overfished waters of the Northwest Atlantic. Spencer was paying just three cents a pound for gutted, head-on fish. Farley listened intently. Years later, he would write *Sea of Slaughter,* his epic chronicle of five hundred years of humans—the most lethal species on the planet—laying waste to the East Coast's marine ecosystem.

Despite the raw weather, Farley and Claire struck out into Nature whenever they needed to recharge their batteries. During a strong southerly gale, they walked to one of the nearby coves to watch the crashing surf. The rain came down so hard that they couldn't raise their faces to it. Spray from the breakers was driven a quarter of a mile inland by sixty-mile-an-hour gusts. Back at the house, they made love and fell into a deep sleep. They awakened at 7:30 p.m., had Brandy Alexanders and pot roast for "breakfast," lit all the fires, and then settled down to work on *Wolves* until dawn. It was a delight to reverse the clock.

The big political story in the country at the time was the debate about nuclear weapons in Canada. In the early 1960s, at the height of the Cold War, protests against nuclear weapons spread around the world. Farley knew that if he were in Toronto, he would be livid about the crisis brewing over A-bombs, and "filled with wild frustration and striking out blindly in all directions." Instead, he was putting the final touches on what would be one of his finest books.

On a brilliant Sunday morning near the end of January, Farley went for a long walk to the Western Sands. There was not much wildlife, but he did spot a solitary raven playing on the wind. "Flying straight and level, then suddenly folding his wings and plummeting, giving a vast gurgle of joy as he did so," he wrote. It was at moments like that Farley the naturalist revelled in being far from the "sullen, endless grey boredom of a Toronto winter."

Claire's first Burgeo birthday arrived on February 5. Farley had written many serious and beautiful love poems to her, but the humorist in him emerged when he penned a fifty-six-line poem "To Claire, My Pretty" to celebrate her thirtieth birthday.

Our little Claire to-day is thirty.
Yet still her ways are pert and flirty.
She still can grace a black silk nightie.
She still remains a trifle flighty...

My Love, on this your natal day,
I have a vital word to say.
So hearken now, and heed me well
While I invoke a birthday spell.
Though time must claim us all some day
And gently steal our youth away,
Yet you will still hold Time at bay
When I am long since old and grey.
Nothing can ever age <u>your</u> charms.
because . . . you're still, a babe-in-arms!
Happy Birthday to my Love,
From Farley—who's your turtle dove.

February was a banner month in Burgeo. The *Swivel* arrived from the mainland with two new residents for the village: a saddle horse for Spencer Lake and an enormous Percheron, who would now deliver groceries and oil by sled or wagon, depending on the season. The CBC showed up in town to record a dramatization of *The Serpent's Coil*, with Farley reading his part. He and Claire decided to install a telephone. And finally, Farley mailed off *Never Cry Wolf* to the publishers. The moment it was gone, he returned to the manuscript that would become *Westviking*. He even began to eat like a Viking. He and Claire dined on venison, but it had not been cured long enough and was as tough as Farley's writing schedule. So they ground it up and made venison meatballs.

March came in like a laudatory lion. When Claire returned from the telegraph office, she burst into the house holding a telegram from Farley's U.S. publisher. Peter Davison had wired that the wolf book was "marvellous." Farley had never known him to gush and was pleasantly surprised. Drawing on their ever-expanding vocabulary of Newfoundland phrases, like "frizzle of frost" and "waller of wind," he said of Davison's praise: "Makes me feel some good."

The editorial news from Toronto was equally enthusiastic. But it was hell to be the rage; Farley would have very little time to revise the manuscript. After that, he would have to return to civilization for the rigours of a book tour. Still, Farley was pleased. "It looks as if we may eat next year," he joked.

The edited manuscript arrived in Burgeo toward the end of March. Farley got through it in jig time, making the corrections and then handing them to Claire for typing. The dedication read "For Angeline—the angel!" Angeline was the female wolf in the book, who coincidentally had many of Claire's characteristics. Angel was also Claire's middle name and her mother's maiden name. As for George, the book's male wolf, he was a version of Farley's well-known alter ego. A wordsmith at play with lupine and libido.

Despite looming trips to Boston and Toronto, Farley wasn't the only person with a busy schedule. In addition to helping get the manuscript together and doing all of her other chores, at the end of March Claire had to host ten members of Burgeo's Mothers Club, sparking a flurry of baking and cleaning. It didn't help that their well had run dry. When the big night arrived, Farley contributed by spiking the punch. The happy guests wobbled home in a gale at 1 o'clock in the morning.

As an early spring burst in Burgeo, Farley's mood darkened. He was worried about the pending April federal election, fearing that if Conservative John Diefenbaker defeated Liberal Lester Pearson, Canada would become a mere satellite of the U.S., complete with nuclear weapons. Nor was he looking forward to his imminent trip to Boston, followed by the hurly-burly of the fall book tour for *Never Cry Wolf* in Canada.

There was only one advantage to leaving the south coast in April. Workers at the nearby Ramea fish plant planned to go on strike on April 8, the same day as the federal election. Had he not been travelling, Farley would have entered the fray on the side of the workers, putting his friendship with Spencer and Margaret Lake on the line.

NEVER CRY WOLF was an immediate hit. On October 11, 1963, the *New York Times* published a glowing review, as did several other big papers in the U.S. and Canada. The *Chicago Daily News* ended its review by saying, "Read this book. You'll never forget it."

The timing of the reviews couldn't have been better for the October 1963 promotional trip to Toronto.

The telephone in Farley and Claire's rented apartment on Avenue Road never stopped ringing. Farley appeared on Pierre Berton's television show, did countless newspaper and radio interviews, and signed books. *Maclean's* magazine published a condensation of *Never Cry Wolf.* In addition to the formal events, there was a spate of parties and other social events.

After a month in Toronto, the Farley caravan moved on to Montreal, where on a single day Farley had half a dozen radio and television interviews and a formal luncheon, followed by a gala party thrown by his publisher. Pierre Berton showed up, and Claire met a young poet who had just returned from living abroad in England and Greece. Surrounded by avid listeners, in a voice like seven miles of gravel road, Leonard Cohen told amusing stories about his destitute days in Montreal. It was rumoured that after Farley and Claire had gone to bed, he tried to get everyone high on marijuana. "Poor Farley was becoming more and more tired with the hectic pace of city life . . . He definitely needs to return to Burgeo soon," Claire wrote.

After a few more visits with family, including one with his mother-in-law, Florence Thornhill, and trips to Palgrave, Farley had one last business meeting with Jack McClelland before leaving Toronto. Then he flew to Ottawa to talk to a movie producer about a film on Newfoundland and to visit a government archaeologist about findings there. Claire drove Farley to the airport after dinner and was all but crying when she got back to the car after his plane had taken off. Another separation.

After two weeks with her family in Toronto, Claire decided that she could never live with them again. Suddenly, with Farley back in Newfoundland, there was a need for letters again. "How, I wonder, could I ever live without you . . . Because you are a reality in my life. Not a daydream, nor a faint hope for the future; but you are real, you exist, you're my man, my love. How it alters the colour of things . . . I could not live without you."

Nor, at times, could she live with him. After they returned to Burgeo in early December, Claire found some of Farley's antics difficult. As a result of the frantic pace of his work, he had a huge need to let off steam. In addition to his books, locals asked him to write letters or petitions for them, paying him with caribou meat. As a celebrity, he was also drawn into local politics, as an advocate for improvements to Burgeo, like a new bridge to Smalls Island. Farley was a handful at the best of times, but he was uncontrollable when he was drinking. He was both the life and the death of many a Burgeo party. And since the social scene was so limited, whatever Farley did became the talk of the town.

When Claire tried to rein him in, Farley just accelerated. She noticed at one get-together that he was again wearing his kilt sans underwear, his favourite party trick. Exactly what sort of pleasure Farley derived from this Claire didn't know. In some mysterious way, he seemed to get great relief from having emotional outbursts in front of a roomful of people.

When she later called him out for his behaviour, Claire was treated to lectures on how she was a spoilsport who specialized in ruining his fun. He also claimed that *her* emotional outbursts interfered with his work and that she didn't understand the creative pressures every writer faces. And there was the little matter of having two families to support. Frances stoked Farley's guilt by sending letters about how Sandy was sick and missed him. Claire was exasperated. "Only 20 nights ago he delivered a sermon to me that I was a frivolous nothing-brain, with nothing on my mind but gadding around parties. I give up. There is no pleasing him."

When Farley later read these entries in Claire's journals, he wrote a footnote confirming that she was dead right, "as can be confirmed by almost anyone who has had to endure me at a party." He wrote Claire a limerick, which included the lines: "And when he gets drunk / He's a skunk." He joked that his funeral would be the one and only gathering at which he behaved himself.

Claire was also coming to realize that she and Farley had vastly different social needs. Farley loved Burgeo for its open spaces and open people. It was easy for him to make friends, much harder for Claire. Nor did he need companionship the way she did, because, next to Claire herself, his great and sustaining passion was his writing. Farley had hoped that her art would consume her in the same way, but for Claire drawing was no substitute for stimulating company.

That was in short supply in Burgeo. The chief topics for ladies were illnesses, church functions, passing dories, and the number of sheep in labour in the Lakes' barn. That left a lonely Claire sitting at home in Burgeo, reading the arts and drama section of the *Globe and Mail*, dreaming of the gay life and social circuit in the city where she had grown up in the privileged class.

Claire longed to get her hair done, get dressed up, and meet interesting people who read books or were witty, flirtatious, or amusing. And every time someone called her Mrs. Mowat, she was reminded of her masquerade as a married woman. The splendid isolation of outport life that so agreed with Farley left Claire sometimes feeling lonely and lost.

Tensions rose between them. Claire said she didn't know what would happen to them if they stayed in Burgeo. She told him flatly that she had to get away because the isolation was destroying her. It was a recurring argument and always ended the same way. Farley would shout, "We'll sell the goddam place and move to Toronto and I hope that satisfies you." Or he would suggest that she leave him for several periods during the year and live it up in Toronto. To Claire, that was impossible in her position. It would mean returning to the city as a single woman, totally at the mercy of every passing seducer. "How is it that Farley, with his truly fine mind can be happy here? . . . I seem to know less and less of what makes him tick."

Farley's frustrations grew. Claire seemed unable to decide what she wanted. When he first met her, she didn't want to run with the pack. Now she claimed that living a different kind of life made her feel lost and rootless. When they left Burgeo she was sometimes shy and uncomfortable, but when she returned she was often lonely. If her own artistic pursuits couldn't sustain her, Farley offered another option: be his dutiful wife and support him in his work. It was a suggestion that took Claire deeper into what was becoming an identity crisis, no doubt stimulated by the writings of Simone de Beauvoir. Claire was a woman with a fine mind caught in the early second wave of feminism.

"Is there a real me hiding below the surface somewhere, nudging to get out under the veneer," she wrote. "I can't seem to make up my mind. No one else can make up my mind either. Not even Farley who knows me better than anyone else. He vacillates between wanting me to fulfill myself through drawing or writing and wanting me to be just a happy housewife with a few hobbies."

Claire couldn't explain to Farley, or anyone else, why she felt compelled to do more with her life. All she knew for certain was that the two of them operated on different planes. Farley only pursued the things that interested him, and his writing seemed to come with less agony than her drawing. "His life has been so free from anxiety," she wrote.

For Claire, burdened with the compulsion to achieve an ineffable something extra, things had never been easy. "I've had to force myself to do everything I've ever done," she wrote. Claire's reflections on the mystery of her own personality took her to a daunting place. "I love Farley. But I wonder if the price I must pay for having him is a bit too much."

Their lives were picking up speed in a downward spiral, as an impulsive and emotional Farley confronted a desperately unhappy Claire. "Farley has just announced that he will not see me degenerate the way Frances did . . . What can I do when depression strikes me? All my energies cease . . . I have depression which comes like a black cloud and just hangs there."

Besides Farley's angry voice arguing about the realities of life in Burgeo, there was another sound in the Mowat household: the ticking of Claire's biological clock. Again, she was conflicted. On the one hand, she bemoaned the fact she had no children. On the other hand, she dreaded the prospect of looking after a child: mountains of soiled diapers to be washed and then hung out to dry, a banging spoon demanding service and attention, cancelled holidays if the child was sick, lack of sleep, lack of money.

But what, in the end, was the use of a childless woman's domestic duties, the hours and hours of preparing for dinner parties, washing clothes that just got dirty again, and the empty repetition of house-work? "Perhaps this is why women want to have children. They at least endure, when all else has vanished."

Proof of the delight of children arrived at Claire's door in the per-son of eleven-year-old Dorothy, a constant visitor. After hearing that Burgeo's most famous residents might be moving on, she had written a song. The chorus went, "Mr. Mowat please don't leave this town, sir . . ."

Claire felt guilty about her complaints. "There are times of course when living in Burgeo can be so delightful." That day, some local chil-dren had brought her flowers. "It would almost be worth having children for moments like these." She noted the children played the same games she had as a child in Toronto and that her mother had played in England.

One day, Farley had taken in the wash and presented her with a large sherry when she got home. The statements had come. They would have enough money to run the two households for two years. Claire felt reassured. A couple of days later, when Farley was working on revisions for *Westviking* and Claire was doing drawings of Norse houses for the book, a troop of six little girls arrived. Claire was "utterly enam-oured with the sight of the children here against the bleak background of the place. It seems to be such a curious blend of nature—human nature and bleak, forceful, windswept nature."

Family members loved visits to Burgeo. Angus and Farley's adopted brother, John, and sister, Mary, arrived in July. The teenagers were readily accepted into the community and had a busy social life. Angus, Claire, and Farley spent quiet evenings together, and Claire was sad to see Angus go: "He is still the best company there is."

Winifred visited in September 1964. During her stay, they went on a picnic on the Sandbanks and sailed to Red Island in the *Happy Adven-ture*. Their friend Lee arrived by float plane and tied up beside them, and they drifted as they shared a picnic. Winnie was delighted with the unusual social call and also got along famously with Margaret and Spencer Lake.

Farley often told Claire that possessions eventually kill their owners. She wondered if that also applied to people. "I am the proud possessor of Farley who was won on a long chance: therefore I clutch him to my bosom and refuse to take any more chances, having won the big prize already; I am afraid to lose now." Maybe he was right that this accounted for her "apparent stodginess. Anyway I am in a bad spot, and frequently unhappy about it. I need security in a way that F. cannot understand."

That security had a name: marriage. As the tumultuous year drew to a close, Farley finally decided to do something about it.

16 | Brothels and Wedding Bells

AT 5 P.M. ON TUESDAY, January 19, 1965, Farley and Claire set out from the wilds of south coast Newfoundland on an odyssey of love and adventure. They had been living together for three years. During their time in Burgeo, Claire wore a wedding ring and was known to the locals as Mrs. Mowat. Now they were determined to make it official. Their destination was Mexico, where the plan was for Farley to get a divorce from his first wife and then marry Claire.

They had to go offshore because Frances still refused to sue for divorce, and in Canada marital breakdown was not yet grounds to end a marriage. There was no other way, unless, that is, Claire wanted to follow her mother's kind suggestion; Winnie had sent her daughter a magazine article proclaiming that marriage was going out of style. Smart people simply lived together nowadays. No sale.

Nana, however, was pleased that they were making the trip, "and it is such a relief to know that you both landed right side up." The two families got along well. Angus had sent his regards to Nana, and she wrote to Claire, "Please tell Angus to keep being fond of me, because I am in love with him, so we are even. I love Farley's mother too. I think she is grand."

Five days before they embarked on their long and complicated trip to Boston and then to Mexico, Claire wrote in her journal, "I am full of apprehensions." Travel was becoming an ordeal for her. She used to love it but now worried about what to take, about flying from Sydney to Boston, about the long drive to Mexico and back. And she worried about arrangements in Mexico going askew. "I am a bundle of nerves and getting worse every year," she wrote. She knew she was little comfort to Farley when she stewed about life all the time. She did not used to be like this. Perhaps it was because she needed "a place to belong, a standard of behaviour to follow, a prescribed list of accomplishments to attain, something to believe in." Farley did not need to follow a standard, "being a strong individual."

Claire didn't want to be seen as an "adventuress living in sin." But that didn't mean she wanted a trip to the divorce factory in a place like Nuevo Laredo either, where you could "walk in at one end of a building with your marriage certificate and walk out the other with your divorce papers."

Claire doubted that any Mexican divorce would be legal in Canada, and Farley wanted something "a little more official." So he engaged a lawyer in Mexico City to do the proper legal work. Claire was thrilled. As one of her closest friends put it, she had always associated legal marriage with "orange blossoms and old lace."

Their timing couldn't have been worse to begin a journey of three thousand miles by boat, plane, train, and car. On the day of their departure, there had been an annihilating blizzard, followed by freezing rain. Glare ice covered everything. When the wind blows in Newfoundland, it seems to come from every direction. No trucks were operating in Burgeo, so they loaded their baggage onto a toboggan and Farley pulled it to a friend's house.

The plan was to meet their boat, the MV *Nonia,* and sail to Port aux Basques that night. Harold Horwood would join them in Boston for the drive to Mexico in his new Comet. Both writers had editing to do with their American publishers. Farley worried a little that although Harold was their best friend, there would be tensions with two writing and one painting on the long drive. "We shall see," he told Claire. "Anyway H loves you. Says he will be standing by when I drown myself or you leave me, whichever comes first."

When they finally reached Boston, Farley and Claire were swept up in a whirlwind of editorial work and cocktail parties. Everyone wanted to meet Farley. He was about to publish *Westviking,* and there were revisions to make with his editor, Peter Davison. Claire also worked with art directors at the Atlantic Monthly Press on the maps that would appear in the book.

Harold Horwood arrived shortly after Farley and Claire had flown in. It was dark by the time he hit one of the most confounding cities in the world to navigate. He knew nothing about Boston traffic and had no route plan. All he had was a street address in Cambridge, which he judged was somewhere to the southwest. It was a clear night with a good view of Sirius, the Dog Star, and Harold reasoned that if he kept the star in the driver's side window, he would eventually reach his destination. He landed at a gas station just six blocks from where Farley and Claire were staying.

Harold also had a book coming out in the U.S., and after Farley finalized his manuscript, they drove to New York, where Harold worked with his editor at Doubleday on the in-house revision of his novel *Tomorrow Will Be Sunday*. Harold burned through his editorial work in a single day.

With Claire curled up in the cramped back seat, they left New York on the morning of February 3 for the long drive south, birdwatching along the way, buying souvenirs, and visiting with friends. Their first birdwatching note as they entered the South was vaguely ominous: "Flock of Vultures."

Waitresses with their easy smiles and southern drawls were friendly enough, but a sign on the wall of a restaurant just outside Emporia, Virginia, delivered a different message: "We reserve the right to refuse service to Anyone."

In South Carolina, Claire noted gangs of Black prisoners doing roadwork under the watchful eye of their armed White custodians. On February 5, she celebrated her thirty-second birthday with her first meal of hominy grits. Near Greenville, Alabama, they finally got some good southern food—fried oysters, yams, eggplant, black-eyed peas, and pecan pie.

Claire wanted to stop in Pensacola, Florida, where her father had grown up and where she hoped to find her paternal grandfather's grave. But they all agreed it would be hopeless to try to find the grave in the sprawling neon city, so they pulled out of Pensacola and headed for the Gulf shore.

After getting their first glimpse of the Gulf of Mexico, they stopped for a beer at a gas station restaurant. When the proprietor found out where her customers were from, she suggested that Canada should join the United States, declaring, "Then we would be really big." They saw the familiar sign reserving the right to refuse service to anyone, but a new one caught their eye: "Wallace for President." The segregationist governor of Alabama would make his run for the White House in 1968.

As they sipped their beer, the TV newscast showed Martin Luther King Jr. being arrested in Selma, Alabama, during a civil rights demonstration. Pretending ignorance, Farley asked the owner what it was all about. She dispassionately replied, "He was trying to get the coloured people registered to vote."

A wealthy fan in New Orleans had invited Farley and Claire to dinner. Harold bristled when Farley told him he would have to wear a tie. He didn't own one, and besides, he had no wish to dine anywhere where one was required, even if it was an antebellum mansion. What Harold really wanted to do was to get into New Orleans by himself and paint the town red.

While Farley and Claire were getting the official tour of the French Quarter from their patrician hosts after dinner, Harold was making his own reconnaissance of the Quarter. He found a rundown restaurant where there was a front entrance for Whites and a side door for "coloureds." Harold chose to enter the "coloured" door and found himself in a room full of befuddled Black people.

The waiter tried to explain that Harold was in the wrong place, but he didn't budge, telling the waiter that he was "coloured," having Indigenous blood on his mother's side. The man replied: "You sure don't look coloured to me, suh." To which Harold replied, "In Canada lots of coloured people have blond hair and blue eyes."

The waiter took his order, and after Harold had his first taste of southern barbecued pork, he spent the rest of the evening drinking orange wine with a Black fellow-diner bemused by the White stranger's antics.

AFTER LEAVING NEW ORLEANS on Sunday, February 7, and travelling through Louisiana, they crossed into Texas that afternoon, where Claire had her first encounter with a stand-up female urinal in the washroom of the tourist bureau.

They stopped for the night at Sabine Pass, Texas. The rental cabins were damp and musty, with peeling linoleum tiles, lit by a single glaring lightbulb hanging from the sagging ceiling. "It was so bad, it was funny," Claire noted. Rather than return to their musty room after dinner, Farley, Claire, and Harold decided to make a night of it in the bar to learn what they could about the local people. Most of the oil workers were Cajuns from Louisiana, drawn to places like Port Arthur, Texas, by high-paying jobs. The big news of the day was President Lyndon Johnson's relentless march toward all-out war in Vietnam, then just a month away. The roughnecks in the bar were not buying Washington's pitch that war against Vietnam was honourable and in the national interest. Farley knew from the beginning it was neither.

Farther south, there were endless fields of rice and cotton. They stopped on Highway 35 near Palacios, Texas, to watch an immense flock of honking Canada geese. Harold estimated their number at more than ten thousand. Just north of Rockport, they saw their first cactus growing in the wild.

Farley and Harold went birding in the Aransas wildlife reserve, famous for its whooping cranes, while Claire luxuriated in their lovely cottage at the Sea Gun Sports Inn, washing her hair, reading, and doing a little mending. At 5 o'clock they all went swimming in the hotel's heated pool. Afterwards, Farley and Claire snuggled and had a drink, while Harold wrote an account of the day's birding for the St. John's *Evening Telegram*.

After a nine-day road trip, they had the car serviced and ate their last American meal at a dime-store lunch counter.

On Friday, February 12, Claire wrote in her diary, "At 1:30 p.m., we girded our loins and crossed the muddy trickle of the Rio Grande River, into Matamoros." For Farley and Claire, it was the land of dreams, a place to say goodbye to an old life and strike out on a new one.

The travellers' first experience in Matamoros was the dead weight of Mexican bureaucracy. The pace of events at the customs and immigration shed was glacial. First, they had to climb three flights of stairs to get their Mexican tourist permit. The authorities declared that photos would be necessary, even for a sixth-month permit. They also wanted to know if the travellers planned to sell anything in Mexico. Farley explained that he was writing a book and that Harold was his "researcher" and Claire was his "typist." When they said that they were from Newfoundland, one of the officials questioned if the group was actually Canadian. As he understood it, Newfoundland was part of Quebec, which he believed had "separated" from Canada.

After Farley gently tutored them, the officials relented on the requirement for photographs and granted their permits. As Harold observed, it all happened without passing over a single one-hundred-peso note. Since the group's baggage had already been inspected before entry into Mexico, they were free to begin the journey to Mexico City.

It was no hardship to leave Matamoros, which the travellers found shabby and more American than Mexican. Claire learned that the residents here worked in Brownsville during the day and returned to Mexico each night—cheap labour for those huge Texas ranches.

At every street corner where they came to a stop as they left Matamoros, the car was surrounded by small boys offering to show them the way to the highway for a few pesos. To the group's surprise, they were directed to a two-lane, macadamized road. They encountered almost no traffic once they put the depressing border city behind them.

It would take five days to reach Mexico City. Their route took them through an array of terrain, some familiar, some breathtakingly exotic. For the first few hours, they might still have been in Texas. The land was flat, and the homes in the tiny villages they passed were grindingly poor. Most were made of wattle and mud.

There was no sign of a postal system and no telephone poles or overhead wires. Each village was identical to the one before, populated by untethered donkeys, emaciated cattle, and groups of people who seemed to be waiting for something that never arrived. As they sped by, both the children and the adults waved languorously at the travellers, saying, "*Hola, hola.*"

After a couple of hours, the monotonous flat lands gave way to rolling hills. Several ancient volcanic cones dotted the countryside. Off in the distance, they could see the gunmetal silhouette of the Sierra Madres. Then a geographic milestone—they crossed the Tropic of Cancer.

At last, the weary travellers stopped at Ciudad Victoria, a city of a hundred thousand at the foot of the Sierra Madres, and checked into the Florida Motel. Dinner at a shabby and empty restaurant was greasy tortillas and baked goat, finished off with a sugary fudge and excellent coffee. They had been directed to the restaurant by "Alfredo," who had attached himself to them outside a restaurant. Harold was so pleased by the cost of the meal—four dollars for all three of them—that he tipped "Freddie" ten pesos.

That night, Claire was awakened at 3 a.m. by the noise of trucks roaring past and roosters crowing from their coops on the balconies of nearby apartment buildings. These became the signature sounds.

Back on the main highway, the landscape remained hilly before flattening out as they headed more deeply into central Mexico. They could see large fields of sisal, used to make rope that produced an unusual specialty product—scratching posts for cats, reputed to be the best in the world. Scattered throughout miles of barren cactus and tumbleweed were villages whose houses, both square and round, were made of thatch and vertical sticks.

With dusk beginning to fall, the group decided to stop in La Quinta Chilla, in the state of Chihuahua, 220 miles northwest of Mexico City. As they passed through a tiny village just outside their destination, they saw a group of masked Mexicans who were doing a kind of step dance in front of a store, a scene that would be repeated all along their route.

When Harold stopped to observe them, the dancers crossed the street and swarmed around the Comet. A few pesos lighter, the travellers continued to La Quinta Chilla. They entered the village through a spectacular tropical valley, at its most magical in the twilight. The restaurant provided a caged monkey and innumerable parrots for the entertainment of diners. After dinner, Claire retired early while Farley and Harold headed out for nearby Tamazunchale to sample the local tequila.

Next morning, the group celebrated Valentine's Day with a visit to the local market, where you could buy anything from a pig's head to magic charms guaranteed to sweeten your love life. At lunch, they met an American, Jim Bullock, who told them about an exotic spot in the mountains, a short distance off the main highway. Who could resist scouting out a place called Xilitla?

The not-so-small village, twenty miles off the beaten track, turned out to have five thousand residents, a good school, and a bus service. The drive took the trio down a stunning trail through the jungle, with bananas and oranges growing by the roadside. They passed a few people on the way into the village, the women carrying parcels on their heads, the men bundles of sticks on their backs. The older children trailed behind, piggybacking their smaller siblings.

The village was situated on a hill, with long, sloping steps as the only means of reaching it. From the village itself, there was a dazzling view of the surrounding valley. Xilitla reminded Farley of the isolated mountain villages in northern Italy that he had seen during the war, a reminiscence that always darkened his mood. As for all soldiers in war, certain memories never faded.

After leaving La Quinta Chilla, the travellers drove through the last of the glorious vistas of the Sierra Madres. It was postcard Mexico. The region was well-populated, with a town every few miles. Entire hillsides were under cultivation. They passed small orange groves and farmers cutting sugar cane on almost vertical slopes.

They reached an elevation of 7,600 feet, the highest point they would hit in the Sierra Madres. Then began the long decent to the plateau below. Although Mexico City was only ninety miles away, they turned off the main highway and travelled instead to an out-of-the-way resort called Tzindejéh.

They called it a rest, but it was more of a delaying tactic. All three of them sensed the stresses of what Mexico City would bring, and decided to enjoy the rural countryside for a few more days. Claire was in low spirits. She blamed it on the altitude, then wrote: "For the first time I can remember, I feel homesick. We all feel rather dis-oriented and tired."

ON THE AFTERNOON of February 17, they drove into Mexico City unprepared for what Claire called "the worst drivers in the world." Everyone raced, honked, swerved around slowpokes, or shook their fist at other drivers and pedestrians, as they hurtled toward their private destinations. "A hair-raising trip that left me shaking all day," Claire wrote.

After checking into the Hotel Versalles, Farley went straight to see his divorce lawyer. Both he and Harold "furiously" hated all cities as soul-sucking cesspools. The plan was to get things over as quickly as possible and vamoose.

It was not to be. The lawyer explained that they would have to stay in Mexico for a month while the divorce papers were processed in Yucatán. Farley signed some documents and paid the lawyer. The price for ending his marriage to Frances was $580.

Farley's editor, Peter Davison, had given them the name of a film producer who lived in Mexico City. Shaken by the drive into the city, Claire broke down in tears at the prospect of getting into a local taxi. It was the equivalent of riding a roller coaster without being strapped in. Farley wisely took her back to their hotel, where she rested while Farley and Harold paid a visit to the film producer, George Pepper, who, along with his wife and many others in Hollywood during the fifties, had been blacklisted as potential communists. As a result, he and his wife had fled to Mexico.

Farley and Harold returned to the hotel shortly after they had left, however, having experienced "the coldest brush-off they had ever encountered." On that first, dismal day in Mexico City, they all went to bed early, feeling out of sorts. Farley slept poorly, as he did throughout their stay in Mexico.

The next morning Harold "abandoned" them after breakfast. Farley went shopping, and Claire got her hair done. They both found the city people curt and unfriendly. After a long search along Avenida Juárez, Claire came across a department store that stocked the thing they so badly needed: typing paper. It had taken half the day to find it.

Exhausted by the heat and smog of the city, they returned to their hotel and had drinks with Harold. Farley and Claire decided to have dinner at the El Refugio restaurant, but Harold declined to go. He missed a sumptuous dinner—beef for Farley, half a chicken for Claire, paired with a perfect Mexican red wine they had never tasted before: Terrasola.

After a day of attempted sightseeing, they discovered that many of the places they wanted to visit were closed. But they did make the thirty-mile trip to the ancient archaeological site at Teotihuacán, which featured the pyramids of the sun and the moon, separated by the Avenue of the Dead. Unfortunately, while they were touring the site, a devil wind suddenly came up, raising clouds of dust in their faces. They were peckish, but the restaurant wasn't open. And although they were curious about the history of the pyramids, no guidebooks in English were available.

The drive back to Mexico City ended with a pleasant surprise. George Pepper, who had been rudely dismissive of Farley and Harold when they showed up at his door, had left a message at their hotel, inviting them up to his apartment for a drink. If it was remorse and an olive branch, Harold wasn't buying it. He refused to go.

Farley and Claire hit it off with George and discovered that they had a mutual interest in archaeology. They also marvelled at George's collection of archaic Indigenous artifacts, beautifully catalogued and filed in a large cabinet.

Despite George Pepper's belated hospitality and the occasional good meal, Mexico City was becoming a horror.

Part of it was the thousands of trucks and their choking diesel exhaust that hung over the city. Part was the grinding poverty of the place—penniless Indigenous people sitting in the streets selling nuts, their children gathered around them, hugging their knees; poor women in front of the Mexico City Cathedral hawking religious charms; and block after block of crumbling buildings in various states of decay.

But there was another reason for their low spirits—there would be no quick escape from Mexico, but rather a dreary month or more of waiting in the sweltering heat for the divorce papers. They began arguing about where they should go to wait. The one thing they agreed on was that they had to get out of Mexico City. Their last night in the Hotel Versalles was uneasy. "Farley and I had a flare-up over nothing, both of us so tired and so tense," Claire wrote.

Exhausted, irritable, and desperate to get off the road and hunker down in one spot, the travellers headed north out of Mexico City. They also needed a municipal address so that they could receive mail. Beautiful as it was, San Miguel de Allende was exactly the kind of tourist trap they dreaded. They continued on to San Juan del Río, where they decided to turn east.

George Pepper had suggested Villa Juárez and Mi Ranchito as good places for a longer stay. Their journey to the northeast took them through tropical valleys with lime and grapefruit trees, exotic flowers, and roadside stands selling fresh melons.

Mi Ranchito, with its excellent food and comfortable bungalows, was a good place to stop for a couple of days, but not the longer-term home they were looking for. Although the birding was good, the weather was wet, foggy, and occasionally cold. Nor were there many interesting people around.

The exception was "Mrs. Keefer," an inveterate nature lover who regularly travelled as far north as Churchill, Manitoba, and as far south as Guatemala to pursue her great passion: birdwatching. She was seventy years old and travelled alone from her home in El Paso, Texas, on her birding odysseys. She and Farley hit it off and birdwatched together. Mrs. Keefer was so impressed with him that she lent him some of her precious birding books.

When they left Mi Ranchito, Mrs. Keefer rode with them as far as Pachuca, where they dropped her at the bus station. They marvelled at her independence, fearlessness, and curiosity. If a seventy-year-old woman could travel the continent alone, they could surely get through a nerve-racking month in Mexico, especially one that would end with wedding bells.

On the advice of a "big Yank" they had dined with at Mi Ranchito, the travellers decided to head to Mexico's Pacific coast. With Farley driving and Harold flaked out in the cramped back seat of the car, they set off yet again.

On February 27, after passing through mountainous terrain and desert plateaus featuring miles and miles of huge cacti, they finally turned into Manzanillo, which Claire described as a "hot, dirty, noisy, little Pacific seaport." There was no town square, not even a church. A large, ornate hotel and several open-to-the-street restaurants dominated the city centre.

After finding other motels booked, the travellers checked in to the Kon Tiki bungalows, situated directly on the beach. For a hundred pesos a day, they got a large, two-bedroom cottage to themselves.

It presented in the usual way: slightly dirty, slightly musty, and poorly equipped. It didn't help that the sink was full of ants. And then there was the curmudgeonly landlady—or, as Claire described her, "a classic penurious, grumbling, and nosy woman with an inept husband." As in nearly all their accommodations, Farley's first job was to fix the bungalow's toilet.

That night, they had dinner at an outdoor patio called La Chiripa, run by "Jean," a cheerful, twice-divorced American woman who, according to Claire, was obsessed with sex and had her eye on Harold. At fifty-five, she was "well-preserved," though Claire noted that she should not be wearing bikinis. She agreed to let them use her post-box number so that they could receive mail.

They all turned in early after having a nightcap with a Canadian couple who were renting the bungalow next door. Instead of being kept awake all night by the din of Mexico's endless traffic, they drifted off to sleep with nothing but the sound of the Pacific Ocean lapping on the beach.

They thought they had found their Sea of Tranquillity and decided to stay, but only if Farley could wangle a move to a newer and less shabby bungalow nearby. He and Harold went into Manzanillo and negotiated with the agent, who was also manager of the local hardware store. After Farley bought two wrought-iron candelabra from him, the agent agreed to let them have the newer bungalow for $120 for the month—a good deal, since it was high season.

They were finally out of the Comet, and they settled in to a long run of days that melted into each other. Sun in the mornings, sun and wind in the afternoons. It was bakingly hot, over a hundred degrees Fahrenheit. Claire wondered what the place would be like in July. They passed the time surf-bathing, shell-hunting, swimming, birdwatching, socializing, and eating and drinking—one of their favourite drinks was green coconut juice mixed with gin.

But bit by bit, boredom, and Montezuma's ever-present revenge, began to poke holes in the protective armour of their routine. None of them were made for either tourism or idleness.

"Time hangs heavily," Claire wrote. "This is about the first time in my adult life that I am anxiously waiting for the time to pass. Normally, I have a million projects pending, but something about the heat and the languorous atmosphere produces boredom. I will be so glad to leave Mexico."

The tedium, inability to write, and uncertainty surrounding the divorce left Farley in an irritable state of mind that occasionally exploded in anger aimed at Claire, especially if he went into one of his post-drinking depressions.

After surf-bathing at Playa de Oro, seventeen miles from the Kon Tiki, they returned to their bungalow after a good day on the beach. They had drinks with friends they had met at the hotel, and everyone got "a trifle tickled." Harold disappeared around 7 p.m., and Farley and Claire stayed in and made their dinner.

"We had been in the best of spirits all day and for some minuscule reason we ended up in a violent quarrel. It was the same old insoluble problem: how am I going to resolve living out my life in that lonely shack-town on the muskeg? Farley wants to stay there forever; to feel it is his permanent home. I can either accept living a life which is wholly to be lived his way, or I can leave. His solution for me? That I spend prolonged holidays with my mother in Toronto, alone and unescorted. Having said all this, he just walked out of the house, more unforgivable really than anything he said to me."

When Farley finally returned and stumbled into bed, he completely ignored Claire. The next morning, she awakened to the sound of a small band and a group of men singing to celebrate one of the many saints' days in Mexico. It was not the time to complain about the noise. Besides, Claire was too depressed by the events of the previous night.

"Just once, I didn't go begging to Farley to say 'I'm sorry'. Just once, I waited to see if he would apologize to me. He didn't."

There is a saying in Newfoundland about the weather: if you don't like it, look again in fifteen minutes. That was also true of Farley's outbursts. After the worst of diatribes, he could be full of remorse in a heartbeat. And so it was that afternoon. They went for a drink at Jean's, where Farley gushed to Claire that pregnancy and motherhood might be good for her, words he knew she longed to hear. They left La Chiripa and rejoined Harold back at their bungalow.

As a rule, they tried to avoid Manzanillo, which they found to be less Mexican than the mountain villages. But when they needed to cash cheques or send telegrams to let various literary friends know their whereabouts, they had no choice. Besides, there was the weekly market in Manzanillo where they did most of their shopping. Claire found the pricing curious, however. Ant repellant cost more than a week's worth of vegetables. She hated the place.

"The market is oppressive and overwhelms me," Claire wrote in her journal. "Crowded, filthy, stinking. Floor covered in squashed fruit, spittle, entrails, and indiscernible wet patches. Farley and Harold thrive on it." To make matters worse, Harold insisted on doing the marketing in his bare feet.

With the mounting pressure of waiting for the divorce papers and putting up with the foibles of the clutch of friends they had given nicknames to—"Bent Bessy," "Ben the Boor," and "Fat Jesus"—their boredom turned into irritability. Farley didn't like the heat and couldn't work, which made him cranky. Claire and Harold tried to do a little writing, but the uncertain electricity—which produced a constantly flickering light that alternated between dim and very bright—made it difficult.

And then there was Jean, who often joined their table when they dined at La Chiripa, except on those nights when her cook was too drunk to work and she had to tend to the kitchen. One night when Farley, Claire, and Harold were sharing a meal of miniature lobsters with their Canadian friends, Jean sat down and triggered the kind of raucous, bawdy, and sex-filled conversation that always distressed Claire.

After dinner, Farley and Claire drove their friends to a vessel they kept, "a seedy, rundown, bug-ridden, converted sailing schooner," where they were joined by American friends, some invited, some not. Claire's mood cratered. She found the party-crashers obnoxious, dull, and loud. "They reminded me of 90% of everyone I knew at the Rosedale United Church. Small wonder the Mexicans despise them. So do I."

After seeing the tipsy sailors off, Farley, Claire, Harold, and Jean returned to the Kon Tiki for more drinks. It was a mistake. Jean, a former journalist with an incisive mind and a cruel streak, commented that Claire had a high, whiny voice. She then irked Farley by claiming that everything Canadians had was a dividend of American benevolence.

When Farley offered rational rebuttals, Jean became even more shrewish and dismissive. As tempers frayed, Harold and Claire withdrew from the verbal dogfight. "I sat there loathing her for what she said, but did not show it," Claire noted. Claire had a great poker face.

Farley, however, was always ready to use his favourite blunt instrument—words—to bludgeon opponents if they got his back up, and he blasted Jean with his vituperative remarks. Claire was there to record the explosion—and to offer a theory of why the brilliant man she had decided to marry sometimes behaved like a vulgarian.

"Farley became loud and dogmatic and punctuated all his conversation with talk of cunts, cocks, Castro, communism, and other guaranteed noise-makers. It is a pity that Farley did not grow to be a very large man. It is as if he were so afraid that no one will see or hear him that, like the small boy at the birthday party, he must shout and kick to be noticed. He belches and sits in a posture reminiscent of a gynae-cological examination. If he could just relax, and know that he will be heard and noticed anyway, having the mind he has, how much easier his life would be."

Harold escorted Jean home at 3:30 a.m., making a prompt exit. Far-ley brooded. The next morning did not begin well.

"Farley crawled in my bed about 8 a.m. but I was so tired and dis-gusted with him, and so full of angry thoughts, that I didn't comply. He went off swimming finally."

That night, Farley remained in a major sulk and refused to go to town for dinner. Harold and Claire went into Manzanillo to see if there were any Mardi Gras celebrations going on. Finding none, they went to the Mauna Kea, an upscale restaurant a short walk from the Kon Tiki bungalows. Harold loved the place. But despite the ornate, tropical decor, featuring palm plants, the usual caged birds, and exotic flowers, all under a huge, circular thatched roof, Claire was in low spirits.

"I felt as hollow and empty as though I were in Toronto again—going out on endless dates to kill loneliness; finding only contrived circumstances and thin companionship."

A letter came to Manzanillo from Claire's mother, who expressed the hope that Farley's divorce proceedings would soon mature. "The very nicest birthday gift you could give me this year, even if only a belated one, is a letter or telegram saying that Farley's divorce is now completed and you are now legally Mrs. Farley Mowat; would get a big thrill out of this, as you would guess . . . a truly happy ending."

THREE DAYS AFTER THAT LETTER, on Monday, March 22, the news they had all been waiting for arrived. Farley's lawyer in Mexico City sent a letter confirming that his divorce had been granted. Their euphoria was short-lived. The lawyer also informed them that he "couldn't guar-antee" when the papers would be signed and delivered. It was Mexico's infernal *mañana* yet again.

With the mercurial Jean in tow, Farley and Claire immediately drove into Manzanillo to ask the *presidente municipal* if they could be married without the official papers. He didn't think so. Luis García, the mayor, later confirmed that their marriage wouldn't be possible without the signed divorce papers.

They tried calling their lawyer on a drugstore telephone. When they couldn't get through, they sent him a telegram and returned to the Kon Tiki. It was the day for the bungalows to be sprayed for malaria-carrying mosquitoes, and the place was in an uproar.

Claire was in a deep funk. Nothing was working out the way she had hoped. Farley's publisher, Jack McClelland, sent a wire saying he wouldn't be joining them in Mexico for the wedding after all. All the public officials said that even though the divorce had been granted, they couldn't get married. Farley accused Claire of complaining too much, which she agreed was true. But she still loathed his idea of a "quickie" wedding as the answer to their predicament.

"After twenty years of anticipating a wedding of some sort, it is heart-breaking to think that I will be married in a stinking, ugly, hot, little seaport town, in a city-hall whose architecture looks like a public washroom, wearing a blouse and skirt clinging with sweat, words spoken in a language I don't understand, and no friends or family but Harold with us. I could only do this for Farley. I cried all afternoon."

To escape from the spraying campaign, which required the removal of all clothing, bedding, and furniture from the bungalows, Farley, Claire, and Harold decided to take a day trip to La Manzanilla, the one place in Mexico where Claire was genuinely happy. Jean tagged along, hoping to break down Harold's indifference to her; she couldn't understand why he preferred birdwatching to more reciprocal activities.

Unlike Manzanillo, with a population of a hundred thousand, the small fishing village was sparsely populated, authentic, and in a way, innocent. The children didn't expect pesos when their photographs were taken, took pleasure in simple things, and were greatly amused at Jean's small dog, Sweetie. They had never seen a dachshund before and wondered what had happened to its legs.

The friendliness of the villagers reminded Claire of outport Newfoundland, where the smiles were real and the generosity reflexive. Pigs and dogs sought out shade for their siestas in front of the stick-and-thatch houses. A herd of cattle, a mixture of Brahman and Holstein, wandered at will between the ramshackle houses. In the middle of the village, there was a stand selling fresh lime juice. The only attendant was a burro, standing motionless by the table.

Claire delighted in the place. She noted that they were constructing a "fairly big church" out of bricks. It was a common sight during their stay in Mexico, and Claire wondered if the Roman Catholic Church was making a comeback. As for the village's existing church, it was the most primitive she had seen in their travels—thatch roof, open stick walls, stone floor (no seats), about thirty feet long. "Crude little altar decked with flowers and plastic Virgin Mary. Large bell hangs outside. I would love to go to church there."

On the way back to the Kon Tiki, the travellers came across a nine-foot boa constrictor sleeping by the side of the road with a large bulge in its middle. Harold was fascinated and wanted to take it home as a pet.

Two things terrified Claire: flying and snakes. She laid down the law. There would be no pet boa constrictors at the Kon Tiki bungalows. The snake was left by the road to digest whatever it was it had swallowed.

Back in Manzanillo, they awaited the 5 o'clock mail. It contained a few letters from Toronto and an invitation to Farley to speak in East Berlin in May. The thing they were all waiting for did not come. Claire was close to the breaking point.

"Nothing from the damn lawyer in Mexico City... The waiting, waiting, waiting is becoming unbearable. So hot, hotter every day. We are debilitated. I am bad-tempered," she wrote.

At 3 a.m., they were awakened by a raucous party hosted by their tireless neighbours. Farley shouted at them, but the uproar continued at an "incredible pitch." Harold stormed down and screamed at the revellers to "shut up." The boozy hullabaloo subsided for a few moments, but soon picked up again and lasted until dawn.

"We got up groggily around 8 a.m., cursing at the inconsiderate behaviour of our friends, including the spineless Canadians, who are easily led into any noisy, drunken venture."

Sleep-deprived and grumpy, the three of them went into Manzanillo, where they sent a last-ditch telegram to Farley's divorce lawyer.

A day or two later, on Thursday, March 25, Jean came to their door with the telegram they had all been waiting for. They gathered around Farley as he read the news. His divorce lawyer informed them that it would be impossible to deliver the divorce papers before they had to leave Mexico in April. Farley had to get back to Canada to correct proofs for his new book, and Claire needed to return to Newfoundland to file their taxes. They decided on the spot to leave Mexico the next day.

Harold slipped out to take some last-minute photographs and then got quietly drunk with Bent Bessy and the Canadian couple. Farley and Claire cooked meat loaf for their last supper and then packed. Afterwards, they all drove down to Jean's to say goodbye.

"We got a strangely cool reception from Jean," Claire wrote in her diary, "who had been so chummy with us for the last month. We conclude that her friendship lasts only as long as our potential patronage. A quick goodbye, leaving her a pile of books (we've read) to sell."

THE ONLY THING STRANGER than Jean's aloofness was the trio's decision to visit a whorehouse.

After leaving La Chiripa, they walked down an unpaved street lined with the worst slum housing they had seen in Mexico. There were five establishments of the sort they wanted to reconnoitre. They entered the largest building, which looked like any other café and dance hall, except that all the women in the place, wearing gaudy, low-cut dresses and heavy makeup, were sitting either alone or at tables full of men "flirting madly."

Farley, Claire, and Harold took a table in the courtyard—which was surrounded on three sides by small bedrooms, each with a door, a window, and a number—and watched the girls "sidling off" with their customers and disappearing into the numbered cubicles. A five-piece band provided the background music for the fleshly transactions going on.

Farley took a look into one of the cubicles and realized that the commercial arrangements were taking place under the watchful eye of Jesus and his apostles: a lithograph of The Last Supper hung on the wall.

Claire recorded that when she saw a man coming out of one of the cubicles doing up his zipper, "I found it hard to hide my astonishment at this open display. Farley and Harold greatly amused at my unveiled reactions."

The three of them visited all five brothels on the street. Their favourite was Casa Blanqueteria, largely because it had an "unbeliev-ably good band." "The sound was amplified and almost blasted us out of the place, but the rhythm and sound was unbelievable for a whore-house band," Claire wrote.

With the clock approaching midnight, there was a final encounter they hadn't anticipated. "A drunken Mexican came along and offered Farley an indecipherable amount to sleep with me," Claire noted. It was, apparently, time to call it a night.

On their last night at the Kon Tiki, they were awakened at 3:30 a.m. by a group of partying Canadians whooping it up in the next bungalow. Farley yelled at them to keep it down, but the best he could do was get them to move the party to another cottage, which was farther away. The roistering went on until morning.

"We got to sleep around 5 a.m., but had to get up at 8 a.m.," Claire noted. "At that point, Farley, Harold, and I made a special point of sing-ing and talking at the top of our voices, thereby rousing the party goers who hadn't quit until 7 a.m." Tired as they were, after forty-five days in the country, they were happy to be leaving Mexico at last.

After passing through Guadalajara, San Luis Potosí, and Lagos de Marengo, a town not listed in any guidebook, they reached Monter-rey, where they spent the night. Claire was exhausted and despondent. What was supposed to have been the beginning of a new life together had turned into an ordeal. And the central issue, their marriage, was still unresolved. That night in Monterrey, she broke down.

"After dinner, I start to cry in exhaustion and in exasperation. Farley wants to do a 'quickie' marriage in Laredo. I don't want to risk the ille-gality. Farley says the entire thing is illegal and farcical. If only he would comfort me when I cry. It's all I want."

The travellers crossed the International Bridge into the United States on the morning of Sunday, March 28. Customs officers made them completely unload the Comet, and even charged them a liquor tax on two half-full bottles of alcohol. Once more, Claire had to stuff her purple tweed winter coat into the small trunk of the car.

They headed north in Texas, bypassing San Antonio and Austin, and stopping for the night just outside Waco. There, they ran into a young couple with "Just married" plastered all over their turquoise Buick. Farley invited them over for a drink. They accepted but abstained from the proffered liquor, sipping on their Dr. Peppers instead, since neither Jim nor Sue drank.

The couple were intelligent, well-read, and sociable. They were also a strange mixture of what Claire called "ignorance and information." Jim was a sports reporter with a local paper, which, he informed them, had supported Lyndon Johnson in the recent U.S. presidential election. But Jim, who had never been out of Texas, had voted for the champion of the far right, Barry Goldwater.

"Both of them were so bright, but were inhibited by the fantastic spiritual isolation of the American south and west," Claire wrote. "Their reluctance to travel and lack of curiosity about the rest of their country, and the rest of the world, seem incongruous with their bright minds."

Jim was later awarded two Purple Hearts after suffering traumatic brain injuries in Vietnam. He had to learn to walk, talk, read, and write again, but he kept faith in God, family, and country.

After Jim and Sue left, Farley fell into one of his post-drinking depressions and became caustic. "He accused me of the usual things: chronic complaining, selfishness, lack of interest in him sexually." Finally, he stopped the diatribe and skulked off to bed.

By morning, he was, as usual, full of remorse, and they "cuddled" and made up. At 7:30, Harold banged on their door to get going. Whether it was the "just married" couple they had socialized with the night before, or an attempt to make sense of their remarkable odyssey, Farley decided they would get married in Texas, papers or no papers.

Acting on the advice of an unlikely enabler, a gas-station attendant, the marriage took place in Corsicana, Texas. When Harold stopped for gas, Farley asked the young man what the procedures were for getting married in the state. As far as the man knew, it was pretty basic. If you could prove you didn't have syphilis and had five dollars to pay for the marriage licence, you could get hitched just down the road. The attendant even gave them directions to a local clinic where they could get their Wassermann tests.

When they arrived at the Medical Arts Clinic, which stood beside the Navarro County hospital, they were turned over to an appropriately named physician, "Dr. Bone," who extracted a pipette of blood from each of them and returned a short time later with forms to sign, attesting that they were free of venereal disease.

After driving thousands of miles and spending forty-five frustrating days in Mexico waiting for divorce papers that never appeared, the big moment had arrived. All they had to do now was show up at the Corsicana town hall, get their marriage licence, and tie the knot. Their Texas marriage had so far cost fifteen dollars—ten dollars for Dr. Bone and five dollars for the marriage certificate.

At 11 a.m. on March 29, 1965, the bridal party arrived at the courthouse, a large, square brick building set in the middle of an expansive lawn. As they walked up the cement steps to the clerk's office, Harold got cold feet. On the pretense of needing to buy nasal spray, he tried to beg off attending the ceremony.

If Harold in fact loved Claire, as Farley had told her he did, it must have been a tough moment. Despite a taxing journey, not only had Farley and Claire not fallen apart, but they were about to get married. Whatever Harold's reluctance was based on, Farley wasn't having it, and neither was Claire. They both insisted that he witness the ceremony, and Harold finally agreed that the nasal spray could wait until a less historic moment. The other witness was a man delivering a package to the courthouse.

The stay in the clerk's office was brief. Farley and Claire presented their papers from Dr. Bone and signed their names twice on the application form. No waiting period, and no questions about previous marriages. Fifteen minutes after arriving in Mrs. Humphries's office, she was leading them to the chambers of the man who would perform the ceremony: Judge Witt "Tip" Tipton. As Mrs. Humphries delivered them to Tip, she remarked to the judge, "It isn't every day we have visitors from Canada getting married here."

With a big smile on his face, Tip shook their hands and then produced a small, leather-bound book and opened it at the wedding ceremony. In a thick, Texas drawl, he explained to the couple that he hadn't been at this job very long and so needed to consult the book. Claire recognized it as an abridged version of the marriage ceremony used in Canadian churches.

It was not exactly a royal wedding. Claire wore a printed cotton blouse, a pleated blue skirt, knee socks, and dirty sneakers. Her hair was straight and unwashed. Farley, whose fingernails were dirty, wore a short-sleeved shirt and corduroy trousers.

The judge asked if it was going to be a ring ceremony. The groom said no, but Claire quickly countermanded him, handing Farley the wedding band she had been wearing for three years so that he could put it on her finger. Tip laboured through the ceremony, referring to Farley as "Mr. Morrt" throughout.

Harold sat in a chair behind the bride and bridegroom, silently taking it all in. Then came the final words from the judge: "In the name of the Father, the Son, and the Holy Spirit, I pronounce that you be man and wife together."

It had taken all of five minutes. Tip explained that he didn't have a set fee for performing the service, so it was just whatever Farley wanted to give him. Counting the five dollars he gave to Tip Tipton, the grand total for Farley and Claire's Texas marriage was twenty dollars. At exactly 11:59, Claire sent her mother a telegram informing her that they had just been officially married.

As they left the courthouse, Mr. and Mrs. Mowat received their first wedding present—a big plastic bag of detergent, starch, Aspirin, and other household items. It was, apparently, a gift provided to all newlyweds, even of the drive-through variety, by the Corsicana merchants association.

Because Corsicana was "dry," the newlyweds couldn't celebrate with a drink after the wedding. It wasn't until they reached the East

Texas city of Texarkana that they raised a glass of champagne to what Claire called the "peculiar day," which they all joked and laughed about.

But on the morning of March 30, when she awoke in their large room in Texarkana's Howard Johnson's motel, Mrs. Claire Mowat recorded her private feelings.

"I awoke early and felt a bit depressed at the recollection of our shoddy marriage yesterday. Farley will be able to laugh it off and think it funny; but I think that my memory of it will always be tinged with sadness. If I had even been wearing clean clothes, let alone pretty ones, it might have helped a little. But it's over and done now and I'm glad. I don't feel one bit different. Perhaps I will when we get to Toronto. Last night I wrote a few funny cards to close friends to announce our marriage. It will be a great relief to no longer have to tell lies."

17 | A Time for Leaving

ON SUNDAY, APRIL 25, 1965, Farley and Claire returned to Burgeo after a three-month absence. Although their steamer arrived at 2 a.m., there was an enthusiastic welcoming party waiting for them at dockside. Their friends Don and Mary MacDonald had the Caulders over for dinner, and the finale of their evening was to meet the boat. Claire was "terribly pleased" to see them all, and everyone sat and drank until most eyelids were at half-mast. It was dawn before the exhausted couple got to bed.

The first few days were full of visitors and news. Claire was appalled to find out that Burgeo now had four jukeboxes and a soft-drink shop, bringing back terrible memories of Texas. There was talk of a new bridge, telephones with private lines, and even a road coming in. Group dancing was being replaced by a new fad called the twist. It was the dreaded cultural pollution Claire feared would ruin the place. "It creeps in like the fog, on little cat feet," she wrote.

The village was also experiencing an epidemic of rheumatic fever. Someone whispered to Claire that a young woman had been locked in her room for the high crime of getting pregnant out of wedlock. A small boy had died in a house fire. Waves of locals were curious to see the Mowats again and hear all about their adventures in far-off places. The children were amazed by the shells Claire brought back from Mexico. Farley barked for them, made faces, and showed them slides from their journey. He also told them he kept a red dragon in the spare room. The assembled ladies were embarrassed when a little boy called his penis a "tassel," a coinage Claire thought brilliant. "I've been looking for a suitable word for it all my life," she told her surprised visitors.

Once the rush of company slowed, the usual chores needed tending to. Farley and Claire came back from the post office with huge bags of mail and a mountain of parcels and magazines. Driving rain had breached one window frame in the house and soaked the carpet to the floorboards. Their friend Sim dried it out for them. There were other repairs to be made, including fixing a break in the oil line. It took two weeks to get the house running smoothly again, at least as smoothly as any house could run where Farley Mowat lived.

Included in the mail was an early birthday present for Farley from Claire's mother. Jack and Elizabeth McClelland had thrown a wedding party for the newlyweds when they arrived back in Toronto from Mexico. Claire used the occasion to make up for her "dirty-sneaker" marriage in Texas and wore a mint-green lace dress with white stockings, the London mod look that was then all the rage. Several celebrities attended the party, including activist June Callwood; Pierre Berton's wife, Janet; novelist Max Braithwaite and his wife, Aileen; meteorologist Percy Saltzman and his wife, Rose; and, of course, author Harold Horwood. Farley and Claire were showered with gifts, including a baby-bottle warmer, records, books, a silver tray, and, as a joke, a branding iron from Harold and Trudy Town. The bad boy of Canadian art also presented the bad boy of Canadian letters with an original triptych he had painted.

Winnie had all the presents picked up the day after the party and paid to have them shipped to Newfoundland. In her accompanying letter, after hearing Farley being interviewed by Pierre Berton, she had some advice. Her "illustrious" son-in-law should not be so openly critical of his fellow Canadians, or how could he expect them to buy his books? "Forgive me dear for being so outspoken . . . if I didn't love you I wouldn't give a tinker's darn."

Winnie's gift had some unintended consequences. Don and Mary MacDonald, the RCMP couple who had become close friends of Farley and Claire's, were over for dinner one evening, and had brought them their mail. Farley opened and decided to share his birthday letter from his mother-in-law. Claire recorded that when Farley read aloud the part about the shipment of their "wedding… (here he stalled)… presents, the word Wedding slipped out." Claire froze.

The MacDonalds, like everyone else in Burgeo, thought Farley and Claire were already married. Claire feared this discovery might affect their relationship, a serious matter, since Mary was her only close friend in town. "This distressed me much more than F reading the word," Claire wrote. She smoked nervously for the rest of the dinner party, and Farley did not drink.

His slip of the tongue wasn't the only possible reason that Farley abstained that night. For several weeks he had been experiencing stomach problems. In the wake of barium and X-ray tests, doctors told him he could neither drink nor smoke. Because they suspected an ulcer, they also put him on a bland diet. The new regimen took the wind out of his sails. When Claire went shopping, everyone asked the same question: "How's Mr. Mowat's stomach?"

They were back in the fishbowl. Ten people showed up in Claire's kitchen one day to watch her make apricot, raisin, and almond chicken, reminding her that there was no such thing as anonymity in outport Newfoundland. In Burgeo, everyone knew everything about everybody, from Farley's stomach to the gossip that a prominent woman in town was in a Lady Chatterley relationship with her barn attendant.

Nursing his sick stomach, Farley wrote a few articles on the Vietnam War and toyed with the idea of doing a book on Peter Easton, the notorious seventeenth-century pirate who haunted Conception Bay. He was also thinking of writing a humorous book about his trials and tribulations with the *Happy Adventure*, an idea that would later become *The Boat Who Wouldn't Float,* one of his most acclaimed books. Claire edited Farley's boys' book *The Curse of the Viking Grave* and tried to establish her regular Burgeo schedule: housework in the morning, art in the afternoon. But with Farley in low spirits, and people constantly dropping by, it was not easy.

The whole town was affected when Mrs. Spence, Burgeo's legendary mother of eighteen children, fell ill. Claire watched six men, including some of Mrs. Spence's grown sons, carry the matriarch on a homemade stretcher down the rocky trail to the truck that would take her to the hospital. It was as solemn as any funeral procession. Earlier that day, a seven-year-old boy had come to the door with lobsters he had caught in his own trap. The going rate was forty cents a pound, and Farley and Claire bought all four for $2.70. Junior Spencer planned to buy a pair of shoes with the money.

In small places, all news is big news, and the sad variety began to roll in like the tide. Claire was distressed to discover that Don MacDonald had been transferred to the RCMP detachment in Corner Brook, on the island's west coast. That meant Mary would soon be leaving, an irreplaceable loss for Claire. When she and Farley went to the post office to pick up the proofs for *Westviking*, there was a letter from *Maclean's* rejecting a piece by Farley that the editors at the magazine considered anti-American. Farley and Claire were infuriated. They later received a telegram from Harold Horwood bearing grim news: Mike Donovan, Farley's librarian friend who had sailed to Saint-Pierre with him, was going under the knife for lung cancer that might be terminal. He was only forty years old and had five daughters, ranging in age from eight to nineteen.

With memories of the rush of social and intellectual stimulation they had enjoyed in Toronto fresh in her mind, Claire was finding it difficult to adjust to the torpid current of day-to-day life in Burgeo. Although she busied herself with running the place, editing Farley's work, and answering his fan mail, which included letters from children in Kansas who loved *Never Cry Wolf*, the familiar doubts about herself and their life crept in. When she was tense, she needed Farley's comforting; instead, he tended to shrink from her when she was needy.

As much as he loved her, Farley seemed not to understand what a sensitive woman he had married.

Claire's unhappiness in Burgeo was the old story after years of life in the outport—no privacy, no paintings, no written work, and no children. Compounding her case of the Burgeo Blues, her lack of productivity had not freed her to enjoy herself in other ways. "I am not having fun," she wrote in her journal on May 25.

When Farley told her to try to enjoy herself, she pointed out that apart from him, there was no one in the village who knew or understood her. Claire could only have fun with people who were simpatico. She was from Rosedale, not Ramea. With Mary on her way to Corner Brook, Claire would soon be facing total isolation. "This is the time I should be doing something with my life, not just diddling it away in this lonely place. Farley is such an idealist that the realities of life depress him."

LIFE SWIRLED ON, carrying them along. Farley worked soddenly on the proofs for *Westviking*. After two years of working on the book, he was bored. The *Star Weekly* called and wanted to publish the piece that *Maclean's* had rejected. The CBC sent a cheque for $650 for Farley's part in the production of *The Serpent's Coil*. Word came from Toronto that Claire's brother, Fred, would be marrying a woman with two children. Farley and Claire were both put on the board of the local library, and the books began flying off the shelf. In one two-hour shift, Claire signed out 130 books. Circulation doubled the first year they pitched in. Claire even painted a new sign for the library.

Farley and Claire never knew who or what might show up at their doorstep. Fresh caribou liver, one of Farley's favourites, arrived courtesy of the milkman. Oni Strickland, who on a single day caught six hundred pounds of cod by himself, gave them fresh fish. Thirteen-year-old Finley Baggs built them a pathway to bridge a hole in the path to their door. Two girls, aged ten and eleven, arrived hoping to be entertained by Farley. Unasked, the girls dried the supper dishes and put them away. They were the seventeenth and eighteenth children in their family. Little Dorothy Spencer wrote a poem about Farley. "Sometimes little folks get ascared . . . Although he has a beard he is very good."

Claire's social unease grew as the spell of Farley's personality beguiled the village. He helped people with their income tax filings and reluctantly entered more deeply into local politics. "Being the dominant character of almost every milieu in which we find ourselves, the success of any gathering largely depends on what he says or does, or what sort of mood he is in . . . I just feel nervous."

Her apprehension was understandable. Ever since she had known him, Farley had had the peculiar habit of insulting everyone he met, as a kind of test. He had alienated the Lakes with his sharp tongue. The town doctor, Ann Caulder, slapped his face for something he said to her and vowed never to speak to him again.

In time, Farley would offend his faithful publisher, Jack McClelland, and even his best friend, Harold Horwood. "I know what he is like when drunk, he is poisonous in what he says, but he won't admit it," Claire observed in her journal. Farley always did his best to smooth things over afterwards, a task he usually managed with his considerable charms. He blamed his verbal outbursts on drinking and the next day could never remember what he had actually said or why people were so upset.

Claire had personal experience with the Farley Treatment. "He did it with me almost as soon as we met. He immediately reminded me of the folly of my middle class career-girl, hopeful wife existence. But I lapped it up. Such a masochist as me loves to be told of her short comings. And my father had preceded Farley with the same technique for 27 years."

Although he disliked Claire's complaining, Farley knew there were problems. Claire seemed to feel that her life lacked purpose and companionable people. He was also deeply troubled by the Vietnam War, which he believed the U.S. was instigating. The prospect of Canada's political leaders selling out for the "Yankee dollar" appalled him. And with the depressing news of Mike Donovan's precarious medical situation, he began to wonder about his own health. Claire suspected that something else was bothering him even more: the reality that marriage couldn't just be a long date.

"I always knew that it wasn't just an idyllic love affair that went on and on, but I think he still believes that that is what it should be. Perhaps that is why he is so loathe to have any children—lest it interrupt the glorious image he has of what marriage should be, but what it can never be. Farley's enthusiasms are so intense, but they are short-lived. I think he is fed up with his schooner, fed up with Burgeo, and although I hope not, he is fed up with me. At this point he doesn't know where else to look for new enthusiasms."

Claire needn't have worried. Farley would never lose his enthusiasm for his Golden Girl. But he was riding the roller coaster of a brilliant and original mind. His life moved at high speed into hairpin turns. He was fired by a fierce instinct to stand up for the underdog, crusade against injustices, protect Nature, and write books. The war had also made him averse to all authority.

When the creative juices flowed, it was wonderful. But when he couldn't write, when doubts and pressures mounted about his ability to support two families, a dark cloud would fall over him and those around him. At such times, creativity turned to mischief. Claire wrote that drinking and blasting out classical music was his "gloom remedy." But no matter how low he might feel, there was always one sure cure for his misery: snuggling with Claire.

Before leaving Burgeo, Don and Mary MacDonald stayed with the Mowats for a week. Farley and Claire were very fond of them and were excellent hosts. They gave the MacDonalds a going-away party, and Farley even wrote them a farewell song. But when their guests left, they made a beeline for the bed, "for a long and licentious afternoon of snuggling and even a drink." It was storming outside and not a soul showed up to interrupt them, which was not always the case.

"It was delightful," Claire wrote. "We talked and talked about our future plans. We joked and played with the dog. We've been together five years now, and we are still great lovers and great friends. Sometimes I can imagine better ways to live than we do, but I could never imagine a better companion than Farley."

A busy summer of visitors buffered their personal ups and downs. Friends from St. John's brought their two children for a visit, and Claire immediately related to nine-year-old Margaret, a shy and sedentary child who seemed to inhabit a dream world created by the books she read. Claire knew what it was like to be a Margaret.

"The Margarets have to suffer so much. We must have our dreamers I trust, but I wish I wasn't one of them." Claire imagined the child would aspire to be a painter or poet, have torturous love affairs, and marry late, "taking her private agonies with her all through life." Claire was also charmed by baby Hamish. An exemplary infant, the eight-month-old ate everything he was offered and slept through the night. "I almost think I could endure a baby if I could have one as good as he."

Claire barely had time to miss Margaret and Hamish before another visitor arrived, in August 1965—Peter Davison, Farley's U.S. publisher and editor, who endured a thirty-hour trip from Boston to Burgeo. A poet as well as a publisher, Davison had been mentored by Robert Frost; Robert Lowell was a friend, and Sylvia Plath was a lover for a brief time. Although Claire and Farley worried about how they would entertain him, Peter turned out to be the perfect guest. Always in a good mood, he would get up at 7:30, make his own breakfast, and take their dog Albert for a long walk.

His visit was a delight. Farley got to know and like Peter in a way he hadn't when they had stayed with the Davisons on their way to Mexico. Claire was impressed with his charm and intelligence. He offered exactly the kind of stimulating companionship she prized, including a sense of fun.

Spying a conch shell on the table, once used by dory fishermen as a foghorn, Peter picked it up and played it along to Farley's recording of Vivaldi. Peter was the life of a social they all attended, enthusiastically joining in the square dancing. He even flirted with Nurse Rene Ellis, the town femme fatale. To the people of Burgeo, Peter was just another benefit of having Farley Mowat living among them; his fame drew new and interesting visitors.

Peter's time in Burgeo ended with a voyage aboard the *Happy Adventure* to Red Island. It was a "wonderful grand time," and Claire was sad to see him go. "I understand Peter very well. We are both urban people. F is not."

While the visits were an enjoyable break from routine, they also made it impossible for either Farley or Claire to work. With Farley not feeling well and unable to write, Claire again found the walls closing in. Farley's antagonistic streak had sparked a feud with the Lakes and the Caulders. Ann Caulder had reported to the Lakes every criticism the Mowats had ever made of them.

Farley and Claire were no longer on speaking terms with the Lakes, and barely with the Caulders. As a result, Claire's social life was reduced to mingling with curious locals, who sometimes didn't speak when they visited. She longed for new faces and the activity that comes with city life. She tried taking tranquillizers, which she called her "happy pills," since they made her feel giddy and sleepy. She felt ostracized and wondered if she had a persecution complex.

Living with Farley was fascinating but rarely simple. His work was solitary and difficult, and his moods came and went like the Newfoundland weather. When she complained, Farley put it down to not knowing what she wanted. "How the hell can anyone know what they want when the situation and the goal changes every few months," Claire wondered. A peasant or a duchess knew what the rules of the game were and where the boundaries lay. But not Farley Mowat's wife.

"The futility of my life . . . I am disintegrating," she recorded in her journal. Claire considered writing a murder mystery, based on who hated who in Burgeo and why. The town's only murder had remained unsolved. An overseer with a reputation for mercilessly pushing his workers was the victim. He was allegedly found strangled with his own scarf at the bottom of Muddy Hole Cove, his pockets full of rocks.

Word that the Mowats were restless began to leak out. Spencer Lake had already asked Farley if he and Claire planned to stay in Burgeo. Farley knew that for Claire's good, and maybe his own, their days in the outport were numbered. He confided as much to Harold Horwood, who was enjoying success with his own writing career.

The corrected galleys for Horwood's novel *Tomorrow Will Be Sunday* were in New York. Work on *The Foxes of Beachy Cove* was in an advanced state and would be ready for a rewrite by October or November. Harold liked his American editor, who even did some research for him on fox behaviour through a friend at the Smithsonian.

"While editors may be jewels, however, ALL publishers are pirates," he wrote. Harold, who had made Farley his literary executor, gave some advice to his best friend. "Your gloomy letters continue to reach me … Don't be hasty about leaving Burgeo. In spite of everything, you've done some of your best work there."

Another person who didn't want Farley Mowat to leave the island was the premier of Newfoundland. Farley had petitioned Joey Small-wood on behalf of the town to have a bridge built to nearby Smalls Island, home to ten families. The children there had to come to school by dory, even in winter. Smallwood sent Farley a telegram informing him that he was sending engineers to see about the much-needed bridge, plus electricity and telephones for the island. He also wrote that the people of Burgeo were "fortunate to have one of Canada's most eloquent voices speak for them."

In early September, the doctors Ann and Mike Caulder resigned their positions in Burgeo. It was yet another blow to Claire. Despite their on-again, off-again relationship, Ann and Mike's leaving would make the place even bleaker for Claire, whose projects had lost all their savour. But there was no time to lament their departure, since Farley and Claire had to leave Burgeo for the two-month national tour for *Westviking*.

They had only a half-hour to pack and catch the float plane to St. John's. Claire was so rushed that she forgot her driver's licence, charge account cards, and bank book. Two hours later, they landed in the city, in Mundy Pond. After visiting Mike Donovan, whose cancer was ter-minal, they drove the forty miles to Russwood Ranch, the private resi-dence of the only living Father of Confederation, Joey Smallwood.

They spent seven hours with the premier, mostly listening, for Smallwood was a world-class raconteur and talker. He confided that his hobby was riding his lawn tractor around the acres of grass at Russ-wood. The phone rang every ten minutes. The premier's deputy min-ister of public works was present to discuss the bridge to Smalls Island. Ever the political horse trader, Smallwood said that the bridge was to keep Farley Mowat happy and in Newfoundland. Favours for favours. Even Farley couldn't stop Joey's relentless monologue.

When Farley and Claire reached Toronto, they found a depressed and lethargic Jack McClelland. He had lost forty pounds in just five weeks and couldn't keep food down. Jack was aware of Farley's own stomach problems and arranged an appointment for him with his internal specialist. The doctor ordered an X-ray, which showed that Farley had a hiatus hernia that was causing his indigestion.

Claire stayed behind in Toronto while Farley did the Winnipeg-to-Vancouver leg of the book tour. It was their longest separation in two years, but it had a silver lining. Farley's love letters to Claire came down like warm spring rain.

"My darling small—Your long and loving letter was waiting at Calgary, and saved my soul... You were right. The Edmonton girl tried a seduction. It was funny, and sad, and I again did what I could to be kind... Do you know, although I love you dearly, I have never before understood how tremendously lucky I am to have you. Trite maybe; but none the less true. I have seen so many nice people, desperately unhappy in their human bondage, on this trip. Now I know you for the greatest good luck the Gods have ever shown me."

One of Claire's worries during the more difficult times in Burgeo was that somehow Farley was losing interest in her. A letter from Calgary—in which Farley admitted that he had sometimes been less than the ideal husband—put that worry to rest. There were even hints of promises to change.

"Sweet golden girl... What is emerging from this trip is the arrow-sharp realization that you are indeed more than life to me. I have assuredly been taking you far too much for granted—that is to say that I have been taking your love of me and all the sweet benefits of that love too much as commonplaces. They are not commonplaces. What I have seen and heard assures me that our love for one another is by way of being unique, or, at least, exceedingly rare. And so I resolve to be more forbearing, if possible more humble, and for certain, more grateful for the love you offer. Darling love, be sure I know you as my own heart's ease. There have been none before you who are comparable; there will be none after... You are my own true love—God almighty, but I do love you so!"

Things were so hectic that when the tour reached Vancouver, Farley barely had time to dash off a brief note, which featured his trademark attempt to make her laugh. "Sorry this so short and incoherent, but then I am short and incoherent! I do love you so much!" And he left no doubt that she was still the one. "I love you exceedingly, adoringly and ferociously. Watch yourself, I shall devour you when I get home . . . Sweet love, Farley."

When they were reunited in Toronto, Farley drove Claire's Morris to Palgrave, where he planned to store it for the winter. The next stop on the tour was Montreal, featuring a feverish rush of events, and a daylong business meeting with Jack. Claire got to meet Irving Layton, who had himself just finished a national book tour, and found the Rabelaisian poet "more pleasant than lecherous."

The *Montreal Star* did an interview with Claire as part of their coverage of Farley's book tour, which appeared under the headline "Marriage Full-Time Job to Writer's Wife." Claire told the paper that she was perfectly happy "keeping house, looking after my husband, and enjoying life as it comes along" and that married women who "are torn between toddlers and typewriters" had her sympathy. She declared that she was never bored and enjoyed the peaceful, quiet life in Burgeo—an Academy Award portrayal of the contented, dutiful wife pulled off by a woman who clearly kept her personal reality to herself and her journal.

ON A MILD, OVERCAST MORNING in November, Farley and Claire returned to Burgeo to the usual display of affection. Someone had already been to the house to light their stove, and five of the Spence children were there to greet them. Nurse Rene, who was leaving Burgeo for a new job in St. Albans, brought them dinner.

As always, the news washed over them like a wave. The new Mountie didn't like fish and his wife didn't like Burgeo. Nurse Rene was supposedly having a torrid love affair with Birch Lake, and Burgeo's leading family was appalled. The town was getting a new brick post office and, of all things, a regular Monday garbage collection. People dropped in all afternoon.

Farley and Claire spent the day unpacking and going through a huge stack of mail. There was a telegram from Joey Smallwood, asking Farley if he wanted to be honoured at a dinner in St. John's. He agreed. Farley's successful bid to get the bridge to Smalls Island had increased his local celebrityhood. The men of the town asked Farley to take part in the launch of a new boat, a sign that he was one of them— something the women of Burgeo had not bestowed on Claire. The Lakes invited them to dinner to thank Farley for his exertions and then encouraged him to lobby the government for a road into the outport. "When the road comes, we go" was Claire's terse response.

Nurse Rene stayed with Farley and Claire for a few days before leaving for her new job. Claire kept her sadness about Rene's departure to herself. She didn't like the way that the Lakes and others portrayed Rene, a single woman in her mid-thirties, as a loose woman. Given her own tendency to present an agreeable facade, she admired Rene's defiance. "I do not have the courage to say what I really think," she wrote.

Claire also believed that the Lakes despised both Rene and Farley because of their ability to defy and rebel—traits she herself did not possess. She rankled under the unfairness of the judgment. It was considered normal for men to be promiscuous but shameful if a woman was. They may not approve of a woman defying conventions, "but at least they will notice." A few months later, Nurse Rene would commit suicide.

Farley's inclination to rebel was on display when he went to church on Christmas Eve. Everyone else wore their Sunday best; Farley appeared in a sweater and rubber boots. "If F and I ever get a divorce it will be entirely because of his lack of grooming," Claire noted in her journal.

That Christmas, gifts arrived from the grateful families on Smalls Island. Santa Claus Farley had given them a bridge, and they returned the favour—a scarf for their benefactor and a handmade tablecloth for Claire.

Claire's complicated relationship with Burgeo rolled on, and she continued to observe the place with an anthropologist's eye. She could not decide whether the beauties of outport life outweighed the loneliness and limitations or not. At times, the authenticity of the people and the place were heartbreakingly beautiful. It could be a simple thing, like Dolph, the Lakes' handyman, bringing a cut Christmas tree to their door; watching Albert, their beloved dog, pull the local children on a sled; or the poignant experience of watching a local wedding. "Why do we [women] want to go and feel the emotion of it all," Claire wrote. "Maybe because life is precious to women. Any life."

Even with an icy wind in her face, Claire couldn't resist walking back to the church to take it all in—the unmatched gowns of the bridesmaids with their plastic corsages, and the bride who was often well along the way to motherhood. The wedding party smiled at Claire as they left the church. She cried, as she always did at weddings and funerals, and wondered why. "Is it that the rest of my life is so glazed and unreal, that the prospect of the beginning and the end shake me until I sob?"

While Farley was hard at work on *The Polar Passion*, volume two of his Arctic trilogy, Claire typed up the entries from the journal she kept in England. She and Farley spent a delightful evening sitting on the floor reading them aloud, laughing about the things they had done in those first few months together after fleeing Ontario.

"Farley was in a lonely agony waiting for me to arrive and really searching his soul. I felt terrible at leaving my parents just when my father was about to die. We had our good moments and our bad, and it brought it all back to read about it."

ON A COLD MARCH DAY, a Sikorsky helicopter landed behind the Burgeo hospital to take Farley and Claire on the four-hour trip to St. John's for the testimonial dinner Smallwood had laid on. On the way, they saw a spectacular herd of caribou scattering wildly at the sound of the aircraft's rotors.

Shortly after their arrival, people began showing up, including Harold Horwood and his girlfriend, Marguerite. Although she was in her mid-thirties, Farley thought she had the innocence of a twenty-year-old. Marguerite told Claire that she didn't think that she could marry Harold because he was her best friend. Claire thought the problem was not Marguerite but her boyfriend. "I suspect that in the realm of courtship, Harold is about as romantic as a clam," she wrote.

Although she always enjoyed Harold's company, Claire found that he was "getting a trifle insufferable about his recently published book" and the success it was enjoying. Farley's own new book, *Westviking*, was selling well in the United States and had hit number two on the hardcover bestseller list in Canada.

When the big day of the testimonial dinner came, Farley and Claire were taken by limousine to Memorial University's banquet hall. Joey met them and introduced them to the two hundred people present, including Spencer and Margaret Lake. A Portuguese chef had prepared a gourmet meal: an entree of fresh sole, followed by a course of orange duck and crème de menthe parfait for dessert. Dinner was served with a delicious white wine, followed by coffee and Newman's port.

Smallwood talked to Farley all evening, studiously ignoring Claire. But Chief Justice Robert Furlong, seated on her left, was witty and entertaining. The premier gave a speech about how proud everyone was that Farley had decided to live in Newfoundland. In turn, Farley served up a chiding address about the dangers of throwing away the province's cultural heritage. Smallwood then presented Claire with a Newfoundland pin and Farley with a set of cufflinks. The evening ended with thunderous applause and a rousing rendition of "Ode to Newfoundland." Farley was uneasy with the huge and calculated fuss that Smallwood had made over him.

In the days that followed, there were interviews and other events involving both Farley and Harold. Harold was riding high on his recent literary success, but Claire was annoyed when he interrupted her conversation with the Lakes to boast about the good reviews and soaring sales of his novel. Farley and Harold had a heart-to-heart, which touched on Harold's personal shortcomings and inspired a remarkable letter from Harold setting out how challenging it was to be in Farley's orbit. The apprentice was chafing under the sorcerer's overwhelming mentorship.

"There are a number of things that tend to make us bristle in each other's presence," Harold wrote, "and perhaps we shouldn't try to force our friendship into protracted periods of intimacy. A week at a time is perhaps as much as we should allow ourselves." Harold acknowledged that the fault was largely his. "I know that I cannot relax, that I am perpetually tense, and that I'm incurably anti-social. But there it is. Society literally disgusts me."

Farley had implored Harold to drop his prickly exterior whenever he found himself in gatherings larger than six people. Harold said he was too old to learn new tricks, but that his difficulties with Farley were a different matter:

"The friction with you is a special case. You are a very strong personality. You are a reformer. You believe you are right about everything. You have a long period of success behind you, and the events of your career have tended to confirm you in your God-like pose. You were an only child. You shot up to the rank of Captain in the army. Your first book was an international best seller. How could anybody survive this without coming to believe in his own infallibility? I have had to fight, in self defence, against your infallibility, against your perhaps unconscious determination to reform me, and Make Something out of me, against the also perhaps unconscious assumption that papa Farley knows best. I hope the last paragraph doesn't sound too nasty, because you're the only living person for whom I have a true feeling of brotherhood."

Harold had nothing to worry about. Being a difficult person himself, Farley knew how to handle talented misfits. The two remained best friends until Horwood's death, in 2006.

AS MUCH AS JOEY SMALLWOOD wanted to keep Farley in Newfoundland, his writing career pulled him into a global orbit. First, there was an extensive trip to the Arctic, and he took Claire as far as Churchill before continuing the journey on his own.

Next, they toured Russia, where Farley's work was immensely popular. To pick up his royalties, they had to travel to Moscow, where three thousand rubles was awaiting him. While on that trip, Farley got to hold the reins as a pair of reindeer pulled his sleigh, and Claire was presented with a coat lined with dog fur, the warmest jacket she had ever worn. The trip produced Farley's book *Sibir*, describing his personal discovery of Siberia, for which Claire typed all the notes.

After five and a half months of travelling around the world, there was no one to meet their coastal boat when they arrived at the wharf in Burgeo on January 15, 1967. Change had left its calling card everywhere. There were now nineteen vehicles in town and more television sets, and the Smalls Island bridge was almost complete. Ann Caulder called to welcome them home, and Nurse Molly King sent over supper. Reverend Mark Genge later played them a tape of the memorial service held for Nurse Rene Ellis. They visited the Lakes, and Spencer assured Farley that he was not biased against Russia and might even go there himself to sell fish.

Farley and Claire had been back only a few days when they heard about the seventy-foot-long whale that was trapped in Aldridge's Pond, a short boat ride from Burgeo. When Farley went to see it, a crowd had gathered and there were several boats in the water. "Then someone saw it—the long black back of him, rising so quietly from the water and then down again and out of sight." Claire noted in her journal that the creature's massive body was pockmarked with bullet holes.

As the whale circled and thrashed, people began throwing rocks at it. Farley screamed at them to stop. He told them that if the whale died, he would write a book about how Burgeo had killed its whale. If they saved it, it would have great publicity value that might lead to better services for the community. "And curiously, they all got in their boats and left," Claire wrote.

The Mowats sent off two telegrams about the whale, one to the Department of Fisheries in St. John's, the other to the Canadian Press. The story was soon on CBC Radio and shortly afterwards shot around the world. Farley put up a lettered sign that Claire had made: "Whale Must Not Be Tormented." She described the people who had injured the animal as "savage, primitive bastards," who should be trapped and filled with buckshot.

Joey Smallwood grasped the enormous opportunity the situation presented. As a result, the Newfoundland legislature voted to adopt the whale and pay up to $1,000 for herring to feed it. The premier said anyone injuring the whale was injuring government property. He also called for donations to save the whale and appointed Farley Mowat to administer the fund as "keeper of the whale." The government ordered the pond closed where "Moby Joe" was trapped, and the RCMP put up signs warning people that harming the whale was illegal.

The story caught fire, and Farley and Claire's telephone never stopped ringing. Photographers flew in to take pictures. Jack McClelland tried to line up an exclusive story about the whale in the *Star Weekly*, but it fell through after he released photographs from Farley to the Canadian Press, meaning that they would not be exclusive to the paper.

Spencer Lake offered to feed the whale herring from his plant, but an effort to trap herring was a failure because the net was old and rotten. A call came in from the world-famous Marine Biological Laboratory at Woods Hole in Massachusetts. Joey Smallwood, who told reporters that the whale was worth $100 million in advertising for the province, arranged transportation for the American scientists. Claire noted Smallwood's shrewdness, calling him a showman rather than a statesman.

Farley and Claire received a frantic call from a fisherman that Moby Joe had breached. The whale was losing blood from the abscesses caused by the two-week-old bullet wounds. Farley tried desperately to obtain antibiotics, which a drug company offered to supply, and a veterinarian offered his services free of charge. It was too late. Three days after Claire's thirty-fourth birthday, the lifeless creature was floating on the surface of Aldridge's Pond, likely the result of septicemia. "Our whale is dead," Claire wrote. "I am distraught. Farley is depressed."

The CBC flew in to do a scathing report on the town that murdered the whale. In the wake of enormous publicity surrounding the tragedy, some residents, including Ann Caulder, blamed Farley for giving Burgeo a bad name. Town members of the Sou'Wester Club turned against him for exposing the story of the whale. Farley the benefactor was suddenly Farley the troublemaker.

Meanwhile, Farley and Claire were both troubled by the ease with which some Newfoundlanders could kill—wiping out the Beothuk people, wiping out wolves, wiping out fish stocks, and now the whale. "Men are beasts," Claire wrote. Farley reached the inevitable conclusion. They had to leave.

Farley announced his decision on July 12, 1967, at a meeting of the library board. Three weeks later, the harbour ringed with well-wishers and the ridge above town lined with children slowly waving goodbye, the *Happy Adventure* left Burgeo harbour for the last time. After a short distance, it became clear that the mooring lines had become tangled in the boat's propeller. Farley dove into the freezing water and cut the *Happy Adventure* free. "The feat of daring amazed all who saw it," Claire wrote.

18 | Finding Eden

"BAD BEGINNING, GOOD ENDING"—so the saying goes.

After stalling in Burgeo harbour, at 3:15 the *Happy Adventure* finally set sail for the coastal community of Grand Bruit in a strong westerly breeze. Farley and Claire hoped the dismal start would mean a smooth voyage. The trip took four hours, and Claire noted that Farley was "eager and tense and happy to be going." She herself was tired, queasy, and frightened by the rough seas. What seemed like the entire community of Grand Bruit met them at the wharf, and a young couple came aboard to give them a jar of bakeapples. They were both exhausted after a frantic month of packing and the choppy voyage, with Claire hanging on to Albert and the boat at the same time.

Their next stop was Port aux Basques, which they decided featured the worst of both Newfoundland and the mainland. It was noisy and crowded, and finding a mooring was like looking for a parking spot in Toronto. The one they got was less than ideal—next to the fish plant's discharge tube. They stayed only long enough to pick up gear for the perilous trip across Cabot Strait. Jack McClelland had sent a rubber lifeboat, but only the oars arrived. He had also sent life jackets, a radio, and airhorns. Farley phoned his friend Captain John Parker, the chief navigational pilot for North Sydney, and asked for his help in making the crossing. In such heavy seas, Farley decided that Claire and their dog would be better off making the voyage on the ferry.

On Saturday, August 5, 1967, Parker showed up for breakfast with Farley and Claire carrying charts. After Claire left to board the *William*

Carson, the two men debated whether or not to sail. Although it was overcast and blustery, they decided to get underway. It was a gruelling voyage in high seas, and the *Happy Adventure* began taking on water, forcing the men to pump her out all the way across to North Sydney. Parker was seasick, but Farley later said he had been too frightened to be sick. The trip took twenty-six hours. At 4 p.m., the *Happy Adventure* landed at the wharf at Kelly's Point in Bras d'Or Lake, a complex of salt-water "lakes" in Cape Breton.

The leak had to be fixed. Captain Parker suggested they go to a boatyard three and a half hours away in Baddeck, Nova Scotia, where the schooner looked crude and dowdy among the expensive yachts moored there. Claire rejoined Farley in Baddeck, where they met an Irish doctor who looked like Jack McClelland and flirted outrageously with Claire—"a fact which seems to amuse Farley," she noted. After cursory repairs, their schooner continued to leak.

The *Happy Adventure* had to be pulled up on a slip so that it could be caulked and the leak checked again. Claire had groceries delivered to the boat, but it felt awkward living on board a vessel on a slip. After living in Burgeo, Claire also felt the culture shock of big money in this Nova Scotia town.

They met some lovely people, including Guido and Faith Perera. "The Pereras are golden people. Rich, talented and uncomplicated. I only feel envy when I meet people like this, not that I want to be like them, only that I had grown up in a similar way with parents who were as sure of themselves," Claire wrote.

The Pereras' daughter-in-law was thrilled to discover that Farley was the author of *Never Cry Wolf,* which her friends had been discussing. In the end, however, Claire judged Baddeck harshly because too many right-wing, loud-mouthed Americans were moored there. "Rich yanks buying up the wilderness," she noted.

Arrangements had been made to meet Jack McClelland in Charlottetown for the sail to Montreal with Farley, while Claire and Albert would take the train. Instead, they hooked up with Jack in Pictou, Nova Scotia, where he was pleased to see how the tourists recognized Farley and swarmed around him for autographs.

The voyage to Montreal had just gotten underway when Farley decided to seek shelter in Grande Rivière because of the weather. "Jack was a little grumpy," Farley wrote. "He would have liked to have held on course until the bottom went out of the boat . . . He mellowed after a few drinks, but was not pleased to find that he had to have his craps on the shingle beach in view of the distant village. Very fussy fellow."

Farley and Jack told some unfriendly locals that they were officers of the USSR merchant marine sailing a small boat from Leningrad to the Expo 67 world's fair in Montreal. If the plan was to inspire sympathy, it didn't work. The locals called the Quebec provincial police to drive the sailors out.

On August 22, they reached Gaspé head. They stripped off their clothes and sunbathed, offending tourists on a nearby boat.

Their reception didn't improve. During the night, when teenagers at L'Anse-à-Valleau tried to overturn the *Happy Adventure*, Jack went aloft to chase them off and was pelted with stones. They set sail for Rimouski, but Jack ran out of time and took a taxi to Gaspé to begin the trek back to Toronto.

Farley was marooned, but not for long. A young southerner named Dale Murray showed up at the schooner with a message from Jack, who had picked him up while he was resting under a bridge. Starting in British Columbia, Murray had been walking across Canada with just his backpack, one change of clothes, a sleeping bag, and a few books.

Knowing Farley needed help, Jack asked Murray if he would like to sail to Quebec in a schooner. Murray had travelled the rails with hobos but had never been on a boat. Although he suspected that Jack was some kind of slick promoter, he agreed. After loading him up with three bottles of rum, Jack sent him by taxi back to Farley.

Whether it was the rum or the raw adventure of it all, Farley made Murray his mate. He gave him a one-hour course in sailing, and they were off. By dawn, Farley was happy to trust him with the schooner. They sailed at night under a full moon, the aurora lights flickering overhead. Under sluggish power, they felt they were on the edge of the Sargasso Sea, moving through seaweed. Then came a grinding moan from the schooner's engine. The reduction gearbox had run dry. After thirty-nine hours at sea, they put in to Rimouski for repairs. Farley called Claire to tell her he had a new companion.

Locals in Rimouski worked to replace the shattered bearings in the *Happy Adventure*'s gearbox. Captain Jules Jourdaine, a master who had the bitter experience of losing three ships, told them that a forty-five-foot boat had nearly been upended by riptides near Saguenay, and shared much-needed information with Farley about the complicated tides and currents in the area. "Local knowledge on the St. Lawrence is priceless," Farley noted. On September 1, their fuel tanks topped up for free, Farley and his first mate were on their way up the St. Lawrence. The marine traffic was heavy, and huge ships loomed out of the night like dinosaurs. One passed so close to the *Happy Adventure* that Farley and his mate saw someone light a match in the wheelhouse.

"This was the wildest passage I have ever made," Farley wrote in his journal. The engine and foresail were full out. They were sailing upstream. Despite his inexperience, Dale remained calm and relaxed. Finally, they arrived at "marina suburbia" in Quebec City, where Dale disembarked and Claire rejoined the voyage.

"I will miss him. As good a shipmate as any I have ever had," Farley wrote. Sadly, the *Happy Adventure* still leaked when under power.

After an epic journey, Farley and Claire finally reached Montreal Harbour on September 8, 1967, in the middle of the afternoon. An RCMP launch gave them the once-over, but after the formalities were dispensed with, they got the royal treatment. The *Happy Adventure* was ushered into the Expo Marina, where they were saluted by signal guns, horns, and bells from hundreds of vessels and given a prime berth. Piped ashore by Expo officials, they were given a fantastic reception "for one dowdy little (sinking) Newfoundland bummer, and two dirty little ex-Newfoundland voyagers." There were many luxury boats in the harbour, and Farley and Claire were offered the thing they needed most: a shower.

The next day, they saw some of Expo 67, but Farley had more pressing work. There was six inches of water over the floorboards, and he had to find out where the leak was. Then, suddenly, she stopped leaking. "Oh bless her soul," he wrote.

Farley was grateful for the enthusiasm of his welcome, but the Expo Marina gave him and the *Happy Adventure* an inferiority complex. "We were certainly the scruffiest, poorest, roughest boat in the lot." They nipped out of the marina on a perfect September morning, into the South Shore Canal of the seaway. There was only one question: Would the boat who wouldn't float make it?

It didn't look like it. By the time they got through the first locks of the seaway, the *Happy Adventure* was taking on water again. Worse, her engine was smoking. A stowaway appeared—a white-footed deer mouse that Claire fed for the remainder of the voyage.

By the middle of September, they were moored at the Kingston Yacht Club, where people looked down their noses at the vessel in a way that sailors in the Down East working harbours never did. In the East, strangers were welcome; in Central Canada, ragamuffins were not.

On the afternoon of September 18, 1967, the *Happy Adventure* moored at the Port Hope Yacht Club. The journey had taken forty-seven days, thirty-seven of them underway, but Farley and Claire had reached their new home in Port Hope, sixty-five miles east of Toronto.

During a winter storm a few months later, while Farley was checking the ice around the *Happy Adventure*, he fell into the frigid water. He climbed out and walked home freezing and soaking wet, thinking about writing a book inspired by his temperamental vessel. *The Boat Who Wouldn't Float* would be published in 1969 and win the Leacock Medal for humour. Farley's fame was growing. There were so many requests for autographs that he ordered a thousand postcards with a photo and room for a message. *A Whale for the Killing*, the book based on his experience with the whale trapped in Aldridge's Pond, would be published in 1972.

Harold Horwood wrote to Farley, sending his love to Claire and expressing surprise that she had not left him yet. He also informed Farley of a new fan, his friend writer Margaret Laurence. She had encouraged Margaret Atwood to treat him seriously and suggested that she publish a study of Farley's work as literature in a literary journal. It might not do much for sales, but Harold thought it might well bring

Farley honours and status. "Are you interested in status?" he asked. "I've never been sure." Farley would later receive the Order of Canada.

IN PORT HOPE, Farley and Claire bought a beautiful old house on John Street, in the centre of town. They lived there for nine years, before moving into 18 King Street in the fall of 1976. The Mowat family home was purchased from Farley's mother, Helen. It was in a much quieter neighbourhood, on a street lined with trees. Helen, now eighty, moved into a one-bedroom apartment in town.

As tumultuous as their lives had become, 1976 was a magical year. Farley and Claire finally found the place they had always looked for, a personal Eden, off the beaten path, and very private. Brick Point, sometimes known as "the Brickery" in River Bourgeois, Cape Breton, was a two-hundred-acre property on the ocean, which they bought as soon as they saw it. The former owners rented the house while they searched for a new home. In July 1977, Farley and Claire towed their Cygnet trailer to Brick Point, where they camped in the living room and in the tiny trailer while they renovated the old farmhouse.

Although they would continue to spend winters in Port Hope, Cape Breton was where Farley and Claire spent their happiest times. Farley drew sustenance from the wild Nature all around him. He engineered a water system and planted an ambitious vegetable garden every year that was carefully planned months ahead. He recorded rainfall with a rain gauge ("July 1 see 2.75" of rain") and made meticulous garden notes during the winter months, sometimes written on the back of page proofs. He noted parsnip seeds that did not germinate. He grew leeks, peas, spinach, cabbage and early beans, potatoes, and squash.

They always left Cape Breton before hunting season began, on November 1. Farley would order seed packages to be sent to his friend Ervin Touesnard so that they would be ready to plant when they got back to Brick Point in the spring. A pale-pink peony bush was there when they bought the property, and Harold Horwood brought them an array of flowers and bushes to plant. It was Harold who planted the Siberian iris at the side of the pond, though Farley was more interested in edible plants. Claire thinned the carrots and peas at Farley's direction, and later in life helped with the weeding. Farley gardened until he was ninety-two. Claire joked that "the world lost a great market gardener when he decided to be a writer."

It had taken them a long time to find Shangri-La. They had looked in Manitoba, owned a farm in Prince Edward Island, and summered in the Magdalen Islands from 1969 to 1975. While staying at Indian Summer, the Mowat family cottage in Ontario, Claire became pregnant. Joy turned to bottomless tragedy when their only child, a boy, was stillborn in March 1969. Claire never got to hold him. Her maternal grandmother, Ethel Winget Angel, had died of complications after childbirth at the age of thirty-five. Farley was afraid he was going to lose Claire as well as their baby, for she needed two operations to stop the bleeding. Claire was inconsolable.

Their great love for each other pulled them through those dark days. They endured. And Farley's ardour for Claire burned on in the letters he wrote when events kept them apart. In one of these letters, after Farley told her that his writing was going well and asked her not to give out his phone number to anyone, the lava of passion for her flowed molten hot.

"The weekend in Toronto was worth a million stings in the ass (or anywhere). It was marvelous, and confirmed my conviction that you are the only woman in the world for me. It is true, I love you mightily, and dearly, and that is a fact, even if I normally don't like facts."

The next day, he wrote again from the Magdalen Islands. "It seems that, at a distance, we can communicate superbly. Got to learn to do it at close quarters, eh? . . . What we have is too damn good to let it slide. We'll make it, kid. We'll make it!"

19 | Creatures Great and Small

FOR YEARS, CLAIRE HAD BEEN LABOURING at a book of her own, and Farley begged her not to let a careless remark by Jack McClelland derail the project. "You are more than capable of doing a good job on it, as witness your journals. Stop brooding about what Jack said, and get the nose to the wheel. Okay?" It was exactly the encouragement she craved from him. "Chin up, lover girl, we'll make it. Remember, most of our distress is not caused by either one of us. We are like the core of a hydrogen bomb, being forced in upon each other by outside pressures until we explode against each other. Main thing is to realize that we mustn't blame each other... Much love, love."

After learning that the remark he had made to her during a visit to the Magdalen Islands had derailed her book, Jack wrote a conciliatory letter to Claire. He had told Claire that if she was looking for a career to offset isolation, writing would be the least suitable for that objective. "But, for god's sake, this does not mean that you should, having started a book, be discouraged from finishing it." He urged her to go on with her manuscript. "Become a painter, a photographer, a collector, a musician—even a hooker... but one writing ego per family is enough." Even so, he said, "it's a matter of record that I have been wrong once or twice in my life. Love, Jack."

Claire was too angry to reply and too wise to send her letter to Jack when she finally answered him. "My God I know what I want to do.

My frustration is in trying to find any time or quietude in which to do it. Why is it I project an image of a vapid, bewildered woman staring into space each morning wondering how to pass the day? Can't anyone, even you, imagine what it is like to be married to this witheringly inconsistent jack-in-the box who never stays in one place long enough to lay in a supply of clean clothes? Wherever we are our life is an open-ended open house."

She wrote that she had as much spare time as the maître d' at Banff Springs Hotel in July. "I never do anything but cook and talk." She never intended to become a writer, but those five years in Burgeo were unique. "Most of it has vanished now." Farley was not interested in writing about it, but she was. The essence of her story was how it was with them in Burgeo. "If we split, the story would be as publishable as the Pierre and Janet cookbook, had they divorced each other."

After eight years, Claire finished her book. *The Outport People* was a rollicking success, with excellent reviews in *Maclean's* and *Saturday Night*. Five more books would follow. When she was on tour for *The Outport People*, Farley wrote from Brick Point and told Claire that she was No. 8 on *Maclean's* bestseller list, and would move up to No. 6 in another week. Jack said Claire's book would lead the spring list and be one of the "biggies" of 1983. Farley joked that people were beginning to call him Mr. Wheeler. "J is very pleased with *Outport* and with you. Says he is counting on you to make up for my laziness in future and to ensure McClelland & Stewart's survival."

Farley saw how exhausted Claire was when she got back from her book tour. It was, he explained, all part of becoming a public figure. "Price of fame and fortune. Other people think you can solve their problems. And turn you into a wailing wall." But he and Claire were lucky. "In a world where almost everyone is besieged by growing fears, doubts, uncertainties about the mere mechanics of survival, we have a lot going for us."

While praising Claire for her phenomenal success, Farley was in Cape Breton working hard on one of his most important books, *Sea of Slaughter*. His writing schedule began at 8 a.m. and ended at noon.

After a couple of hours of outside work, he returned to the typewriter for two more hours of writing in the late afternoon. He was getting a thousand words a day, but it was tough sledding. He told Claire he was "so sick of it that I have great difficulty keeping on." But he had to either finish the book or quit writing entirely. Claire, meanwhile, wondered if Farley wasn't "content" being separated from her. He most decidedly was not.

"It's an old problem with us, one we had right from the start I think, but we've handled it so far, which ought to mean we can handle it the rest of the way. But you are wrong about one thing. I am NOT content to be away from you, down here. Yes I am happier in Cape Breton than in Port Hope, as far as the environment is concerned . . . but I am unhappy at being separated from you. It is lonely and unsatisfying. You are, and remain, my dearest and bestest friend, and my companion, and without you I suffer a sense of loss and inadequacy."

After a month apart, and facing nine more days of separation, Farley wrote, "I feel specially missing of you . . . Hang in there. I love you, need you, and miss you all at once."

IN 1985, AUTHOR GRAEME GIBSON wrote that he was organizing a series of birdwatching trips to Cuba that winter and invited Farley and Claire to come along. Gibson had become a birdwatcher after a large bird flew directly over his head in the Don Valley Ravine, and he had bought a guide and a pair of binoculars to discover that it was a red-tailed hawk. In his book *The Bedside Book of Birds*, Gibson wrote: "One of the rewards of birdwatching is the brief escape it affords from our ancient and compelling need to make Nature useful." Farley had just spent five years writing *Sea of Slaughter*, his lament for how humankind has mistreated the other creatures of the Earth.

Gibson, Margaret Atwood (called Peggy by friends), their daughter, Jessie, and other writers who were close friends of the couple would also be going. Atwood's father, Dr. Carl Atwood, who was an entomologist, and her mother, Margaret, would join them as well. Farley had wanted to go to Cuba for thirty years and happily accepted the invitation.

He had been interested in Cuba since the days when Castro was trying to defeat Batista, and had been an early member of the Fair Play for Cuba Committee when the U.S. was making every effort to reverse the revolution. Farley had even lured Pierre Berton to one of the public meetings. Berton was annoyed when he realized the meeting could be construed as a "communist" activity.

The first public meeting of the Toronto branch of the Fair Play for Cuba Committee had been held at the First Unitarian Church on February 19, 1961. There were three hundred people in the audience, largely members of the church and students for nuclear disarmament. The principal speaker, Professor Samuel Shapiro of Michigan State University, urged Canada to remain neutral and keep trading with Cuba, in the hope that the country would remain independent of Soviet control. Pressure was building in Washington to stop normal contact between Canada and Cuba, testing Canada's independence.

The next day, a report naming Farley Mowat had been sent to the U.S. State Department and CIA from the consulate general in Toronto: "A message was read from the well-known Canadian author, Farley MOWAT, in which he offered the use of his name 'in any manner that would counter the scurrilous policies of the United States toward Cuba.'" The U.S. embassy in Ottawa was copied, and the U.S. invasion at the Bay of Pigs was launched on April 17, 1961.

On December 7, 1985, the birders met in the international departure lounge of Pearson International Airport. The group included historian Ramsay Cook and his wife, Eleanor, writer Ron Graham, and politician Judy Erola. Members of the diplomatic corps and several Americans flying to Cuba on business were also on the chartered Air Canada flight. They landed at a small airport near Varadero and were met by the first secretary of the Canadian embassy, as well as professional ornithologist Orlando Garrido, considered Cuba's greatest living naturalist. Also a former tennis star, Garrido had played at Wimbledon several times.

The group boarded a bus and set off in the sudden semi-tropical darkness for the Bay of Pigs. The bar at the back of the swaying bus made the trip memorable as they passed through the provincial towns of Cárdenas and Jovellanos. The crowds outside were on foot, and there were many horse-drawn vehicles.

Their small resort consisted of about thirty cabanas, a dining hall, and a bar. Most of the guests at Playa Larga Resort were Cuban. Farley and Claire's toilet exploded in the middle of the night, and Farley joked that a suggested headline could be "Mowat Killed by Exploding Toilet in Cuba. CIA plot suspected." The beach was unpretentious but well-kept, and the waters calm. The resort itself was pleasant and quiet, and according to Farley, all the meals were good "but straightforward and simple." The next day after lunch, while their companions sweated in the noonday sun looking for birds, Farley and Claire decided to go back to their cabana for a snooze.

Orlando Garrido joined Farley and Claire for a drink and was surprised to be talking to the author of *Never Cry Wolf*. They enjoyed a good dinner of red snapper. Breakfast was at 6:30, and then they were off in a tarp-covered truck, which Farley christened "the Big Blue Machine." As they travelled through the Zapata wildlife refuge, the rattle under the truck was greeted by most of the birders with amusement.

Atwood and Cook were the really enthusiastic birders. Ron Graham, like Farley and Claire, was more interested in Cuba. Jessie and her grandparents joined Farley and Claire in exploring Santo Tomás, once the poorest community in Cuba, while Orlando took the rest of the party in search of the minute bee hummingbird, with its nest the size of a golf ball and eggs the size of a coffee bean.

They visited the local school, where the children were bright and polite. The teaching aids included charts of native birds and animals and material about conservation. In the front yard, there was a stone bust of a Cuban writer, not a politician. An enormous sow had taken up residence in an unused bomb shelter, built after the Bay of Pigs invasion, to protect the schoolchildren from U.S. bombs. Concrete machine-gun posts and pillars intended for roadblocks reminded Farley of the south coast of England in 1942, under the threat of Nazi invasion.

The tour leaders had been ordered to show the group a bee hummingbird, so Farley and company had to abandon the village and follow the others into the bush. A mile up a dirt road, they entered a small clearing surrounded by yellow and red flowering mahogany trees, where Cuban emerald hummingbirds were sipping the nectar. And then they saw the bee hummingbird—the smallest bird in the world.

On the edge of the swamp, they had a lunch of cold chicken and potato chips, washed down by excellent Cuban beer. Orlando roused them at 6 the next morning to see a Cuban grassquit, endemic to the island. After breakfast, they set off in the Big Blue Machine through low, dense jungle in pursuit of more bee hummingbirds and quail doves. They also sighted some Cuban trogons, the national bird, whose colours reflect the Cuban flag.

Stopping by a bridge, they saw hundreds of coots, little blue herons, and masked ducks. The Bay of Pigs invasion museum at Playa Girón was closed that day, so Farley and Claire took a siesta, had a swim, and hosted a convivial gathering of Cubans in their cabana for drinks. A pig roast was held by the light of a bonfire that night, and an enormous cake, decorated with endemic birds made of coloured icing sugar, was baked in honour of the visitors.

The next day, they visited the museum in Girón. Outside was a wrecked U.S. fighter-bomber, a U.S. tank, and various U.S. assault boats and medium guns. Inside, they showed a film about the invasion, and people standing up in defence of their country. The invaders had counted on the local people rallying to their cause, which of course did not happen. In fact, 150 Cuban defenders were killed, including civilians.

Before a planned visit to Havana, they were briefed that they should be aware of communist seductions. Margaret Atwood was the president of PEN Canada, so they were also briefed by the Canadian embassy that they should take a strong stand on behalf of Amnesty International for writers and human rights in general.

The next day, they toured Treasure Lake by boat and saw clusters of snake-backed anhingas and ducks. The lake and its swampy islands had been the last refuge of the Indigenous Cuban people when the Spaniards came seeking gold. At the resort, the Canadian travellers were served a buffet. Alligator was on the menu—and to Farley it tasted like "tough elderly beef." They all enjoyed a "marvelous star-lit" boat ride back to Big Blue.

Farley and Claire took a day off from birdwatching to lounge on the beach and swim with Jess and her grandmother. "Jess is a remarkable child, with the brains of her parents," Farley wrote. Jess had fond memories of the trip, and in later years, when her parents wrote the Mowats, she would always send her best.

Tipping was not allowed in Cuba, so Claire gave the staff a sheaf of ballpoint pens. Their hosts at Playa Larga were overwhelmingly willing and enthusiastic.

They were then bused to the Hotel Comodoro on the west coast of Havana, a second-rate hotel reserved usually for tourists from communist countries. After a buffet dinner of chicken, which was free range and excellent, they were taken by minibus to a reception at the Cuban writers' union headquarters in what had once been the palatial home of a sugar baron. Expected at 5:30 p.m., they were three hours late because of travel delays. Only a handful of Cuban writers were still there, an intoxicated one celebrating his birthday, and another who became quite enamoured of Judy Erola. The senior members acted like any other functionaries.

The Canadian group was led by Peggy and Graeme. The visit was depressing except for the fact they were served excellent rum punch. Farley presented the union with several of his books and a copy of Claire's *The Outport People*. That night, Peggy, Graeme, and Jess were guests at the Canadian ambassador's residence while the others returned to the Hotel Comodoro.

After breakfast, they set off on a guided tour of Havana. They visited Castillo de San Salvador de la Punta, a restored section of the city, and the cathedral. They were impressed by the fossils in the limestone used to build the church and the little stray dogs in the cathedral square. Claire wanted to adopt them all. They were also impressed by the cleanliness of the streets and the amicability of the people. There was an air of vitality. Claire bought some funny anti-U.S. T-shirts for Farley.

After lunch, most of the group visited Hemingway's former home, but Farley and Claire elected to go for a swim instead in the lagoon behind the hotel. That evening, there was a reception at the Canadian embassy. After being greeted by the first secretary of the embassy and his wife, Farley found himself talking to Ramón Castro, who looked like his younger brother, dressed like him, and smoked a big cigar. They hit it off and had a long conversation. Farley gave him a copy of his new book, *My Discovery of America,* and Ramón insisted it be autographed "To the Three Castro Brothers—Ramon, Fidel and Raoul." He would read it first and pass it on to his brothers.

Ramón suggested that Farley return to Cuba as a guest and write a book about the Canadian cows that had revolutionized Cuban agriculture. A fabulous Canadian Holstein had won an international award for Cuba, for milk production. Ubra Blanco, "White Udder," was now dead, but in 1982 she had set a Guinness world record for most milk production in a single day. She was descended from Rosafe Signet, a champion Canadian bull.

Ramón overstayed his usual visiting time and embraced Farley before he left, telling one of the embassy officials that Farley was already a Cuban because he had a good sense of humour. The first secretary took Farley aside to warn him to be careful and not let the Cubans "use me."

The rest of the group elected to go to the Tropicana, but Farley and Claire decided to go back to the hotel and bed. In the lobby they met an Armenian writer who was familiar with Farley's books in Russian, and those of Stephen Leacock. The next morning, they got a call with an invitation from Ramón to visit a show cattle farm en route to Varadero. They would have to leave the hotel an hour earlier than planned. That prompted groans from others in the group, most of whom had hangovers. The elevators were not working, so they lugged their suitcases down the stairs.

A modern highway skirted the coast. They passed guava orchards and fishing villages, then headed inland to a high, rolling plateau with a view of the sea. The manager of the collective farm had served with Castro in the Sierra Maestra campaign. The farm now had seven thousand milking cows. Before the revolution, only the children of the rich could afford to drink milk.

UNDER NORMAL CIRCUMSTANCES, both Farley and Claire preferred a cold winter day to the tropical heat. But when they returned to the bracing winter weather in Port Hope, there was an unpleasant surprise waiting for them: the Canadian Wildlife Federation was launching a $13 million lawsuit against Farley, along with the CBC, CTV, and several newspapers. Farley would spend $20,000 on legal fees before the suit was dropped after two and a half years and a carefully worded apology worked out by both lawyers.

But there was also some very good news. Early in 1986, Jack McClelland called with an exceptional proposal for a new book. Time Warner wanted Farley to write a biography of Dian Fossey, the American primatologist who had been murdered in an especially brutal way, with a *panga*, a machete-like African tool.

Farley was still soul-sick from writing *Sea of Slaughter* and the exhausting tour that followed. But as an eco-warrior himself, Farley knew how important it was to stand up for like-minded activists, who often put themselves at risk to advance their causes. He took on the project.

With the help of friend and neighbour Wade Rowland, a senior producer at CBC, who gathered much of the research from three continents, Farley finished *Virunga: The Passion of Dian Fossey* in June 1987. Much of the book was in Fossey's own words from her letters and diaries. After it was published that fall to international acclaim, the Mowat household in Port Hope became busier than usual.

Adrienne Clarkson and John Ralston Saul came to visit Farley and Claire for dinner on March 19, 1988, and stayed overnight. Like Farley and Claire, they were both passionate nationalists and opponents of free trade, a subject of political debate at the time. It was a frigid weekend perfectly suited to relaxing in front of the fire. The next morning, Adrienne and Claire went to church at St. Mark's, where Adrienne the famous TV personality caused a stir among parishioners.

That afternoon, just two hours after Adrienne and John had gone, Sigourney Weaver, who was playing Dian Fossey in a forthcoming movie, showed up in a limousine, looking dazzling in a red wool dress. She was so tall that she almost had to duck under the door frame as she entered the old house. Weaver was in Toronto to reshoot some of the earlier scenes of the movie, set in Kentucky, where Fossey had been a physiotherapist. The director was filming the retakes in Canada because it looked like the U.S. and was a cheaper to place to film. Farley and Claire were flattered that Sigourney had taken a few hours out of her packed schedule in Toronto to visit them.

Sigourney was every bit as charming as they remembered her from their first meeting the previous April. She said Farley's information in the spring had been a great help to her in playing the role of Dian in the film, which was released in September 1988 as *Gorillas in the Mist*. The film would garner five Academy Award nominations and earn Weaver the Golden Globe Award for best actress.

Her brief visit was a delight. They had dinner at the Carlyle, which was great fun. "We all had filet, lots of wine and lots of talk," Claire reported. Farley was energized as they talked about Dian, Sigourney, the nature of fame, and Canada, which Sigourney loved. "This lady is an aristocrat, the best of the best Americans—unaffected, well-educated, well intentioned and very nice," Claire observed. "Would that they had more political clout in their own land."

Claire knew Sigourney would be great in the role of Dian. She even looked like Fossey, but prettier. "And she was full of tales about the gorillas, the very same ones that Dian knew so well." Time flew by. When they arrived back from the Carlyle, Sigourney's limousine was waiting for her. After expressing warm wishes and hopes for another visit soon, she was whisked back to the Sutton Place Hotel and the work still ahead of her.

In the spring of 1988, Farley and Claire took a road trip to Palgrave to visit Sandy, who had become an executive producer at CBC Radio, and his wife, Kim. They spent the afternoon sitting in the garden surrounded by flowering lilacs. After breakfast the next morning, the four of them went to visit Frances, who lived nearby. Sandy saw his mother about once a week, but the visits were usually short.

Frances gave them a warm welcome. Claire always felt odd going there. The house still had mementos of Fran and Farley's years together as husband and wife—there were pictures and books everywhere.

Frances offered Claire and Kim some earrings she no longer wore, the screw-on variety, which was now hard to find. Claire did not have pierced ears and gladly accepted two pairs.

"We saw all of the house, the first time I'd been beyond the living room and the kitchen. There was the room, and the bed, which F. once occupied," Claire wrote in her journal. There were the two tiny rooms at the back, which had housed the two boys when they were growing up. An avid reader, Frances had volunteered at the school and the local library while the boys were being raised. She remained in her house in Palgrave until her death in 2001.

After Farley and Claire left Ontario and returned to Brick Point, their first visit was an evening with long-time friends Ervin and Janice Touesnard and their children. Claire recorded in a 1988 diary entry just how drawn she was to the life they enjoyed as a big, close family: "I'd give everything I have to trade places with them . . . They're surrounded by brothers, sisters, nieces, nephews, aunts, cousins and parents on both sides. As well as their own kids. I have absolutely no one. No one." But she did have Farley, and as she noted in her journal, he was becoming nicer to her as he grew older.

In early September 1988, Farley was hard at work. He flew off to the Magdalen Islands to begin filming a two-part episode for the CBC TV series *The Nature of Things*, based on his book *Sea of Slaughter*. Claire knew the film mattered to Farley far more than the one he had done on Siberia, or even *The New North*, a documentary on seven Arctic nations that came out in 1987. Farley won a Gemini Award for his documentary script. While he was gone, Claire worked daily on her new manuscript, incorporating editorial suggestions from Adrienne Clarkson, who had just left Brick Point. Farley phoned several times to say that the filming was going well and they were actually a day ahead of schedule.

Although publicity trips were often gruelling, Farley was a seasoned professional and handled them well. On September 22, 1988, he and Claire left home in Cape Breton at 1:30 p.m., dropped their pets at a dog motel in Marble Mountain, and then headed to the Halifax airport, boarding at 9:50 p.m. for a flight to St. John's and then on to Heathrow Airport in England. Once landed, they stood in the immigration line for over an hour. To Farley's delight, the young man at the immigration counter opened his passport and said, "Ah ha, I have read several of your books and seen two of your movies."

Farley and Claire were picked up by two promotion agents and whisked off through London traffic to their Knightsbridge-district hotel, a short walk from Hyde Park Corner. Farley barely had time to register and drop his bags. They were running late, and Farley was scheduled to do a BBC broadcast at 11:30 a.m., an hour-long program about Dian Fossey. "It went well and was quite pleasant," he reported. Later, he did a fifteen-minute promotional video for his book in one take. The first workday ended, and Farley and Claire were in bed by 10 p.m. after an excellent meal in the small hotel dining room. They slept through until 10:30 the next morning. Although arduous, the publicity trip to England, Scotland, and Ireland was a rollicking success.

In September 1989, Farley did an unusual thing: he turned down an offer of $925,000 from Bantam and Key Porter to write a three-volume autobiography. Farley had always preferred to earn royalties from published books, rather than take large advances for books he had not yet written. He was also concerned about what would happen to his backlist if he left McClelland & Stewart for a new publisher.

A happy and creatively productive period continued. In 1991, Farley began work on *My Father's Son: Memories of War and Peace,* which would be published in 1992. *Born Naked* was published in 1993, followed by *Aftermath* in 1995. Claire was also hard at work on her own writing. Even if she stayed up with friends talking until 3 a.m., she got up the next morning and went down to her office by 9 a.m. Her efforts were rewarded, for Lily Miller, Claire's editor at M&S, wrote to her on December 20, 1988: "As I already mentioned to you, your manuscript of POMP AND CIRCUMSTANCES was a delight to read—entertaining, informative and charming. I really think it will be a hit."

In 1989, Claire published an account of the viceregal tour of Scandinavia she and Farley had taken with Governor General Ed Schreyer and his wife, Lily, in 1981. Farley had done some editing for Claire, and she wrote that "he is my very best helper and critic. I'd be sunk without him."

They used Indian Summer, the old family cottage built by Angus, to get away from the phone calls, meetings, and steady stream of visitors to their doorstep in Port Hope. Claire loved the dumpy old cottage that asked nothing of her. There, she could read all through a rainy day and listen to music, and she delighted in pumping water and using a cold outhouse in winter. She also enjoyed "just looking out at trees in winter, the dark sky over Lake Ontario in winter."

20 | Saturday Night and Sunday Morning

IN 1996, FARLEY WAS THE AUTHOR of thirty-four books and was at the height of his powers, a known crusader for Indigenous rights and the environment. He took up the cause of "the others": whales, polar bears, seals, birds—any creature that had the misfortune of trying to share Nature with humans. He had been anti–nuclear bomb, against the Vietnam War, and for Canadian independence from the U.S. when it was dangerous to hold such beliefs. *Never Cry Wolf* had been made into a Disney movie.

On May 3, 1996, *Saturday Night* published a cover story on Farley Mowat, depicting him as Pinocchio with a long nose with the heading: "Oops! A Real Whopper." The title page said, "Farley Mowat shocked the world with his best-selling accounts of life in the North. Now, from the archives, comes the real story." The inside photo was even worse than the cover shot. The story accused Mowat of lying about starving Inuit and wolves in his early books about the North, which had made his international reputation. But the real impact was from the cover, which caused a sensation, even for those who didn't read the article.

A major Canadian publication was going after the reputation of a major Canadian writer who had sold millions of books worldwide, many of them based on his experiences in the North, which were considerable.

In a journal entry dated April 3, 1996, Claire had noted a call to Farley from John Goddard, "the journalist from *Saturday Night* who is trying to write a nasty article about Farley." Farley was curt with him, she wrote, and told him this sounded like an FBI investigation. "I hate to think what they are going to do with him. SATURDAY NIGHT is now a neoconservative magazine, owned by Conrad Black, that sour, verbose, billionaire who despises anyone on the political left."

On Easter Sunday, April 7, 1996, Farley had planned to go to church with Claire, something he rarely did. In the morning he said, "I've got a problem. I can't walk straight. It's like I was drunk without the fun." He told her to go off to church. He'd be fine. "No way," Claire said.

Claire drove Farley to the Port Hope hospital. At 10:30 Easter Sunday morning, it was deserted except for one other patient, so Farley was seen right away. The good news was that he hadn't had a heart attack, and the young doctor prescribed a strong aspirin. He believed it might be an embolism. Farley needed further tests, however, and he was to see his family doctor as soon as possible. They drove home and Farley insisted that Claire go to a planned lunch at the Carlyle with friends. He wanted to rest.

On Easter Monday, a family friend, a retired doctor, came to check on Farley. He suspected that Farley had had a transient ischemic attack, a brief mini-stroke. On Tuesday, their family doctor made a house call and said it was important that Farley see a neurologist as soon as possible. They arranged an appointment in Peterborough on Thursday, April 11. After the examination, a diagnosis was made of Wallenberg syndrome, caused by a brief stroke. Treatment would include drugs, blood tests, and a CAT scan. A bit of good news: the current symptoms might diminish with time. It was a relief when the doctor said it was all right for Farley to go to Cape Breton, where he was to be honoured at the Cape Breton University convocation in May.

Fortunately, the book Claire was writing, *Last Summer in Louisbourg*, was almost finished. It was at the point where their executive assistant, Mary Talbot, could type a first draft and mail it to Claire at Brick Point. During this time, Farley was regularly talking on the phone to his publisher, Anna Porter, about the pending article in *Saturday Night*.

"It was terrible not knowing what was going to be said, or implied... We know that the journalist John Goddard was out to get him, that he had an agenda of some sort," Claire wrote in her journal. "Anna managed to get a look at an advance copy through a connection at *Saturday Night*. Despite Farley's best efforts to play down the article, Farley is upset about this impending attack I know. He shrugs and says it doesn't matter, but I know at heart, that it is bothering him."

But there was also some very good news in the family. Claire wrote to Harold Horwood: "Our grandchild Justin is thriving. The last time we saw him, just a few weeks ago, he continues to look like Farley!" Sandy and Kim's son was now almost five months old.

The right was on a roll in 1996. Stephen Harper took charge of the influential National Citizens Coalition and mastered the use of U.S.-style attack ads. The Reform Party was gaining strength and would win sixty seats in June 1997 to become the official opposition. When publisher Conrad Black hired an editor to launch the *National Post,* he would choose his *Saturday Night* magazine editor Kenneth Whyte. Whyte had also worked at the *Alberta Report,* a catalyst for the rise of western social conservatism that led to the founding of the Reform Party in 1987.

Taking out a major environmentalist who was one of the first writers in Canada to champion the rights of Indigenous people would certainly be good for the cause.

On April 9, 1996, just two days after his health scare, Farley had written a registered letter to Ken Whyte telling him that in November 1995, his publicist at Key Porter had asked him to do an interview with a writer from *Saturday Night,* John Goddard, about his new book, *Aftermath*. Farley had agreed to do an interview on that understanding. Since Goddard had already approached *Saturday Night* with his story proposal, dated September 14, 1995, this arguably implied bad faith, when the interview was supposed to be about *Aftermath*.

The interview was to have taken place in Toronto, but Goddard had called to say he was working on a deadline and had to see Farley at once. Wanting to be helpful, Farley and Claire invited him to Port Hope for the day. Then Farley was told the article would be about his entire literary career.

Subsequently, Goddard urgently requested a second interview at the Key Porter offices in Toronto, in the presence of Farley's publicist.

"What ensued was not an interview," Farley wrote, "but a taped inter-rogation during which I was accused . . . of misrepresenting aspects of *People of the Deer*, and was forcefully urged to admit as much."

Farley wrote to Whyte that on the evening of April 4, 1996, God-dard had phoned, "requiring me to account for my actions in central Keewatin during June 1947." Goddard also told Mowat he had retained the services of a private investigator. Farley noted that it was evident that Goddard wanted "to charge me with having played fast and loose with the truth in *People of the Deer*," and no effort or expense had been spared.

Farley also commented that "*People of the Deer* was published 45 years ago to expose the unconscionable and barbarous treatment of a group of Canada's Inuit at the hands of government, the missions, the RCMP, the traders, and, in the last analysis, all those of us who permitted this atrocious human situation to exist." The book was not written as an anthropological text: "It was an activist tract designed to reveal, and blow the lid off, a situation amounting to something close to genocide."

In a foreword to a 1975 edition of the book, which he enclosed in his letter to Whyte, Farley explained that he had altered some things, such as names and places, and gave the reasons why he was forced to do so. "I believe I have been manipulated and misled by your writer, but assume he is only doing what he is paid to do. So be it." Farley asked that the photos, taken on the clear understanding they would be used for the publicity of *Aftermath*, not be used.

On April 9, Farley sent a copy of his letter to Ken Whyte to his editor, Susan Renouf, and told her that "these hyaenas are still trying to nip the ass end of the old lion. It's quite clear that *Saturday Night*, whether or not they are acting directly under Conrad Black's instruc-tions, are out to get me." Farley also confided that he had just had a minor embolism and wasn't feeling at the peak of perfection, "but the old lion still has a growl left in him."

Farley then wrote to the McMaster University archives, asking why Goddard was given access to his personal journals and letters when most of the material was supposed to be embargoed. He wanted an explanation of how this had happened. On May 6, 1996, McMaster issued a press release saying that Goddard was not given access to letters, journals, or papers that were supposed to remain private. "Goddard saw nothing that Mr. Mowat had not already given his permission for the public to see." The Goddard article had quoted extensively from what Goddard described as "journals" written by Mowat in 1947 and 1948. He actually saw what Farley had referred to as "field notes" and "log books." His "journals" were locked in a vault. "They have not been seen by Goddard or anyone else," the release said.

The May issue of *Saturday Night* was distributed with the Toronto edition of the *Globe and Mail* on May 3, 1996, and would be on the newsstands in a couple of days. Both Farley and Claire knew it was going to happen, but the reality was still a shock. "We never had a gutter press, or the sort that existed in Britain where politicians and the royal family are spied upon and their private lives held up to ridicule," Claire wrote. "We now have this in Canada, being done cleverly under the banner of a magazine that used to be thoughtful, reflective, respectable and a little boring... Their main theme is to discredit anyone on the ideological Left, to promote neoconservatism and the sanctity of the Corporate Takeover of the World. I can see why Farley Mowat would be an obvious target."

The phone rang constantly. Calls came from the media and supporters who were outraged by the article. Farley and Claire appreciated their answering machine more than ever.

To show their support, Sandy, Kim, and Justin came for a visit the day after the article appeared. "Justin still looks like Farley!" Claire noted. "Maybe he'll change as time goes by—but it makes me feel so good to look at him, to know that some fragment of Farley will live on; a genetic fragment." Nothing of her would ever exist after her death. Claire also noted that Sandy and Kim were wonderful parents.

Sandy gave his father some advice about what he should and should not say in his reply to the article, which he intended to send to the *Globe*. Long-time friend and fellow writer Ronald Wright had also given some advice the day before. What had upset Farley the most was that God-dard had left the impression that people did not starve and that there wasn't a program to cut the wolf population.

On May 6, the *Globe and Mail* ran Farley's reply to *Saturday Night*. He noted that in 1952, when he was attacked in *Saturday Night* for his exposure of the sometimes fatal neglect of the Inuit by the Arctic estab-lishments, he was given equal space in the same issue to reply. This time he was not offered that opportunity. Farley was also upset that Goddard had used private material in the archives that had caused con-siderable anguish to his first wife, including information that was not in the books. He said a full account of his travels in the North from 1947 to 1953 would be the subject of a future book.

As Ronald Wright notes in the following paragraph, Farley had brought information about the Ihalmiut in the North to the attention of the public for the first time through his books, which had a profound effect, inspiring the work of others, such as David Suzuki and Wright himself, who took up the cause for Indigenous rights.

Wright's letter to the *Globe* was published on May 7, 1996: "What (or who) can have possessed *Saturday Night* to mount a squalid attack on Farley Mowat's work of half a century ago? The books in ques-tion—Mr. Mowat's landmark *People of the Deer, Never Cry Wolf,* and *The Desperate People*—were fully debated at the time... Could it be that the real purpose is the attempted character assassination of a great Canadian who remains a sharp thorn in the surprisingly tender flesh of the Jurassic right? The only reputation likely to be damaged by such a transparently desperate piece of muckraking is what lit-tle remains of *Saturday Night's* good name since it was colonized by Conrad Black."

On May 18, George Galt—the former senior literary editor of *Sat-urday Night* magazine, who had left when Conrad Black took over—wrote in the *Globe and Mail* that Mowat was neither a journalist nor a science writer:

"In the books under scrutiny Mowat employs the techniques of dra-matic narrative. On some pages he is writing in the first person, mixing memory and impression and sharp observation with his passionately held views on the natural world. He binds it all with a powerful narrative voice." For years critics had accused him of writing subjective non-fiction, but readers kept reading him because they did not see dramatic licence as fabrication.

"First-person narratives are by definition filtered through heart and memory, two faculties not known for infallible factual precision," Galt continued. Dramatic narratives may "exhibit a polemical streak in which hard evidence plays second fiddle to impassioned and lyrical expression. That may make Mowat a romantic. It does *not* make him a fraud." Galt noted that Herodotus wrote *The Histories,* the first great non-fiction narrative, in the fifth century BC. He also had his critics, but we are still reading him.

Claire was worried about Farley's state of health. She would always wonder if the incident had brought on his mild stroke. The good news was that he was gradually improving. He needed a cane but was once again walking the dog. There was a welcome outpouring of support for Farley, including calls from broadcaster and humorist Stuart McLean, June Callwood, and many people he didn't even know.

The CBC Radio show *Morningside* aired a debate with author Maggie Siggins taking Farley's side and editor Robert Fulford speaking against him. Journalist and author Silver Donald Cameron later remembered doing a script and interviews for a *Life and Times* CBC documentary about Farley in the fall of 1996. In one scene, Farley was splitting beans from his garden at Brick Point. As he split a bean, he sang out, "Robert Fulford, take that!"

Michael Enright of the current-affairs program *As It Happens* interviewed John Goddard and asked why he had written the piece. Goddard said he had read Farley as a young man, then reread some of his work when he lived in Yellowknife and didn't believe it. Claire had darker thoughts: "I don't know what his agenda was, or is. I think he's trying to heighten his own profile, like some nut case who assassinates a pope or a president." Farley was almost seventy-five; Goddard was forty-five. Claire noted that most of the people who had the knife put into them by *Saturday Night* were older: Mother Teresa, Irving Layton, Earle Birney, Jean Chrétien, for example. And now Farley.

Some thought Farley should sue *Saturday Night*, but he decided against it. It was not his style. A decade earlier, he had written to Harold Horwood, "Never fall into the hands of the legal trade. Both sides batten on you with unique impartiality."

On May 8, 1996, their great friend and neighbour David Brooks drove Farley and Claire to the airport for the flight to Nova Scotia. At the newsstand, when Claire saw a pile of *Saturday Night* magazines, she felt angry that she had been nice to Goddard when he had come to their house. "I should have put poison in his soup if only I had known what he was up to," she joked.

Claire was ecstatic when they landed in Halifax and a friend picked them up for the three-hour drive back to Brick Point. "We were here. We were away from the recent horrors. Farley was alive and reasonably well. We had a whole summer ahead of us . . . I felt I was coming home. So did Farley." As they passed by Antigonish, it began to snow. Snow in May. "I loved the barren look of the late winter landscape," Claire wrote. "It could snow all summer for all I care."

The house looked wonderful. They poured a drink to celebrate their homecoming and carried some of their luggage upstairs. "Imagine being here this early. Not even a trace of the rhodora to come, no foliage on the Tamarac trees, only the skeletons of the wild rose bushes that abound. I was so happy, so relieved." Claire was pleased that they would be there for the Canadian census. The envelope was already on the table.

Farley loved getting things done at Brick Point—gardening, fixing things, building—but Claire was still worried about him. "And it turned out to be the best place possible, to be here. He got better and better as the weeks passed." On Saturday, May 11, Farley received an honorary doctorate from Cape Breton University, an institution that *Maclean's* ranked as Canada's poorest in endowments and resources. Farley also had an honorary doctorate from Canada's wealthiest university in endowments, the University of Toronto. He had nine medals, and now nine honorary degrees.

Farley's keynote speech generated a lot of affection from the audience, but Claire worried that his voice sounded stressed in a way it had not the previous fall, before the article. The university presented Farley with a huge birthday cake topped with a howling wolf made of icing sugar.

Claire prepared a small dinner party for Farley's seventy-fifth birthday, on May 12. Activist and Green Party leader Elizabeth May and her daughter, Victoria Cate, neighbours Ervin and Janice Touesnard, and Silver Don Cameron and his son, Mark, attended. The mood was subdued. Only a month earlier, Cameron's beloved wife, Lulu, had died after a long illness.

There was, however, some lighthearted chatter about the dreadful article about Farley. "They kidded him about it, which was the right approach," Claire recalled. It was a dismal, rainy night, but no one cared. "Farley and I were so glad to be here." Claire treasured every day they had together. She loved the Atlantic provinces and dearly wished she had family there.

A week later, they dropped in to Ervin and Janice's house for a visit; family and friends were there for supper. No one had seen the magazine, which had not yet arrived at the local drugstore where it was sold. Friends had heard the debate on *Morningside* and followed the news, but they did not take it seriously. Claire observed that "the hot air emanating from Toronto is diffused by the time it gets to the Maritimes."

When Claire finally read the article, she realized it wasn't all that bad, "just a catalogue of minor, nit-picking insinuations." What was damaging was the cover picture of Farley as Pinocchio and a photo inside in which he looked sneaky and arrogant. And, of course, there was the title: "A Real Whopper." Claire believed, correctly, that many people would conclude that Farley was a liar without actually reading the article. Friends kept calling from Ontario about supportive articles in the *Globe* and the *Star*. Farley told Claire he could put it behind him now. On May 25 it snowed.

Claire spent the month writing letters, making sure that everyone who had written or phoned with a message of support was answered. She wanted people to know that Farley was all right and that the agenda of the magazine was to discredit the left. She wouldn't be surprised if they went after David Suzuki in the near future. Or Bob Rae. Or Alexa McDonough. Or Elizabeth May.

A letter from a friend wishing Farley congratulations on his feast day included an injection of humour. "Bill thinks you must be having a good chuckle at the thought of the forests that will now be preserved due to the cancellation of all those *Saturday Night* subscriptions."

There was also a letter from a lawyer who had roomed with Farley during the 1966 Spence Bay murder trial of Shooyook and Aiyoot, two young Inuit men charged with the death of Soosee, who had been driven mad and become a danger to her tribe. He had had the honour of being thrown into a bathtub with Farley at "the great shirt-ripping party after the verdict. I have the cut off end of your suspenders framed on my memento wall." He said that *Saturday Night* was in keeping with the "Canadian obsession with hurling acid in the face of its heroes." Farley, Pierre Berton, and Peter Newman had awakened Canadians to their own country. "I, for one, don't give a damn how much literary license you might have taken along the way... I know you are not very tall, but take comfort in the fact that at least one of your readers knows that everyone at *Saturday Night* is a lot smaller than you."

Artist Ron Bolt may have said it best in a letter to the editor of the *Globe and Mail*. "For fifty years, Farley Mowat has been needling the pompous and the powerful, focusing public awareness on environmental issues and raging against the stupidity of war. He has done this with style, wit and passion. Factual or otherwise, his is a much needed voice in an often complacent country. *Saturday Night* used to have a similar kind of voice until it saved its skin by selling its soul. The unbalanced and personally hurtful article on Mowat raises one question. So what? His books remain, his influence on the young is invaluable, and he continues to afflict the comfortable."

Another supporter agreed in a personal letter to Farley. "Screw the critics. I started my 'relationship' with your stories of life in the North when I was a child in London, Ontario. '*Lost in the Barrens*' hauled me out of the Wonder Bread conservatism of a life insurance town into the world of caribou and canoes and bug infested tundra. You gave a kid something to dream about, and I am grateful. Later in life I became a park naturalist in the Rockies, tracking wolves and bears, wriggling through the mud to find rare Calypso orchids. I think I have an idea what kept you warm writing '*Never Cry Wolf*'... I'm sufficiently satisfied from your writing and experience to know you speak with an honest voice... Thanks for your work. Stay proud and raise your kilt to any who would wish to bring you down."

A letter came from a field biologist who had spent two years alone on a remote lake. "I certainly know that your books are a wonderfully accurate representation of northern life and the work and passion of biologists. I don't care how 'authentically' you arrived at those insights, but you did and I am glad you did. In February 1981, I was flown into a remote lake in northern Saskatchewan to conduct research on northern pike. With 12 sled dogs, a tent, canoe and pile of assorted junk, I lived alone at this lake until sledding out in April of 1983. The resulting M.Sc. thesis... is no work of literature, but the field work follows the theme of your book '*Never Cry Wolf*' to a tee... Your writing has shown this natural world and its problems to the public in far better style and language than any of us could ever hope. Thank you."

An undated card made a boxing analogy. "From everything I've seen or heard and despite a cheap sucker punch before the opening bell it's been no contest; Mowat all ten rounds with none to Goddard or Black... Certainly everyone I've talked to has judged the Goddard 'piece' as vindictive and fatuous and not worth the trouble of reading."

Hugh Murray wrote to John Goddard, and copied Farley. Murray had admired Goddard as a journalist but was very upset by the *Saturday Night* piece. "Your piece on Farley Mowat in *Saturday Night* devastated me. What was your point?... No record had urgent need of being set straight, and even people who like flogging dead horses have the decency to wait till the horse is dead." Murray searched for a legitimate motive for the story, and all he could come up with was money. "The article came across to me as so mean spirited it saddened me beyond words, not just for Mowat, who is well able to look after himself, but for you and the career you might have had."

On May 28, 1996, journalist John Bacher wrote a rebuttal to *Saturday Night* for *Now Magazine*. He pointed out that documents quoted by Goddard actually confirmed that Mowat did visit the area and had reliable Inuit informants. Formerly classified documents in the recently published scholarly book *Tammarniit* revealed similar government arrogance and indifference in the eastern Arctic. "Mowat's writings in the 1950s were prophetic," Bacher said. "They popularized the findings of experts whose works would have otherwise been known by only a handful of specialists. Rather than ridicule the prophet, connections should be made to his profound vision and the many contemporary struggles to defend a nature revering way of life based on millions of caribou migrating over thousands of miles."

BY THE END OF JUNE, Claire remained worried about Farley. His legs were giving out, and he felt weak and wondered if it was his medication. He also admitted that he was depressed. Claire treasured every day and every night.

By mid-July, Farley was feeling much better. He even installed a new system of eavestroughs and rain barrels. Although Claire did not like him going up the ladder, it was a joy to see him so enthusiastic and pleased with what he was doing.

At the end of July, they went chanterelle hunting on a hillside across from their beach. In August, Ervin and Janice organized a corn roast on the shore, the local equivalent of a cocktail party, with simple food and unpretentious people. The important thing was just to be there with each other, and there was no name-dropping or attention paid to expensive clothes or flashy watches. As Claire observed, "This is a nearly classless society."

The visitors that summer came in like the tide. Harold Horwood brought Farley and Claire an assortment of annuals from his garden in Annapolis Royal. He also helped them dig out the irises he had given them six or seven years before, to replant them with more space. "Crusty, grumpy Harold—I always enjoy having him here for a visit, even though at times it gets a bit tense," Claire wrote in her journal. "Just having two males in the same house, especially two authors, brings on a kind of friction." They saved a nest of baby red squirrels that Marc Touesnard, the son of Ervin and Janice, had found in the manure pile and brought to the house. Farley and Harold knew just what to do, and the mother moved them to a new nest.

September was a month for new beginnings. Silver Don Cameron had a new lady in his life, British Columbian author and journalist Marjorie Simmins. Farley and Claire met her on a very cold, wet, and stormy Thanksgiving weekend. They sat in front of the fire after dining on *coq au vin*, eggplant, rice, and cucumber salad, with upside-down cake for dessert. "She's lovely," Claire wrote in her diary. "I knew the moment I met her. So did Farley."

Claire looked forward to knowing Marjorie, who was lively and smart, as well as good-looking. "I tried to tell Farley that what Marjorie wants, primarily, from her relationship with Don is a lot more than just sex. As a woman she needs companionship, protection, respectability, a place in the sun, and—children, all of which matter as much as mere screwing. Farley wouldn't hear of it. It has taken me a lifetime to fathom the male agenda and try to understand, intellectually, how much the mere act of fucking means to a man . . . He wins every time just by his fury and anger. My father did exactly the same thing. Are all men the same?"

On September 19 a film crew arrived at Brick Point for three and a half days to do interviews for a documentary about Farley's life. Silver Don Cameron was the interviewer. "It was reassuring to have Don as the script writer-interviewer, to know he wouldn't stab Farley in the back. Ever since the SATURDAY NIGHT article last May we will never be so trusting again," wrote Claire, whose photograph albums from Port Hope were used in the film. "I can't wait to see the film and see what they used. Goodness I've spent a lot of my life just keeping track of our life together—what with this endless journal and all those photo albums. I wonder why I have done it? Truly—most people don't record their daily lives the way I have. Why did I?"

On October 26, their neighbour Marc drove them to the airport in Halifax for the trip back to Port Hope. Their nephews Brian and Matthew Mowat met them at the airport in Toronto for the drive home. Sandy, Kim, and baby Justin, who was one week from his first birthday, also arrived for a short visit at the airport. Farley took everyone out to the Railside restaurant for dinner when they got back to Port Hope.

In November, they visited Dr. Tovich, Farley's neurologist. He had some good news. The Wallenberg syndrome symptoms were almost completely gone, and Farley was prescribed a daily mild aspirin. They had lunch with Ron Wright and his wife, Janice, and talked about the takeover of the media by the forces of fascism and censorship. "How strange to live in an age of Lies," Claire noted in her diary.

On November 23 and 24, they had a visit from Sandy, Kim, and Justin. "How wonderful. Sometimes I have to pinch myself that it really happened, that they are now parents." Justin was now thirteen months old and still resembled Farley more than his parents. Claire was amazed at how much they loved him. She had obtained a two-year loan of a crib from David Brooks's family, which was set up at Farley's office for Justin to use. "Farley is a wonderful grandfather and has far more rapport with the baby than I do—making funny faces, playing little finger games. I've never known the love of an infant which is very sad for me."

That month, they were also invited to dinner with Governor General Roméo LeBlanc and his wife, Diana, who wanted to meet Farley. He and Claire had not been to the residence since 1984. The place had been redecorated during the Jeanne Sauvé years and looked even more beautiful. In the sitting room, the paintings of Colville, Lemieux, Riopelle, and Milne had been replaced by nineteenth-century portraits of the wives of past Governors General.

LeBlanc apologized for being five minutes late. There was a crisis upstairs; his wife's sister was visiting with her six-month-old baby, and the baby was crying. "I liked Romeo and Diana from the start," Claire wrote. "Unpretentious and smart, both of them." Diana told Farley she had enjoyed reading Claire's book *Pomp and Circumstances,* with Claire as lady-in-waiting to the Governor General's wife, Lily Schreyer.

Ed Schreyer invited them to go to Montreal the next day to have lunch with Pierre Trudeau at his club, but they decided it would be too difficult to rearrange train tickets and reservations. Claire wrote in her journal that she would always admire Trudeau: "a man of principles and intellect the likes of which we have not had as prime minister since he stepped down in 1984." Farley and Claire were also planning a birthday party for Lily on Friday in Port Hope.

Despite the *Saturday Night* fiasco, Farley's work was going well. Claire wrote that "Farley is on a roll with his work, his book about 'Albans,'" the pre-Viking Europeans who Farley believed came to North America. "He usually is, in December. He's hitting his stride, just when I have to deal with bloody Christmas and all that entails, he acts as if he'd never heard of Christmas and just wants to get down to serious work." *The Farfarers* would be published in 1998.

From December 24 to 28, 1996, they attended six parties in five days, the process that linked them to other people in the community. The literary anthropologist in Claire observed, "I suppose it's no different than carnival time in Rio or the religious feasts of the middle ages in Europe."

Despite the snow and traffic, Sandy, Kim, and Justin arrived to join John Mowat, Farley's adopted brother, and the rest of the family for dinner on Boxing Day. Claire had been preparing the dinner for twelve for three days. Everyone in the family had talked to one another and gotten along. "I like people to get along with one another," Claire wrote.

On December 27, 1996, they attended a lively house party with sumptuous food until 3 a.m. Claire talked with an eighty-year-old English lady from Herefordshire who said the party seemed like a scene out of *Brideshead Revisited*.

The following day, Farley was too tired to go to yet another party and stayed home, but Claire went. The next morning, she went to church but was exhausted and glad there were no more events to attend. She had a nap in the afternoon, a dark, wet day in which nothing much got done. "Farley was feeling better though, and got on with his latest book."

They had a quiet New Year's Eve. "Nobody over a certain age bothers with New Year's Eve anymore," Claire noted. "The best part for us was the television—two solid hours of Canadian comedy. First The Royal Canadian Air Farce followed by This Hour Has 22 Minutes. Thank God for our own humour. The best New Years Eve we could imagine. It was very cold—0 degrees F. with lots of snow—the kind of weather I love."

OVER TWENTY YEARS before the *Saturday Night* article appeared, Farley had written a preface for his collection of papers at McMaster University, dated August 22, 1974. "A bit like writing one's own obituary while sitting in a cemetery." He writes that he does not trust facts. "My experiences in many fields of human activity suggest that facts generally conceal, or at least becloud as much as, or more than, they reveal. They are far too easily contrived and, once contrived, are treated as sacrosanct in a society dedicated to the deification of data." Farley believed in a subjective approach rather than an objective one. "My battle cry has been: Never Let the Facts Interfere With the Truth."

As a result, the academic world regarded him as a queer fish. "I am convinced that, in the unlikely event some future researcher may try to discover the real me, he will be so misled by all those facts that the essential Mowat will get quite lost in the process." His métier was between fact and fiction, and he would not take the easy way out by writing fiction.

"The truth was... that I was simply ahead of my time. When Truman Capote finally 'discovered' the middle ground it became respectable and acquired a name so that, at last, it could be charted. The void I had been swimming in for lo, these many years, became known as subjective non-fiction. At last I had been pinned down like the somewhat tattered butterfly I was."

He still received plaintive requests from librarians asking to which categories his books belonged. "This pleases me. It proves that I can still wiggle even though pinned to the board... I was content from the first to be a simple saga man, a teller of tales which, preferably, had a moral of some sort."

The Ihalmiut whom Farley wrote about in *People of the Deer* were forcibly removed from their camps at Ennadai Lake in the 1950s. Despite their deep knowledge and attachment to the land, which some consider the most beautiful place in Nunavut, they were removed from their homes and relocated five times in one decade to unfamiliar lands. Unable to hunt, they suffered starvation and exposure. During an anthropological workshop held in Arviat in May 2006, survivors of the camps spoke about their memories, some for the first time. The resulting paper concluded that "the relocation effectively became a deportation causing great economic and cultural distress as well as loss of life to the Ahiarmiut." (The modern spelling of *Ihalmiut* is *Ahiarmiut*.)

Job Muqyunnik, one of those evicted, recalled that it was "the saddest time of my life. It was around May in 1949 [perhaps 1950]. The Qallunaat [white man] came to the weather station at Ennadai Lake. They had a large vehicle up there. The bulldozer came to our tent. The driver told us to leave our tent so we went out. He went back to his vehicle and drove over our tent, back and forth. He broke everything we had. He drove over them and destroyed everything. That was the hardest time of my life because we didn't have anything to survive anymore." The people were ordered onto a yellow two-engine plane by a man with a stick. They could not speak the language, and they were not told where they were going or why. "He said that we were garbage. That's all I remember. He said everything was garbage." They were flown to an island, and the women started to cry, knowing they might not survive. They had no axes, no knives, no place to sleep.

According to Inuk elder Mary Anowtalik, who was a child at the time, they used trees as shelters because they didn't have anything else. People started to get sick. Four of the elders died, and the others were unable to give them a proper burial. They spent eight months on the island and knew they would die that winter if they stayed. It took them three months to walk back to Ennadai Lake on foot, only to face relocation once again in 1957.

In September 2018, seventy years after Farley first brought the world's attention to the Ihalmiut, the people who didn't exist, they and their descendants received a $5 million settlement from the federal government. They were also recognized as a distinct group of Inuit.

Four months after the settlement, on January 22, 2019, the Ihalmiut also received a formal apology from the Honourable Carolyn Bennett, the minister of Crown-Indigenous relations, on behalf of the government and all Canadians. The special ceremony was held in Arviat, once known as Eskimo Point. Bennett called it "a dark chapter in our history" and apologized, saying, "We are sorry. Mamiapugut."

She said the relocation had been carried out "without explanation, without consultation and without consent." The only assistance they had came from Dene hunters in the area, who shared some food, even though they had been traditional enemies of the Ihalmiut.

Survivors had walked for three months through wind, ice, and snow to return home, where "they knew the lands and waters," Bennett said. "The relocations of the Ahiarmiut between 1950 and 1960 were misguided, mishandled, and tragic . . . we are sorry that the Ahiarmiut suffered so immensely—experiencing indignity, starvation and death—as a result of our actions." A colonial mindset "ignored your deep ties to the lands and the wisdom gleaned from your ancestors."

News reports of the settlement noted that Farley Mowat had first drawn attention to their plight in *People of the Deer*.

On September 10, 2018, Ron Wright wrote to Claire that he had been listening to the CBC in the car "and heard that Ottawa has finally forked over some millions in compensation . . . to descendants of the Ihalmiut whom Farley wrote about in *People of the Deer*. The news story mentioned how influential he and the book had been. I let out a cheer!"

Claire replied to Ron on September 18. "Thanks so much for your letter . . . I did see and hear media items about the Inuit settlement and they mentioned Farley's name. If only he had lived to witness this. He might have felt there was some justice in the country. It is just terrible the way those people were moved around like pawns. The settlement isn't all that much when you consider that many generations have been born since re-locations took place back in the 50's and 60's. At least it's an acknowledgement of wrongdoing."

21 | The Long Sleep

FARLEY MOWAT BEGAN 2014 as he had so many other years in his long and remarkable life. He was working on a new book, bringing morning tea and the newspaper to his Golden Girl, and planning a return to Cape Breton in the spring. He was also regularly entertaining the host of friends who came to the door of their home in Port Hope for a drink or a talk, or just to say hello to the famous couple.

The new book told the story of the first people who lived between the forest and the ocean in Britain, the Orkney and Shetland beach people—what he called the "strand lopers," early humans who, while hunting and gathering on land, also used the resources of the sea close to their beach or strand. Farley closely followed the work of archaeologists like Patricia Sutherland and Thomas E. Lee, and he believed it was possible that Europeans had come to North America much earlier than the Vikings—possibly in the sixth century. During research at habitation sites on Baffin Island and in Labrador, Sutherland had found evidence of yarns made from Arctic hare and white fox, indicating the presence of women, as well as tally sticks, whetstones, and the fur of a house rat not native to North America. Lee had found low-walled, boat-shaped stone structures. Roofed with an overturned boat sheathed in walrus hide, they could have been inhabited by early Europeans. Similar structures had been used in northern Britain.

Farley would have been fascinated by the recent work of international scientists who may have discovered evidence that the Solutrean people had migrated to North America from what is now France, Portugal, and Spain. The hypothesis is that during the last ice age, possibly twenty thousand years ago, people travelled along a massive ice bridge from mainland Europe, using skin boats.

Farley's book already had an editor-publisher, Susan Renouf of ECW Press. Farley had decided against publishing with McClelland & Stewart because they wanted him to work with an editor who, although excellent, had a reputation for nitpicking over every sentence. "Farley wouldn't last long with that," Claire noted. As for her opinion of the new book, she didn't quite know what to make of it.

"Of course one wonders if Farley will ever finish this damn book he's been labouring over for five years . . . I don't know if the book is good or not," she wrote. "I worry that he has laboured over it too much, that it will lack spontaneity. I suppose any book with his name on it will sell well. It's so hard to grasp the changes in the world of book publishing. There was indeed a Golden Age from about 1965 to 1990, in Canada. After that US corporations took over most of the publishers . . . Hard to recall the days of Jack McClelland and all the other high flyers."

It occurred to Claire that Farley might be the oldest author still actively working in Canada. Even Alice Munro, who won the Nobel Prize in Literature in 2013, had stopped writing, saying, "And perhaps, when you are my age, you don't wish to be alone as much as a writer has to be." Claire noted that writing books was hard work and was unrewarding.

The world of publishing wasn't the only thing changing. Each year cost Farley another irreplaceable friend—Harold Horwood, Jack McClelland, and Peter Davison were all gone now. But that didn't stop him, at age ninety-two, from strapping metal ice-clamps on his boots and making his way from the house, where the windows were frosted over in the arctic temperatures that winter, to his office, where the old Underwood typewriter was waiting for him. Even though she wondered about what sort of book it would turn out to be, Claire understood his compulsion to write. "I do think he'd be lost without it."

ONE OF THE FIRST VISITORS that year was Green Party leader Elizabeth May and her daughter, Cate. After arriving on the train from Toronto, they had tea by the fire and a lunch of Claire's homemade soup. Elizabeth and her daughter played Scrabble. Inside the box was the score of a game Elizabeth and Claire had played with Elizabeth's parents, Stephanie and John May, in 1991. Farley was Cate's godfather.

Elizabeth and Farley had been friends since the 1970s, when a teenage May led the fight against giant corporations who were spraying forests with toxins during the spruce budworm infestation in the Maritimes—Joan of Arc versus Agent Orange. They first met in person at Brick Point in the summer of 1988. When Elizabeth was in her mid-thirties and wondering if she should have a child, she turned to Farley for advice.

"He said, 'Kid, there are a lot of kinds of regrets,'" she remembered. "'You can handle a lot of regrets, but you can't handle biological regrets.' And he said Claire-a-Belle had lost that baby, but he said she couldn't face it again. She never got over really being sad." Nearly fifty years later, that memory still brought tears to Claire's eyes. She was further tormented by the thought that today, with the latest medical advancements, her baby might have been saved.

Elizabeth loved Farley like a second father. "He was a hundred percent loving, supportive, caring, generous, kind. I never saw a mean streak in Farley." He was also "really smart, but very, very kind." Asked if Farley and Claire's relationship was romantic, Elizabeth smiled. "Well, I think anyone who brings tea to bed every morning is, I think, romantic." Farley also picked wildflowers for Claire, and they still held hands on walks. One of their favourite subjects was the passion and romance of their early days on the *Happy Adventure*.

Another visitor was Louise "Lou" Pamenter, then owner of Furby House Books in Port Hope. She had bought the shop just to keep a bookstore open in town. The store had been selling first editions of Farley's books, and Lou dropped off a check for $2,700. The store received the same amount, and they were gradually winnowing down the cartons of Farley's books stored at his office, which helped keep the bookstore open. "Farley genuinely likes Lou Pamenter and he is very fussy about who he likes and trusts," Claire noted.

George and Julia Boileau dropped by to show the couple photos of the statue that George had made of Farley, now cast in bronze and to be housed at the University of Saskatchewan in Saskatoon. "Quite wonderful," Claire noted. The university wanted to make a big event of the unveiling and invited Farley and Claire to attend. Sitting in the comfort of his living room, Farley thought that would be fine, but Claire worried that he might not be able to endure the airport and the mobs of people. "I have a feeling that he might agree to go and then back out at the last minute."

On February 5, they celebrated Claire's birthday at the Railside restaurant, along with John Mowat, who almost shared a birthday with her. As they were leaving, two young women asked to have their photographs taken with Farley. They were thrilled when he agreed. "Even though he is 92 he is still the same fellow they must have read about somewhere or seen on TV, etc. I was glad this happened," Claire wrote.

The previous year had been a milestone birthday for Claire. "Last year it seemed a bit novel—turning 80. I could hardly believe it, that I'd left my 70s behind. This year it came like a thud," she observed. "I am in my eighties. It is likely the final decade of my life. People tell me I don't look my age, which is nice. But what I do know is that my energy level is that of an 81-year-old person. I get tired so easily. There is so much that I want to do before I become a senior incapacitated or dead."

Three days later, she got the best birthday present of all. Despite the winter storms, Sandy, Kim, and Justin Mowat came to celebrate Claire's big day. Among their gifts was a 1971 National Film Board documentary about Angus Mowat, narrated by Farley. "It is a beautiful film," Claire wrote. Justin taught Claire how to play a DVD in the box connected to their television, and she made notes of his directions. "The whole process is so illogical. I truly thought I'd more easily learn to play the violin."

Claire was deeply grateful for the film, and for the patience of her grandson in teaching her how to replay it. There was Angus as she knew him, making maple syrup, restoring an old boat, singing and playing his banjo. Larger than life—like Farley, Claire thought. And how fascinating it must have been for Justin to watch his great-grandfather. "It occurred to me how rare it is for anyone to see a film about his great-grandfather. I certainly never did and never even saw a photograph of any of mine."

During dinner Clair talked about how they learned of Angus's death, in 1977, when they were in the Magdalens preparing to move to Brick Point. In telling the story, Claire started to cry and could barely speak as she remembered Angus. "All of the emotions came flooding back." She had loved Farley's father, as had her mother and grandmother, "with all his quirks and his stellar personality."

ALTHOUGH 2014 WAS MUCH LIKE all of their other years together, there was a dark difference too. Farley was undergoing changes. For five years, he had been living under the shadow of an aneurysm, having decided against a new surgical procedure that was risky. He also suffered from a narrowing heart valve. He wasn't eating as much and now weighed 152 pounds, ten pounds less than his normal weight.

Their social life remained busy, but there too changes were taking place. While dining with George and Julia Boileau, Claire could see that the evening was a little too much for Farley. He was fading, picked at his food, and wanted to go home. She decided to limit visits from friends and well-wishers to two hours. "I worried about him," she wrote.

On Thursday, February 20, Farley was feeling tired and stayed in bed, forgoing the morning ritual of bringing Claire tea. Liz Prower Brooks, a neighbour and the couple's guardian angel, came to clean while Claire went to the supermarket. When she returned, Farley told her he had fainted in the bathroom. "I was alarmed. He said he thought he had taken the wrong medication that morning, that it had lowered his blood pressure too much." By suppertime he seemed himself again and ate dinner.

At 4 a.m. on Friday, February 21, Farley fainted again in the bathroom. Claire heard him call out, "Are you awake?" and rushed in to help him. Luckily, he had been able to break his fall by grabbing the door frame and the edge of the bathtub and was not injured. Claire helped him back to bed, but he still felt dizzy. They agreed that he should try to sleep and if he felt no better in the morning, they would call an ambulance. The next morning, Farley was still dizzy. For the first time in her life, Claire called 911. Sobbing into the phone, she blurted out that they needed an ambulance.

Despite freezing rain, it arrived ten minutes later. Claire stood outside to alert the paramedics to the right house and led them upstairs. "They were amazing. They asked Farley for his first name right away and spoke clearly and kindly to him. They asked for all the details of what happened."

As they talked, they took his pulse, blood pressure, and heart rate. Claire gathered Farley's pills in a bag, as the attendants covered him with a blanket and his rain jacket and then wheeled him out to the ambulance. Douglas Brooks, a young boy whom Farley had taught to howl like a wolf, was home from school that day because of the weather and watched the proceedings from a window next door. Dougie ran to the door, and before Farley was lifted into the ambulance, he waved to the child, reassuring him he was just going to the hospital and would be okay. The ambulance moved off slowly down the icy road for the Northumberland Hills Hospital in Cobourg. That morning, Claire made her own tea.

The next morning, John Mowat drove Claire to the hospital to see Farley, who had a room to himself. "He was in good spirits," she observed. "He was chummy with the nurses and apparently liked the doctor who had treated him." Farley said they had given him every test known to man. The doctors changed his medication daily by eliminating one pill. They wanted him to stay another night to make sure he didn't faint again. He agreed, and John drove Claire home.

Farley came home the next day in "good spirits," though he had no appetite. He was in and out of bed all day. Two days later, he kept a long-standing appointment in Peterborough for skin cancer treatment, which included a minor surgery. Ken Stock, a retired veterinarian who lived next door, offered to help Farley change the bandages after his surgery, saying that there was not much difference between bandaging a horse, a dog, or a person. He also took note of how Farley was healing.

"He's really good at it, and came every day... This was a great help... He was a tower of strength," Claire wrote. "Also it was good for Farley to have some company, another man, especially." But the wear and tear was beginning to show. "He really didn't seem that old until the last few months," she noted.

On Monday, March 3, Claire drove Farley to the hospital in Cobourg, where he saw Dr. Brian Mackenzie again. Claire got the feeling that the fainting spells were now a permanent part of his life. The only treatment was a complex procedure that included inserting a stent in the groin. Claire detected from the doctor's tone of voice that Farley might not be able to endure the procedure. He also said that the likely cause of the fainting was a narrowed heart valve rather than the drugs. Nevertheless, some drugs were being eliminated and others reduced.

Farley now weighed a shocking 145 pounds, a drop of seven pounds from less than two weeks before. He had been picking at his meals, sometimes skipping them altogether, despite the fact that Claire was a seductive cook. She took Farley to Dr. Paul Hazell, who had been a family doctor in Port Hope for forty-six years. After a checkup, both the doctor and his nurse thought that Farley may have been right about having picked up a virus while he was in hospital.

BY MID-MARCH, Farley began to improve. He stopped losing weight, and his appetite returned. At night, he enjoyed a small nip of Islay Mist, a whisky he had developed a fondness for late in life. They even began driving down to the lakeshore hiking trail for walks, something they had done for years with their various dogs. Even though Farley still had a driver's licence, Claire was now the chauffeur, for the doctors worried that Farley could have a fainting spell behind the wheel.

With his improved health, their social life resumed. Their friend Debra Kerby and her dog, Farley, dropped by for a visit. Debra told them of her late father's final years. He had had a major operation that went terribly wrong. He lived another year and a half as a pain-stricken invalid. "If our Farley had undergone a huge operation as was recommended about 4 or 5 years ago, he would never have survived," Claire wrote. "He lives with an aneurysm, and with a narrowing heart valve—but he is alive!"

The day after Debra's visit, Farley and Claire arranged for Leah, the eleven-year-old girl who lived across the street, to dress up in Farley's old caribou parka and Claire's Greenland sealskin boots. Together with Sarah, Leah's mother, they drove down to the end of Gage Creek road, where there were still frozen waves to serve as a backdrop. "It looks as if it could be the far frozen north," Claire wrote. They took photographs and a video of Leah interviewing Farley about his book *Lost in the Barrens* for a school project—her equivalent of a book report.

On March 29, their good friends John and Mary Shaw-Rimmington came over for a visit. It happened to be an important day for Farley and Claire. "This is actually our wedding anniversary although we never celebrate it," Claire wrote. "We were married in 1965. How many years ago is that?"

Their visitors had a new dog, Farley. Claire was amused. The sheepdog in the beloved comic strip *For Better or for Worse* by Lynn Johnston was named after Farley Mowat. "How many dogs are there in this country named 'Farley'? Maybe hundreds." The puppy was well-behaved and friendly, and they were happy to let him amble around the house. "How I miss having a dog! It's just that at our ages it's a question of who is going to die first," Claire wrote. "Or what happens when we cannot look after the dog?"

On the last day of March, Claire drove Farley to the hospital in Cobourg for his appointment with his cardiologist, Dr. Mackenzie. He was very thorough and explained everything to them in meticulous detail. The upshot was that he thought Farley could make the trip to Cape Breton that summer. Farley was a little apprehensive about being away from the doctors who knew his case. If they did go, it would not be until June. Farley had gained back four pounds. "This is good news," Claire noted.

Claire herself had been having heart palpitations and periods when she felt she would faint. Nothing showed up in extensive tests, however. For exercise, she had been walking down the ninety-one steps of Jacob's Ladder, along Highway 28 for a block, then up the lower steps back to King Street. She had also returned to her fitness class. "I want to feel fit again," she wrote.

The day after Sandy Mowat's sixtieth birthday, he and his family arrived for lunch at the Vault, their favourite restaurant. Justin brought a recording on his laptop of a Queen's Park reception he had attended, celebrating the restoration of the portrait of Sir Oliver Mowat. Both Farley—who was descended from Reverend Professor John Mowat, the brother of Sir Oliver—and Sandy had been invited, but Justin went in their place to represent the Mowat family.

Justin had given a brief talk about his first awareness of Sir Oliver in Grade 8, from a history book about Confederation. It had triggered his interest in politics. "He spoke so well [at the reception]. It was brief; not a trace of nervousness. He has some of Farley in him for sure, which Sandy Mowat doesn't have," Claire observed. The direct descendants of Sir Oliver, who had had seven children, were also there in force. Claire noted that Justin, who was about to finish his first year at Ryerson University, was more sure of himself than he had been just six months previously. "He will do well in this life I am sure."

Farley felt well enough to visit the Furby House bookstore, where he signed hundreds of books for sale both in the store and online. "Hard to believe some of these books, if they are first editions of F.'s work will sell for one or two hundred dollars each," Claire noted.

On Palm Sunday, neighbours invited them to attend a matinee movie in Cobourg, *Tim's Vermeer*, about a man obsessed with the techniques of the seventeenth-century Dutch master. "I was fascinated, having had 4 years of art training nearly 60 years ago. Wish I'd known about the mirrors and the geometry of it," Claire wrote. But Farley found it hard to breathe in the theatre and afterwards wanted to go home and lie down. But he rallied, and they had dinner with the Stocks as planned, though Farley took a brief time-out, resting on their chesterfield.

ON MAY 6, the last day of his life, Farley was in good spirits, and he and Claire went out to run some errands. They drove to the drugstore for his supply of pills for the summer migration to Cape Breton, the bulk food store for his favourite dark chocolate, and the liquor store for six bottles of wine. He was just six days away from completing his ninety-third trip around the sun, and people would likely be dropping by with birthday greetings. Farley also picked up a new switch for his desk lamp at the hardware store.

Because Farley and Claire had been out all afternoon, they decided to get Chinese food for supper from a new place that had opened. When they got home, Farley repaired his desk lamp. "I can still fix things," he said. They watched the TVO channel for a few minutes, but Farley said he had a pain in his side and went to bed early, which he sometimes did. A well-marked copy of *A Short History of Progress* by his great friend Ron Wright was on the table beside his bed.

Claire was in the kitchen cleaning up the dishes and making soup for lunch the next day when she heard a terrible thud. She raced upstairs and found Farley on the floor. He had been listening to his favourite pianist, Angela Hewitt, playing his favourite composer, Bach. "Farley, can you hear me?" she cried. He looked terrible and could barely speak. Claire turned off the disc player and called 911.

Liz Brooks saw the ambulance arrive at the house and hurried over. Claire met the paramedics at the door. Because it was a lovely evening, neighbours were outside and quickly gathered around. Claire was crying and sobbed, "He's going to die tonight." Liz tried to reassure her that they would not know until the doctors checked him out. But Claire knew.

The paramedics put an oxygen mask over Farley's face and carried him down the stairs on a stretcher. "This is serious," they told Claire. Farley was alert by the time they arrived at the hospital in Cobourg.

He was down to his last two hours on earth. Liz drove Claire to the hospital. Another neighbour, Sarah, looked after Dougie. Their friend Ken Stock drove to the hospital as well. Claire, Liz, and Ken were ushered into a waiting area adjoining the emergency examination room, where Farley lay on a gurney surrounded by the emergency room doctor and a number of nurses and technicians. The doctor kept talking to both Claire and Liz, perhaps thinking Liz was their daughter.

Farley and Claire asked if surgery was possible, and if so, what the odds were that Farley would survive. The ER doctor phoned the surgeon, who said there was at best a twenty-five percent chance of survival. "What's my other option?" Farley asked. "We can make you comfortable." When Farley chose to be comfortable, Liz Brooks left Claire in the room with the love of her life.

As he slipped the lines, Farley asked, "Claire are you here? Where's Claire?" He put out his hand and she took it. "I leaned over to Farley who said two things feebly from inside his oxygen mask. 'I love you', he said. And then 'I want to go to sleep now.'"

In the waiting room, Claire used Liz's cellphone to call Sandy and Kim, who were just getting ready for bed. The words tumbled out. "Hello, Kim. It's Claire. I'm sorry to disturb you late at night. I'm in the Cobourg hospital. Farley is about to die."

After Claire spoke briefly to Sandy, whom she asked not to come because she didn't want him driving at night, the nurse summoned her back to Farley's side.

"The oxygen mask was gone. Farley lay unconscious gasping his last breaths. There was no colour in his face. I don't know how long we sat there—was it a few minutes? Or longer? Finally he stopped breathing. I turned to the nurse and said 'he's gone isn't he?' 'Yes,' she said."

In 1961, Farley had written Claire a prophetic letter about a vision of his own death, which was remarkably like his real passing. "I have a recurring dream, rather stark, that I am in your arms, and dying. Not with pain, but gladly. The long sleep."

Late that night, Claire returned home accompanied by John Mowat and two neighbours, Ken Stock and David Brooks. They nursed a drink together, and the men talked nervously about banal things.

"I just sat there stunned. I had watched the most important person in my life die just an hour or two earlier." Claire was grateful for the moral support, but she didn't want to hear about vintage cars. "Here I learned my first lesson about death and bereavement. Most people don't know what to say about it. It's somewhat like sex or childbirth; a matter so profound we cannot talk about the feelings involved. We can talk about the mechanics of it. That's easy. But not the deep emotions."

When the mail came over the next few days, it was a surreal mixture of birthday greetings and condolences.

22 | Ashes to Ashes

ON THE NIGHT OF FARLEY'S DEATH, John Mowat insisted on staying with Claire and bedded down on the chesterfield. She protested that she would be all right on her own, but he insisted. "John might not have been able to articulate how he felt, but he wanted to protect me," Claire wrote. Luckily, the couch was fairly comfortable, complete with the pillow and blanket Farley used when he lay down for a rest.

Claire climbed the stairs to bed around midnight, numb with the shock of fresh grief and a disbelief in Farley's death that would never diminish. She was up early the next morning to get breakfast for John, who headed home to clean up and change his clothes before returning with his wife, Dianne. Then Sandy and Kim Mowat arrived, and Claire served them the soup she had been preparing the previous evening for Farley's lunch. She called the minister to tell her that Farley had died and then tried to call Mary Talbot, Farley's steadfast typist and executive assistant for thirty-one years, to tell her before the news broke. Claire had to leave a message for her to call.

Coincidentally, Mary came by to drop off a birthday card and some typing she had done for Farley. It was rare for her to arrive unannounced. "Come in, come in," John said to her. Claire came to the door with the dread news: "Did you know Farley died last night?"

The blood drained from Mary's face. The two women hugged each other and cried. John escorted Mary to the dining room and seated her in Farley's chair. "Of course I couldn't keep the tears away," she later said.

The family hoped to have a day without publicity, but word inevitably got out. By lunchtime, the phone was ringing off the hook. They had wanted to keep Farley's death quiet until they could reach Farley's son David Mowat, in Calgary, and Farley's sister, Rosemary Mowat, in Barrie, but the media were relentless. The family wasn't prepared for the avalanche of press interest in Farley's passing, and in the absence of a family statement, they were worried that the media would go to the author of the 1996 *Saturday Night* article for a comment.

Elizabeth May rode to the rescue. She was happy to go on air with anyone she could, carrying the message that Farley had been very wounded by his portrayal as Pinocchio in *Saturday Night*.

"There was nothing about Farley that was dishonest. Farley was valiant and I don't know, whatever words they used. Farley was scrupulously honest, but he liked a good story... And he was absolutely passionate, directed, and ethical in every way in the fight to save the world. So I was angry. And losing him was so hard. And I talked about it. We are talking about a war hero, by the way. Let's not forget," May later recalled in an interview.

Three days after Farley's death, the 1996 *Saturday Night* article was posted on a blog site, along with a photo of the author, John Goddard, and the added line: "Farley Mowat proved to be about as trustworthy as Rob Ford and as distinguished a Canadian as Ben Johnson." The posting has since been taken down.

In contrast, former Governor General Adrienne Clarkson and her husband, acclaimed writer John Ralston Saul, gave a glowing tribute to Farley on CBC Radio. It would be one of many. In thanking them later, Claire wrote, "I am blessed that he lived so long but his sudden death is a terrible shock. Now I must figure out a way to live my life without Farley in it."

When Mary Talbot returned home shaken to her core, there were messages from the press. "I soon had the experience of being interviewed, on live television, by the CBC in Peterborough. At least I felt I was doing something, even if whatever I said was undoubtedly mixed up."

Mary had been hired by Farley in 1983 to work on his new book, *Sea of Slaughter*. He gave her a few instructions about formatting the manuscript, but joked, "Don't worry, it doesn't have to look like a bride going to her wedding, you know." She, of course, fussed over each and every page. Farley invited her to the splashy launch party for the book at the Sutton Place Hotel in Toronto.

After *Sea of Slaughter* was published, Jack McClelland had presented Farley with an early version of Apple's Macintosh computer. Farley tried it just once, when he used MacPaint to draw an enormous heart with a squiggly arrow through it, asking Claire to be his valentine. He then declared there was no way he would let that thing in his house. So it took up residence in Mary's office. (As for Claire, she always sent Farley the same valentine, disguised as a bill or a cheque.)

Others were also shocked by Farley's death. Mary Shaw-Rimmington and her husband, John, became good friends with Farley and Claire after they moved to Port Hope, in 2003. John, a master stonemason, proposed building a stone boat-roofed house, based on Farley's 1998 work *The Farfarers*. He wanted to honour Farley during his lifetime. The undertaking required forty tons of chocolate limestone and used a replica of a walrus-hide boat as a roof, just as the people did in *The Farfarers*. An international team of volunteers came to build it. The project was finished in 2006 and later moved to what is now Farley Mowat Park in Port Hope.

The day Farley died, Mary Shaw-Rimmington was out having lunch with friends. A mutual friend came to her house and broke the news to Mary's daughter, Mattie, who drove to the restaurant where her mother was having lunch. "She said to me, 'Mom, come outside with me please. I need to tell you something,'" Mary recalled. Her daughter was very upset.

"We went outside, and we stood on the corner. She said, 'Mom, Farley has died.' And I looked at her and said, 'He's just a nine-month-old puppy, what are you talking about?' I said, 'Have you told your father? He's going to be so upset.' And she grabbed me by the shoulders and she said, 'Mom, it's not the dog.' That's how eternal Farley was to me," Mary recalled.

Mary Talbot noted that Farley's concern and generosity had extended far beyond his family and friends. He had had a lifelong dedication to protecting the underdog and all living creatures and had changed many lives with his writing. He often said, "Writing is my function. If I cease to write, I cease to function."

At ninety-two, Farley was working on his forty-third book. At the time of his death, he had sold over fourteen million books worldwide, with more than 550 editions of his work, which had been translated into twenty-six languages. He was also Canada's first writer of creative or subjective non-fiction, true stories told with a personal voice—a storyteller who revealed universal truths.

FARLEY'S BROTHER, JOHN, and his wife helped with the funeral arrangements. At some point during the day, the funeral director called and talked about what a fine person Farley had been. Beyond thanking him, Claire didn't know what to say. The phone rang for two days straight. The last thing Claire wanted was to talk on the telephone. She thought phone calls to a bereaved person were a mistake and was happy to let most of them go to the answering machine.

People also arrived at the Mowat door, including Reverend Marg Tandy, to set a date for the funeral—Tuesday, May 13, the day after what would have been Farley's ninety-third birthday. As a last gift to his family, Farley had left funeral instructions, including his preference to be cremated.

The telephone mailbox at the Mowat household was full, and the flowers arrived non-stop. Claire gave some of the overflow to Liz Prower Brooks. One beautiful bouquet arrived from a couple Farley and Claire had allowed to camp on their beach on the Magdalen Islands forty years earlier, and with whom they had shared a lobster supper. Food arrived—cookies, fruit, homemade meals. Claire appreciated every bit of the outpouring of love, but nothing was registering in the normal way. Stretching out in front of her was the loneliness of the long-distance lover—to extinction and beyond.

"Most days I am in a state of shock," she wrote in her journal. "I guess it takes a long time to realize that this person who shared my life for 54 years is dead. It's a strange feeling to see all his clothes in the closet, his toothbrush & pills in the bathroom, his favourite CD's and his books all over the house."

Farley and Claire's street was under construction at the time of his death, and the foreman asked Claire's friend Liz to let him know the date of the funeral. He said he would move construction to another street on the day of the funeral, clear out all the cars, and keep people from parking there. Respect for Farley came in many forms, including work gloves and hard hats.

The funeral was private. The church was small, and only close friends and family were invited. The pews were nevertheless packed. Elizabeth May and Cate circulated through the mourners, welcoming and comforting them.

Elizabeth McClelland, Jack's widow, called. She said family members would have been there if they had known the details about the funeral. David Mowat was located in Calgary and, to everyone's surprise, showed up. At one point in his life, David had been estranged from Farley and the rest of the family, but he called periodically. The black sheep of the family because of his long absences and checkered past, David sat anonymously in the back row of the church. When Claire saw him, she insisted that he join the family in the front row. Sandy had not seen his brother for forty years, and it was the first time Kim and Justin had met David.

After the funeral, David left a letter for Claire, saying, "Thank you so much for all these years of uncompromising care which you extended to my father and the hospitality you always extended to me . . . Call if you ever need me. All my love and respect, David."

It was a traditional Anglican funeral, which began with the organist playing Bach. Justin's remembrance was stirring. He mentioned the huge ash tree just outside the church, which Farley had always stopped to put his hands on when he walked the dog in the mornings. Chester would wait patiently for him. Was Farley just catching his breath, or was it something else? Liz Prower Brooks believed he had a "connection" with the great tree. "When Justin mentioned that tree . . ." They put their heads down. "The tears just . . . We know the tree because we'd all walked with him in the morning," Liz remembered. Claire thought Farley had a "transcendental" connection to the towering ash. This was, after all, the man who swam with the capelin.

Mary Talbot was "incredibly honoured" to be the other speaker at Farley's funeral. Mary had known Farley better than most people and described him as she found him. "He was, quite simply, wonderful to work with—considerate, complimentary, grateful." He was also uncompromising and outspoken. "He railed at the destructive power of human greed and materialism we inflicted on the planet long before others did."

Mary urged the people in the pews of St. Mark's to honour Farley's legacy by continuing his good works—protecting animals and the environment, planting trees, reconnecting to the natural world every day, and being kind and compassionate to one another. "Things like this will help bring comfort to his family and particularly to Claire, his steadfast love, his rock, his mainstay." Claire was touched by Mary's words.

When the choral portion of the service came, Claire enthusiastically joined in. "Maybe it was some kind of release for this the most terrible loss of my entire life." Whatever it was, she was able to sing with gusto the hymns she had chosen. Reverend Tandy made an allegory of one of Farley's last acts, repairing his writing lamp. She reminded the mourners "that Farley had shed light on so many important issues and injustices during his long life."

When it was all over, Justin escorted Claire as the family led the procession out of St. Mark's. To be arm-in-arm with the grandson she adored and who reminded her so much of Farley was a pleasure. "Even though we are not related by blood I really do claim him as my grandson," she wrote in her journal. In his address, he had referred to her as Gramma Claire.

An urn containing half of Farley's ashes was placed in the ground at St. Mark's Church cemetery. The other half was reserved for a memorial service for Farley at Brick Point, planned for a few close friends that summer. Mourners who wanted to were invited to throw a handful of earth into the grave. Everyone at the funeral remembered a bright-red cardinal sitting in a tree above them, its piercing, single-note birdsong filling the air. The murmur went around that it was the spirit of Farley.

When Claire chose Farley's headstone, she had it engraved with a cardinal.

23 | The Crazy Love

IN LIFE, FARLEY MOWAT WAS NO STRANGER to public honours: his own place on Canada's Walk of Fame in Toronto, the Governor General's Award in 1956, the Leacock Medal in 1972, induction into the Order of Canada in 1981, and a school named after him, not to mention hundreds of dogs. At the official 2006 opening of Farley Mowat Public School in Nepean, Ontario, Farley and Justin gave a wolf howl to commemorate the event.

In death, the memorials were overwhelming: a statue of Farley and his dog Chester unveiled at the University of Saskatchewan, the province where he lived from age twelve to sixteen and the place he returned to the day after he got out of the army; two scholarships bearing his name; the new ship of the Sea Shepherd Conservation Society christened the *Farley Mowat II*; a tribute at McMaster University entitled "The Truths of Farley"; and a musical tribute in Port Hope put on by the Friends of Music, featuring world-renowned pianist Angela Hewitt. There was a celebration of his life at Cape Breton University, and the Farley Mowat Chair in the Environment was endowed in his honour. A memorial service was held at Christ Church Cathedral in Ottawa, where Margaret Atwood read from her book *The Year of the Flood*, in which a new religion has a "Saint Farley of Wolves."

At the time of the Ottawa memorial, organized by Elizabeth May, the then Green Party leader had recently used a well-known, all-purpose Scottish word in a speech at the Press Gallery Dinner. The incident touched off puritanical outrage at her language. According to Justin Mowat, who sat beside Margaret Atwood at Christ Church Cathedral, Canada's most famous author had no time for this little tempest. "Why the fuck can't people use the word *fuck*?" she asked.

But the public imprint only tells part of the story. It is the private pathways that often reveal the person behind the list of accomplishments, the public reputation. Very few people had seen Farley and Claire up close and personal the way Janice and Ervin Touesnard had.

When Farley and Claire came to live at Brick Point, in 1977, the Touesnards extended the first invitation they received—to their wedding. The Touesnards and the Mowats remained "family" for nearly forty years. Farley became so close to their son Marc that he would occasionally ask him to read chapters of his works in progress. Sometimes Marc was also their chauffeur on the drive between Port Hope and River Bourgeois in Cape Breton, with Claire as navigator when they hit the labyrinths of Montreal.

According to Janice Touesnard, Farley was always the big personality at the table, doing most of the talking and keeping the conversation going. Claire had influence in the background. "Claire had her opinions and she said them, but she just kind of let him, she was happy to let him take the lead in it. I mean, Claire was very smart . . . She would disagree with Farley. . . 'Oh Farley.'" Ervin felt that Farley was basically a shy person who put on an act. "Claire is reserved," he said, but "she has the knowledge to go out and talk to anyone, celebrities included . . . To the heart, to the core, she is a very good person. An honest person. Would never do anything to harm anyone."

Janice remembered a heated discussion over the dinner table about seals, which were a plague to fishermen because of the damage they caused to their nets and to fish stocks. Farley was staunchly against the seal hunt on environmental grounds and loudly proclaimed it. Janice recalled saying to him, "Would you like it if seals ate books?" Farley stomped off to bed. "He didn't back down; we didn't. The next day he was fine."

When Farley wanted to leave after an evening at the Touesnards', he'd say to Claire, "'Okay, old dear, it's time to put you to bed.' Meaning he wanted to go to bed." Janice laughed as she remembered one night when Farley was carrying on, only to have Claire rein him in. "She said, 'Come on, you old fool. I'm taking you home.' Not something she said on a regular basis."

Despite his antics, and their occasional disagreements, the Touesnards knew how much Farley and Claire cared about them and their family. Without being asked, Farley lent Ervin the money to buy a lobster licence. The licence cost $12,000, which at the time was five years' salary for the Touesnards. They had no collateral and no way of getting a loan from the bank. Ervin recalled the terms of the loan as laid out by Farley. "No interest. Pay me back whenever you can, if you can. If you can't, it doesn't matter."

They paid him back. "He was loyal to his friends and to all of the people who depended on him," Ervin said. After Farley's death, the only time Claire asked Ervin and Janice for help was after she found a snake on her car's windshield. Claire was even more terrified of snakes than she was of flying.

According to another long-time friend of the couple, Silver Donald Cameron, Farley enjoyed being the star of the show. "Farley certainly wanted to give the impression that he was the dominant figure, and Claire seemed quite happy to let him be that . . . certainly in public, and to a large extent in private too."

But Cameron, who died in 2020, also knew that when Farley crossed certain red lines, "there was a steel spine in Claire . . . There would be certain points where she would say, 'No, no, this is the way it is going to be.' She wouldn't do it often, but when she did, it would be done."

Farley had had a reputation as a womanizer, and it hurt. But, Cameron said, "I never got the sense that Claire worried overly much about that." Claire knew that many women were attracted to Farley. Asked about this in an interview, she insisted that Farley did not have an affair—dalliances, but not an affair.

Cameron was adamant that Claire did not break up Farley's first marriage, noting that Frances was clearly not the woman "that wanted to be doing the stuff that Farley needed to do... the marriage was already in trouble." Cameron also noted that Claire was always very loving and respectful of Farley's relationship with Sandy.

Asked what the core of their relationship was, Cameron replied: "Obviously, they loved each other very deeply. They counted on each other's company. They did a lot of stuff together. They would go off with the canoe, in the waters of Cape Breton, after a morning's work. They spent a lot of time trying out ideas on one another. Discussing books with one another... They really did live one life together. With her keeping records on one hand, and him keeping records on the other... I think that really does give you a sense of who they were together. And I think he counted very heavily on her perceptions too... And her opinions and her insights were very important to him."

Cameron remembered vividly when Farley paid him a visit in D'Escousse, Cape Breton, after completing his war book *And No Birds Sang*. Farley had gone through a dry spell in the mid-1970s, and finishing a new book, especially about the war, was an emotional moment. He read some passages from the manuscript to Cameron and his wife. "And that's the second time, I guess, of the three times I saw him cry, was when he finished that book. He said it was important to him that he have our approval... He was in tears when he finished the reading."

Asked if he saw Farley and Claire as Canada's first "green" couple, Cameron said, "I think for Farley you can see a fairly clear line from the Second World War on the destructiveness of human beings. *And No Birds Sang* is a title that really speaks directly to this. That Farley would be writing about the war in terms of the birds. Be using that image. So I think you can see where Farley, and also go back to his boyhood in Saskatchewan, and the experience with *Owls in the Family*, and all that kind of thing. Clearly, it's part of Farley as far back as you can really make sense of the question."

Although Cameron was not aware of Claire's background in the same detail, he believed that her views on the environment were as strongly held as Farley's. "I've had the sense all the way along that she was absolutely, one hundred percent there with him on all of that. She had a very similar kind of appreciation for Nature, which probably comes out of her artistry." In Cameron's opinion, Farley needed Claire, but he gave as well as took. "And he supported her too. I think that's important. This was a very mutual relationship."

Cameron said that Farley needed a mate with the kind of psychological brilliance that Claire possessed. She didn't judge Farley, but instead allowed him to be what he was. But she was definitely not intellectually submissive. Cameron's wife, Marjorie Simmins, recalled how Farley appreciated Claire's wicked sense of humour: "Just to see him looking at her, when she cracked one of her 'little nice wife' jokes... he'd just look over and almost chuckle. He really loved that about her."

Farley could say things that made people deeply uncomfortable, and Cameron thought he took a certain pleasure in it. He believed it was rooted in Farley's unwillingness to settle for anything less than the full truth. "So that things that people would rather not talk about, Farley would manage to get them to talk about... Partly I suspect there is also a curiosity there. What will happen? He was like a little boy in a way. 'Gee, if I put these two elements together...' George Woodcock once referred to Irving Layton as a 'Ring-Tailed Roarer' in the little zoo of Canadian letters. I think that's not a bad description of Farley too. I think being the perpetual bad boy of Canadian letters was certainly, it was part of his persona. It was part of what he sold."

Farley was one of the first in the country to write about the environment, though as a visionary and naturalist, not a scientist. Cameron noted that he had an uncanny knack for getting the big shapes right. "And he is a storyteller, so you don't necessarily have to run after him for factual information and details. He's right on the big issues."

Is Farley's work a quintessential record? "Yes," Cameron replied. "It absolutely is. I think that a number of the books that he wrote were just magnificent. There's nothing really like them. And I would say his absolute masterpiece is *Sea of Slaughter*. One of the most chilling and terrifying books." In an updated edition of that work, Farley wrote, "The living world is dying in our time."

RONALD WRIGHT AND HIS THEN WIFE, Janice Boddy, met Farley and Claire in 1987 in Port Hope. Farley invited Ron over for a drink after he and Claire got back from Fiji, where they had read Wright's great classic *On Fiji Islands*. The two men drank vodka together. The third time they met over a drink, Farley quipped, "You know, we don't have to get drunk every time."

Wright was in awe of Farley and his writing. He had moved from Britain to Canada when he was twenty-one, and had read a wonderful passage from *People of the Deer* in a collection of Canadian literature published in Britain. Wright had no idea who Farley was, but when he read the whole book after coming to Canada he was profoundly impressed. "I am sure that contributed to my own desire to write about Indigenous people," he said.

Ron and Farley would go to lunch together, usually for steak-and-kidney pie at the Beamish Pub on John Street, and talk about the terrible state of the world. Farley could read body language forty feet away and was always right. Wright believes he got that skill from studying animals. Farley talked to Ron about the war, which had affected him profoundly. Years later, Ron said "it was the carnage of Italy that made him go to the North and go to places where there were very few people around." Farley was unsettled by civilization.

In 2004, the Wrights moved to British Columbia and Janice landed a job at the University of British Columbia. Their departure left a large hole in Farley and Claire's lives. In 2005, Farley wrote to them, saying, "Life without you two tends to be blunt at both ends. Almost worth burning the rest of my candle on a flit to BC."

The Wrights remained good long-distance friends, writing letters, calling, and visiting Cape Breton three times. They talked about books, drank vodka, and skinny-dipped in the Mowats' pond.

Wright knew that Farley could sometimes be wilful and hard to handle. He was known to shout out "Masturbation" at parties or moon people when dressed in his kilt. But Wright also knew it was not necessarily the essential man, just the public performer—drunken, outrageous, and very funny. The other, and arguably more genuine, Farley was the introspective thinker and writer. Wright remembered Farley saying to him once, "Oh, that Farley the buffoon that everyone enjoyed in public, I don't need him anymore. I created him."

Wright described Farley as an excellent friend. "I felt I could always turn to him. A drunken chat about any life crisis. Also for the problems of writing. Just soak up the experience of someone who had been at the game so much longer. He was never too busy to talk to you."

Wright observed the deep mutual respect between Farley and Claire: "Comfort levels that only come from years and years of happy life together. There was just one Claire. Her warmth and charm were genuine." Farley was by nature gregarious and a charmer. "But Claire has a great deal of ease and *savoir faire*. She's very good in a group, funny stories extremely good. Can talk to people she has nothing in common with. Gracious." Both of them had a wonderful sense of humour.

Wright noted that the couple's idea of fun was going to Cape Breton and living in a lovely old farmhouse, "just being together in Nature." They loved the cold and the North.

Ron Wright was one of the first people to reach out to Claire after Farley's death. In a letter thanking him for his condolences, Claire spoke about the shock of what had happened and the belief most people have that their loved ones will never die. "Sudden death is, what many people are telling me, preferable. But I am wondering if that's true. Right now I wish Farley was maybe in a hospital bed and I could visit him and tell him simple things. I think that's what I miss most; not being able to tell him about some bird I noticed, or that they now have fiddleheads in the supermarket, or that I got him new typewriter ribbons for his birthday."

Cate May Burton sent Claire a special remembrance of her godfather. "I've been thinking about the way Farley in particular influenced me and how wonderful it was to know him ... I always saw that you were a great joy to one another and that was a beacon for how good relationships can be. The greatest thing I learned from Farley was to be playful and sometimes not allow other people's opinion of you to prevent you from having fun and speaking your mind. Whenever he was making fun, I wanted to be in on the joke with him. He was as real and unpretentious as anyone could be."

Cate believed that Farley had a kind of prescience about the dark phase civilization was entering, a forbidding perception that spoke to her generation. "I think a lot of young people now feel like maybe there isn't a lot of hope for civilization as it stands now."

Environmental activist Mary Gorman had met Farley in 2011 when she and a film crew came to do an interview about oil drilling in the imperilled Gulf of St. Lawrence. "And Farley, you talk about emotional intelligence. That guy could just read anybody in a nanosecond." Mary, the wife of a lobster fisherman, was exhausted and unable to sleep because of a growing sense that the anti-drilling protesters were losing the battle. Farley helped her to define herself as "the one giving voice to those creatures whose language we don't speak."

When Farley told her that, Mary was so emotional she thought she was going to cry. Farley sensed her fragility and her need. "He pulls me aside and he takes out one of his little postcards. I'll never forget this; it really touched me. He wrote this, and he said, 'This is for you.' Now, can you make out his writing? It said, 'For Mary, never despair, with affection. Love Farley' . . . He knew. Yes, he did. He picked right up on me. And he understood. It's like he could read your soul."

It was not until she met Claire without Farley that Mary realized how passionate Claire was on environmental issues. "They were very much an equal partnership. It's just that I didn't realize that when I first met them . . . She's just a lot like Farley, she can read you right away. And she knows."

Asked if the "Crazy Love" of the Van Morrison classic song existed between Farley and Claire, Mary replied, "Oh yes, yes, yes . . . That was definitely the Crazy Love. That was it. And she said it was instant, when he looked up at her from that boat there and walked up, that was it . . . It's just one of those blessed relationships, where there's a simpatico there, and adaptability. I would say she is a phenomenon as a woman . . . I just think Claire is one of those rare types of women that can retain her identity, and femininity, and she is not subservient, and yet she's just highly adaptable."

It took a special person to adapt to Farley Mowat in all of his roaring splendour over a fifty-four-year relationship. Adapting to life without him proved much harder.

24 | The Cold Days of Life

ON JUNE 27, 2014, less than two months after Farley's death, John Mowat drove Claire to the Via Rail train that would connect in Montreal with the train to Nova Scotia. It was her first trip to Brick Point as a widow. She started to cry when she said goodbye to John. He had been remarkably helpful and attentive, a "guardian angel."

"John truly surprised me," Claire wrote in her journal. "He seemed to genuinely care how I was faring after the death of Farley. He's not a bit demonstrative but in his way I could sense that he cared about my well-being." Marc Touesnard picked her up at the train station in Truro and drove her to River Bourgeois and down Grand Gully Road to the farmhouse, "without Farley."

On her first night there, Claire was awakened by a call from a friend to say that Vi Warren, a long-time friend, had just died. In 1943, Vi had joined the Air Transport Auxiliary in England, where she delivered planes to maintenance units and military bases; there is a postage stamp in her honour. At five foot two, she had to sit on her parachute to see out the window. Claire was learning that death was ubiquitous and endlessly accommodating.

The next morning, she got up and got on with life, unpacking and making decisions about what to keep and what to discard from thirty-six summers together at Brick Point. Claire found it very difficult to part with Farley's clothes. When she saw his T-shirts and worn-out pants, it was as if he might come around the corner and put them on again. Clearing up the workshop was equally painful. Farley was a worse "pack rat" than Claire was, hanging on to anything that might be useful in the future. All told, she filled four bags, under the watchful eye of a character that Farley had painted over the years, by wiping off paintbrushes on the workshop door.

Claire bought some marigolds and tomato plants, which she was determined to grow. Her back wasn't strong enough to plant and tend Farley's extensive vegetable patch. Janice Touesnard brought over a huge pot of begonias, explaining that they were in lieu of sending flowers to the house when Farley died. Claire appreciated every act of kindness, but she still felt isolated and alone. Grief was a chill wind blowing over the old bones of remembered love.

"It is very hard, impossible really, for people to understand my grief. Only those few who have lost their loved life partner know what it's like. I find people telling me about the time their father died, or mother or grandfather. It's not the same thing. People don't know what to say to a person mourning," she said. In Cape Breton, many people just gave her a silent hug. "This I like. This is a way to share sorrow without saying a word."

Farley, though gone, was omnipresent. There are thirteen steps up to the loft, Farley's writing room at Brick Point. On the bulletin board, there are two pictures of Claire and the *Happy Adventure*. The nameplate of the boat, painted by Claire, hangs over the doorway. On the photo of the *Happy Adventure* in dry dock is a sticky note with the words "Who am I? Who knows."

There is a Sanford Chicago pencil sharpener, and above it, the skull of some creature. Farley's old Underwood typewriter commands the desk, flanked by a manuscript with a carbon sheet beside it. There is an Ella Fitzgerald cassette and a tape player, along with the usual writer's tools—paper clips, pens, a magnifying glass, and scissors. Twenty of Farley's books are on a shelf behind his writing chair, plus an Oxford dictionary and *Roget's Thesaurus*.

Also on the bulletin board is a list of contents for the book he was working on. "Part one Introductory Session. Not yet written as of August 1 2013... Part 7 (First footers/strand lopers/Orkney/Shetland

Beach people etc.)"—people from the mesolithic era ten thousand to six thousand years ago that Farley called the First Farers.

He had been working on a grand, speculative book on a subject that had always fascinated him, the very early migration to North America from Europe, and his own roots, a follow-up to *The Farfarers*. He was particularly interested in the Alban people of northern Scotland, who may have preceded the Norse. Within that narrative, he also planned to tell his and Claire's early love story, while they were in England and Scotland in 1962. Farley worked on the book until the day he died.

Claire was all but overwhelmed with gathering Farley's records, making decisions about financial matters and the complex issue of rights to his books, and running two households. And there was the pressing need to answer the flood of condolences from hundreds of Farley's friends and admirers. In replying to legendary editor Doug Gibson, who wrote to her about Farley's remarkable life, Claire revealed just how hard it was to get through all the tributes to her husband. One of the hardest was the unveiling of the statue of Farley and Chester at the University of Saskatchewan:

"It was an eerie experience for me. Only five weeks after he died I saw a replica of him, in bronze, standing there (with his dog) in a beautiful setting amid trees and the classical, stone buildings of the University of Saskatchewan . . . It is the ordinary day-to-day things that aggrieve me the most; his raincoat hanging by the door, his favourite marmalade in the fridge, the clutter of pens and pencils on his desk and this ancient typewriter. The world has lost a singular author. But I have lost my very best friend whom I first met 54 years ago in St. Pierre and Miquelon. I am blessed that he lived so long but it's no easy task to figure out how to live without him."

ON JULY 25, 2014, thirty people gathered at Brick Point for a final memorial to Farley. Sandy, John, and Justin Mowat were there, along with intimate friends like Elizabeth May and Cate. Ronald Wright and his partner, Deborah Campbell, travelled from British Columbia to pay their respects. The family had hoped to scatter the other half of

Farley's ashes from the top of the hill behind the house, but the path was steep, hopelessly overgrown, and full of ants. The trees were now so big, you could barely see the ocean. What had once been open fields was now being reclaimed by Nature.

Claire decided they would scatter the ashes in the large patch of wild roses beyond the lawn. Chester and another of their dogs, Tom, were buried nearby, which Claire thought would have delighted Farley. Elizabeth May was eloquent in her remembrance of the man she often turned to for guidance, as was Justin Mowat. John presided over the spreading of the ashes, and Claire found herself more moved than she had been at Farley's funeral in Port Hope. "I was in a kind of daze, still unbelieving that Farley is dead, and these ashes are all that is left of him."

Claire sent thank-you notes to all of the people "who scattered Farley's ashes in a place he loved so much." She told Ronald Wright and Deborah Campbell she regretted that their visit was so brief, given they'd come all the way from British Columbia. Wright wrote a reply from the heart. "I can imagine how bereft you must be feeling. Farley leaves behind a huge Farley-shaped hole in the world, in this nation, in so many lives—and yours above all. But he also lives on in everything he did and wrote and said. He was such a great soul & spirit that it's no wonder you're still grieving deeply. Those we love live within us until we go ourselves," Wright told her. "It meant so much seeing you in July and being able to say goodbye to Farley in that perfect way. A short visit, but poignant and lovely."

It was August before Claire took up writing in her journal again, a gap of four months since Farley's death. The immense wave of practical demands and business details was just part of the reason for all the blank pages.

"I was, and still am, in a state of shock and incredulity. Farley is dead. He is gone forever. Every once in a while the full impact hits me." She missed telling him things like the fact that Pottersfield Press in Nova Scotia was about to publish a paperback edition of her book *Travels With Farley*. Or letting him know she was growing a few small tomato plants in the little greenhouse he built. There was so much in the house in Cape Breton that had been put together by his inventive mind. Everywhere she turned, there was Farley.

Although people were very kind to her, on social occasions with local friends there was no real escape from her grief: "I find myself oddly out of things when I'm in a group... When Farley was with me the conversation would somehow evolve in a way that included him, or some subject dear to him. Now that he's gone the same doesn't apply to me." She saw herself as a displaced person, someone who had no relatives there and no children of her own.

Despite the sense of isolation, Claire attended Ervin's sixtieth birthday party, as she had all of his birthdays since he was in his twenties. The Touesnards were a big, close-knit family, and Ervin and Janice now had six grandchildren. In the midst of the celebration, Claire felt a keen and familiar sadness.

"At times like this I nearly cry. Why did my life turn out like it did? Why couldn't I have been part of a scene like this? It really is what I hoped for. Why was I subjected to two men, my father and then Farley, who did not want me to have children? Why was my own inner voice stifled, amid all the crap about education and careers and over-coming the inconvenience of being female?"

IT WAS BEAUTIFUL but bittersweet to be at Brick Point alone. Claire thought that if she dropped dead there, no one would notice. So that autumn she was glad to take the train back to Port Hope. She was immediately plunged into the enormous task of preparing Farley's papers for the McMaster University archives. She had invented a new life for herself; her mission was now to ensure that Farley's legacy was honoured in all the right places.

There was a lot of snow that winter, and it had always been Farley who fed the birds. Claire located the feeder, but not the tall iron rod from which he hung it. She found an odd hook in the basement and hung it on the clothesline. In the morning, there were birds on the feeder. "Slate coloured juncos, I think. I was so pleased."

On her first New Year's Eve without Farley, she turned on the comedy hour with Ron James. At the end of the show, James urged the Canadian public not to just gaze into their cellphones, but to be involved and aware of what was happening in the world today. "Take Farley Mowat, famed author who died last May at the age of ninety-two," he said. "Just a week before he died, he was admonishing the government to get the Wi-Fi out of our national parks." It was true, and Claire went to bed with a smile on her face. She found herself wishing that Farley were still alive, even if he had been an invalid.

In early January, a team of archivists from McMaster University arrived in Port Hope, where John Mowat helped Claire prepare ten big boxes of material for the archivists. Farley was one of the first Canadian authors whose work had been collected by the archive, in the 1970s.

"Farley, thank goodness, was tidy and methodical but it is still up to me to get it all together," Claire wrote. "So much of a woman/wife's life is blended with that man after a long time together. You knew his favourite food, music, jacket, toothpaste, wine, books. Suddenly all those things are unimportant in your own life. Yes, these are the cold days of life. I do wonder if they will last forever."

Despite a heavy snowstorm, the two archivists from McMaster later returned to sort and pack Farley's office. They assembled thirty-three Bankers Boxes of books, manuscripts, photos, and tapes. Claire was unnerved when they began to cart it off.

"What a strange feeling—to see so much of Farley's work packed up and leaving this house. I'm glad it's going to a safe place where someone, some day, may make use of it. It's just that I still think, in my heart, that Farley needs all that material. I still feel that Farley is alive," Claire wrote.

Claire wrote to Ronald Wright about how difficult it was to see Farley's manuscripts and research material on their way to McMaster and how much shelf space in his normally jam-packed office was now empty. But there was still a lot more that needed to be sifted through and sorted. "No one else can really do it so I just hope I live to be 90-something to get it all despatched (or discarded) appropriately. It's rewarding that so many people cared so much about Farley."

Claire had a clear purpose in life as the keeper of Farley's legacy, but her emotions were tested on every special day without him—Easter, Thanksgiving, Christmas, and birthdays. She had a particularly hard time on March 29, 2015, on what would have been their fiftieth wedding anniversary. Even though they almost never celebrated the event, the date carried Claire back to their beginnings on the magic carpet of memories.

"He didn't care about birthdays or anniversaries. And I have always doubted that we actually were legally married... Farley always thought it was comical, this befuddled judge who had never married any two people before. But to me it means a degree of legitimacy, my surname the same as Farley's on my passport, and my driver's license. I had, of course, dreamed of being a bride in a white dress, or any colour dress, but I knew it would never happen."

She couldn't help thinking of all the photos she had seen of people celebrating their fiftieth anniversary surrounded by children and grandchildren. "It was always what I wanted: from the time I was a girl... Of course once I met Farley I put it all behind me. God had been good to me after all and I found my true love and had a spectacular life with him. But our only child died at birth."

Claire had always had the feeling that she was an outsider. Among many other things, Farley had provided an oasis of spiritual and intellectual comfort. Now, when the world wounded her, or her own self-doubts or regrets mounted, she was without safe harbour, without Farley. She was alone.

"Part of the problem is that while I have often been in the company of people who are selfish, or stupid or insensitive or boring—I could always go home to Farley. He was always interesting. Not always sympathetic but that didn't matter. It was simply that he was wise and intelligent and most people, I am discovering, are not... Some days I hope to live long enough to make sure every shred of Farley's legacy gets channelled to the right place. Then days I just want to die, soon."

For three consecutive years, Claire returned to Brick Point by herself. It was the place Farley loved more than any other. He kept a pair of binoculars by his chair in the living room and a ledger of sea birds and other creatures he saw from the window.

Brick Point was sacred ground to him. His detailed records measured the environmental impact of humans on the area. He noted the subtle declines made by that impact in his ledger. Claire had done coloured botanical drawings of all the wild plants they found at their property when they first arrived. It was a magical place. If Farley were to reappear anywhere, it would be at the two-hundred-acre property that he and Claire left to the Nova Scotia Nature Trust as a permanent nature preserve.

"I still find it hard to believe that Farley is dead. It is so strange. He filled all the corners of my life for 54 years. I still have the feeling I will see him return. Does this feeling ever go away? I wish I could believe in Heaven and that I would see him again there."

The lane into their Cape Breton property is perfectly curved so that the old white farmhouse is not visible from the road. Nelson DeWolfe was just eighteen when he began mowing the lawns at Brick Point, and he had sometimes helped Farley with the gardens. Nelson enjoyed talking to the writer about the wildlife he saw in the woods. Bobcats were coming back to Cape Breton, and the deer population was doing much better. Nelson had even seen a doe with three fawns. At first, he didn't know how Farley, the protector of all animals, would react when he found out that Nelson was a hunter. "After I got to talk to him, it wasn't an issue. He could judge the kind of person you were, what your intentions were with that kind of stuff. We always got along great. An understanding of Nature."

After Farley's death, Nelson kept the lawns trimmed and the path down to the swimming hole cleared for Claire. He was also a beekeeper, and set up his colourful hives in what used to be Farley's vegetable garden. Farley's father, Angus, had kept bees in Trenton from 1921 to 1923, when the family subsisted on porridge, crackers, and honey, and Farley's earliest memory was of watching a bee.

In spring, the first flowers at Brick Point are apple blossoms. A large crabapple tree, its blossoms aquiver with foraging bees, shades the corner of the side-yard by the farmhouse. There are banks of wild roses, and honeysuckle for the hummingbirds. Huge blue dragonflies hover over the bulrushes in the pond. In early July, the blackberries and raspberries come into blossom, and that's when the bees really start piling on the honey. There is not a lot of nectar in August, but that changes when the fall flowers bloom in early September, the goldenrod and wild asters. Then the otherwise perfect silence vibrates with the deep thrumming of bees.

Photo by Peyton Harris.

Acknowledgements

THANK YOU to the exceptional staff at Greystone Books. Your early enthusiasm for *Farley and Claire* was a delight. Editorial director Jennifer Croll kept us all on the same page, and creative director Jessica Sullivan has shown an artist's eye in her jacket and text design. A bow to my editor, Nancy Flight, and to copy editor Brian Lynch, whose careful attention to detail continues to amaze me. Proofreader Jennifer Stewart's queries show how much she loves words.

Rick Stapleton and the staff of the William Ready Division of Archives and Research Collections at McMaster University, where the Claire Mowat and Farley Mowat fonds are stored, made research at the archives a pleasure. They also helped navigate the extensive collections, opening embargoed letters and journals for the first time. Their timely help with photographs was also appreciated.

Allison Wagner, Senior Rare Books and Manuscript Advisor, Archives and Special Collections at the University of Calgary, facilitated access to the Harold Horwood collection. She proved once again why archivists and librarians are among my favourite people.

The list of Mowat family and friends and others who helped make this book by sitting down for interviews or providing insights and photos includes:

Liz Prower Brooks and David Brooks
Nelson DeWolfe
Stephen Ernst of S. A. Ernst Photography, who rescued photos
     from old negatives

Mary Gorman

Andrew Horwood

Rosemary Kilbourn

Elizabeth May and her daughter, Cate May Burton

John Mowat and his son Matthew Mowat, who also provided
    technical expertise and some excellent winter driving skills

Mary Shaw-Rimmington

Marjorie Simmins and Silver Donald Cameron

David Suzuki

Mary Talbot

Janice and Ervin Touesnard and their son Marc Touesnard

Ronald Wright

James King's fine 2002 biography *Farley: The Life of Farley Mowat* was a much-appreciated reference for this book.

Thanks to Margaret Atwood for a vivid foreword that brought her friends Farley and Claire to life as only a master wordsmith could.

I also wish to thank the Canada Council for the Arts for their writer's grant in support of this project.

Finally. The incomparable Lynda Harris, whose work on this book proves once again that this is a woman who could have built the Pyramids all by herself.

DAVID
SUZUKI
INSTITUTE